To Mary Ann.

THE ROAD TO
RESPECTABILITY

MURRAY WILLIAMSON'S ROLE IN US HOCKEY

By JOHN SCHAIDLER with MURRAY WILLIAMSON

FOREWORD by LOU NANNE

BEAVER'S
POND
PRESS

Editor: Paige Polinsky
Production editor: Alicia Ester

ISBN 13: 978-1-64343-753-8

Library of Congress Catalog Number: 2021925544

Printed in Canada
First Printing: 2022
26 25 24 23 22   5 4 3 2 1

Book design and typesetting by James Monroe Design LLC
jamesmonroedesign.com

Typeface: Athelas and Pill Gothic

Beaver's Pond Press
939 Seventh Street West
St. Paul, MN 55102
(952) 829-8818
www.BeaversPondPress.com

Contact Murray Williamson at murray-williamson.com for book club discussions and interviews.

CONTENTS

Murray Williamson's Legends behind the Scenes | v

Foreword | xiii

Introduction | 1

Chapter One: Trials and Tribulations:
The First Three Decades of US National and Olympic Teams 7

Chapter Two: Don't Expect Any Miracles:
Mariucci Wins Silver at the 1956 Winter Olympic Games 13

Chapter Three: A Barber's Son with a Dream:
Winnipeg Youth Standout and Montréal Canadiens Prospect 25

Chapter Four: Williamson Meets Mariucci in an Eveleth Pool Hall 39

Chapter Five: Williamson Becomes a Gopher 45

Chapter Six: St. Paul Johnson Wins the 1955 State Tournament 49

Chapter Seven: Mariucci Lays Out His Vision for Minnesota Hockey. 53

Chapter Eight: Mariucci, Ridder, and Bush Bring Hockey to Iowa 59

Chapter Nine: Vic Heyliger Launches the
NCAA National Championship Tournament. 63

Chapter Ten: Williamson and Brooks: Gopher Freshman Teammates 71

Chapter Eleven: The Paper Salesman Who Brought Down the WIHL 77

Chapter Twelve: Walter Bush Lays the Foundation of the USHL 89

Chapter Thirteen: From the St. Paul Steers to the US National Team 97

Chapter Fourteen: The Man Who Hired and Fired John Mariucci 103

Chapter Fifteen: On to Vienna 111

Chapter Sixteen: The Road to Grenoble 119

Chapter Seventeen: Restoring US Hockey to a Position of Respectability 133

Chapter Eighteen: Fighting to Get into the 1972 Olympics 147

Chapter Nineteen: Tutelage Under Tarasov 159

Chapter Twenty: Silver in Sapporo 175

Chapter Twenty-One: I'm Not Here for My Health:
The WHA Changes the Game 191

Chapter Twenty-Two: The Midwest Junior Hockey League
and the NCAA 203

Epilogue | 215

Index | 217

Contributors | 225

MURRAY WILLIAMSON'S LEGENDS BEHIND THE SCENES

Players and coaches bask in the glory of medals and championships. This book hopes to pay tribute to those legendary folks behind the scenes that helped make US amateur and college hockey the thriving sport it is today.

Austin, Ken

A former goalie for both the Roseau Rams and the Minnesota Gophers, Ken Austin later served as the first commissioner of the Midwest Junior Hockey League (MJHL).

Blatnik, John

Representative John Blatnik was elected to Congress fourteen times, proudly representing Minnesota's Iron Range. He was an early and active supporter of the national team concept and helped sponsor the Congressional act that granted Lou Nanne US citizenship prior to the 1968 Olympic Games.

Brooks, Herb

Herb Brooks is famous for assembling and coaching the "Miracle on Ice" gold medal team, but his contributions to US hockey go far beyond that. Brooks represented his country as a player seven times (second only to John Mayasich), including in five world championships and the 1964 and 1968 US Olympic teams. (Also, he and Nanne were never quite as clever as they thought. I usually knew when they were sneaking out and where they were going.)

Brown, Harry

After playing hockey for the University of Minnesota's freshman squad and serving in the US Naval Coast Guard, Harry Brown coached high school hockey for many years. He led Patrick Henry High School to a third-place finish at the 1964 Minnesota State Tournament and compiled a career record of 70-49-8. He also won a landmark lawsuit that allowed high school hockey players to practice and play in the off-season. Perhaps most importantly, he founded an American Junior A league that predated the MnJHL. Harry Brown was inducted into the Minnesota High School Hockey Coaches Hall of Fame in 2012.

Brown, Walter

Walter Brown made significant contributions to US amateur hockey and continued to raise the bar throughout the 1930s and '40s. He coached the US national team to a record of 44-3-3 during the 1932-33 season, capping things off with Team USA's first international championship in Prague, Czechoslovakia. He also served as chairman of the US Olympic Ice Hockey Committee for the 1960 US Olympic hockey team, which made history by winning their first Olympic gold medal. The Walter A. Brown International Hockey Tournament was held in his honor at Broadmoor World Arena from 1964-68.

Brown, Warren

Warren Brown was the deputy director of the National Collegiate Athletic Association (NCAA) when they tried to eliminate college hockey as a varsity sport. His attempts only spurred the Amateur Hockey Association of the United States (AHAUS) to action, prompting them to get involved in US Junior A hockey. Ironically, US Junior A became a popular intermediary step for young prospects who wanted to play for top NCAA teams.

Bush, Walter

From 1963-74 Walter Bush served on four US Olympic Hockey Committees, also serving as general manager for the 1964 team. He is probably best known as the primary founder and co-owner of the Minnesota North Stars. Somehow, he also found time to serve as president of the Minnesota Amateur Hockey Association (MAHA) and director of AHAUS. He was inducted into the US Hockey Hall of Fame in 1980.

Clark, Don

Don Clark was a founding member of the Minnesota Amateur Hockey Association (MAHA) in 1947. The United States Hockey League (USHL) championship trophy is named in honor of him. Clark was inducted into the US Hockey Hall of Fame in 1978.

Fleming, Bob

Bob Fleming was the chairman of the US Olympic Hockey Committee for ten years, beginning in 1970. He was the driving force behind the 1972 Olympic silver medal team and the 1980 gold medal team. Though he received the Lester Patrick Award for his outstanding service to US Hockey, he has yet to be inducted into the US Hockey Hall of Fame.

Heyliger, Vic

Vic Heyliger was the impetus behind the first NCAA National Ice Hockey Championship at the Broadmoor Arena in Colorado Springs. As head coach of the Michigan Wolverines he was legendary, leading his teams to six NCAA National Championships in a span of thirteen years. For years he was a fixture at the Broadmoor Arena's Golden Bee pub, chomping an unlit cigar as he told stories late into the night. Heyliger was inducted in the US Hockey Hall of Fame in 1974.

Kennedy, John F.

John F. Kennedy was the US president who, in 1963, questioned the respectability of the US Hockey program after they had a disastrous showing in international competition.

Lockhart, Tom

Tom Lockhart founded AHAUS in 1937. Decades later, AHAUS became USA Hockey, which is the primary governing body for organized hockey in the United States and a member of the International Ice Hockey Federation. Lockhart was inducted into the US Hockey Hall of Fame in 1973.

Martin, Gordon

Martin Gordon was the Boston-based attorney who successfully fought the NCAA, guaranteeing amateur status for young prospects who played in the Midwest Junior Hockey League.

Marvin, Cal

Warroad, Minnesota, is known as Hockeytown USA. thanks in large part to Cal Marvin. He founded the legendary Warroad Lakers, a top-level senior league team, and went on to coach the squad for most of the next forty-five years. He also coached the 1958 US national team and managed the 1965 US national team. Over a dozen of his players competed on US national teams, including Bill and Roger Christian and Henry Boucha. He was inducted into the US Hockey Hall of Fame in 1982 and the Manitoba Hockey Hall of Fame in 1997.

Mariucci, John

John Mariucci is the godfather of Minnesota hockey. Before going on to coach the Minnesota Gophers hockey team for fourteen years, "Maroosh" was a bruising, defensive-minded player for the Gophers and the Chicago Blackhawks, whom he played for five years. He also coached the US Olympic team to a silver medal at Cortina d'Ampezzo, Italy, in 1956. He was famous for championing Minnesota-born players and always built his teams around homegrown talent. He was inducted in the US Hockey Hall of Fame in 1973 and the National Hockey League (NHL) Hall of Fame in 1985.

Mayasich, John

John Mayasich was one of the most prolific scorers to ever play the game of hockey. As a Minnesota Gopher he won the Western Collegiate Hockey Association scoring title twice and was named All-American three years in a row. Mayasich played on six different US national and two US Olympic teams, winning Olympic silver in 1956 and Olympic gold in 1960. His eight appearances at international tournaments are more than any other US-born player. Mayasich was inducted into the US Hockey Hall of Fame in 1976.

Nagobads, George V. (Doc)

Doc Nagobads was the team doctor for the Minnesota Golden Gophers hockey team for thirty-four years and performed that same role for eight US Olympic teams and sixteen national teams, including the first-ever US women's team. He was inducted into the US Hockey Hall of Fame in 2010 and was awarded the Paul Loicq Award in 2010 for his outstanding contributions to International Ice Hockey Federation (IIHF) hockey.

Peters, Bob

After serving a mere two years as head coach at the University of North Dakota, Bob Peters stunned hockey insiders by moving across the border to Bemidji State University, an NCAA Division III program at the time. In his second season at BSU, he led the team to its first of thirteen national championship titles. In his thirty-five years as head coach of the Beavers, Peters became the first collegiate coach to win seven hundred games behind the bench with a single club and the only coach to lead his team to the Final Four in NCAA Division I, Division II, and Division III national championship tournaments. He was always a gracious host at Bemidji State when our national and Olympic hockey teams camped out there. He also helped co-found and run the Bemidji International Hockey Camp, one of the finest summer youth hockey schools in the world. In 2001 Peters was named a Hobey Baker Legend of Hockey.

Ridder, Bob

Bob Ridder was the founding president of the Minnesota Amateur Hockey Association (MAHA) in 1947. He also managed the 1952 and 1956 US Olympic hockey teams. Ridder was one of the original eight co-owners of the Minnesota North Stars and a prominent supporter of Olympic and international hockey. He was inducted into the US Hockey Hall of Fame in 1976 and the International Ice Hockey Federation (IIHF) Hall of Fame in 2010. The Kathleen C. and B. Ridder Scholarship is awarded annually to an outstanding student athlete who plays on the Minnesota Gophers women's hockey team.

Sonmor, Glen

Glen Sonmor was a fellow Canadian brought to the University of Minnesota by John Mariucci after suffering a fluke eye injury that ended his playing career. Ironically, he later replaced Mariucci as head coach of the Gophers, followed by a brief stint as skipper for the Minnesota Fighting Saints. He was also a talented scout, hard-nosed general manager, and legendary storyteller, enthralling radio audiences with countless anecdotes as an analyst for Gopher hockey. Sonmor was awarded the Lester Patrick Trophy for outstanding service to hockey in the United States in 2006.

Tarasov, Anatoly

Anatoly Tarasov is known as the father of Russian ice hockey. He established the Soviet Union as the dominant force in international hockey. He coached too many Soviet national teams to world championships and Olympic gold medals to mention here. He was also one of the first Russian nationals to be inducted into the Hockey Hall of Fame in Toronto, Canada.

Trumble, Hal

Hal Trumble first got involved in international hockey as a referee. He later went on to manage the 1972 US Olympic team that won the silver medal in Sapporo, Japan. Trumble was the first person to serve as executive director for USA Hockey in a full-time capacity, from 1972–87, increasing the number of registered teams from about 7,000 to over 11,500. He was inducted into the US Hockey Hall of Fame in 1985 and the International Ice Hockey Federation (IIHF) Hall of Fame in 1999.

Tutt, Thayer

Thayer Tutt was president of both the El Pomar Foundation and the Broadmoor Hotel in Colorado Springs. He was instrumental in organizing the first NCAA Hockey Tournament in 1948. He later served as chairman of the International Ice Hockey Federation (IIHF) from 1959-72. He was inducted into the US Hockey Hall of Fame in 1973.

FOREWORD

BY LOU NANNE

I'm excited and honored to write the foreword to Murray William-son's book, *The Road to Respectability*. Murray is one of the most influ-ential people in Minnesota hockey history. His accomplishments throughout the 1960s and '70s have left a lasting imprint on US ama-teur hockey.

Murray first came to Minnesota to play for the Gophers. From 1957 to 1959, he played under Coach John Mariucci at the U. He capped off his college career by winning All-American honors his senior year as well as being named the Gophers' MVP.

After a short stint with the Port Colborne Sailors in Ontario's top senior league, Murray came back home. From 1962 to 1966, he coached and managed the St. Paul Steers of the United States Hockey League, one of the top senior teams in the country. It's in that context I first met him. His passion for the game was evident immediately.

I graduated from the University of Minnesota in the spring of 1962. That fall, I joined the Steers' biggest opponent: the Rochester Mustangs. The Steers–Mustangs rivalry was as tough and intense as it gets, and we played some incredible games. A lot of the players knew each other. Some of us were former teammates. Once the puck dropped and the game began, however, none of that mattered. We fought to the final buzzer. Then we'd go across the street and have a drink at the Golden Steer.

In 1967, Murray and Walter Bush began putting together the ros-ter for the 1968 US Olympic team. They wanted me on the squad, but I wasn't a US citizen. Murray and Walter asked me if I was willing to become one, and I told them yes. That's when Murray got down to business. Working tirelessly with Representative John Blatnik, he helped push through an Act of Congress that granted me immediate citizenship and made me eligible to join the US Olympic team.

Playing for my country in the 1968 Olympics is an experience I'll always treasure. Nothing else quite compares. We finished sixth that year even though we were a very talented team. Murray spent the next three years refining the national team's training program, which included a trip to Moscow to see Tarasov's innovative dryland drills and grueling practices. Murray's plan must have worked, because he led the 1972 US Olympic team to the silver medal in Sapporo, Japan, second only to the perennially dominant Soviets.

In 1973, Murray turned his attention toward the US National Junior program. Not many people know the lasting impact he had on the US junior program and the United States Hockey League (USHL). Murray assembled and coached the first National Junior team and helped turn USHL into the country's top junior league. Today, the USHL is the major feeder program for US college and professional players. Without the dedication and efforts by Murray and Walter Bush, I'm not sure we'd even have that league.

To nobody's surprise, in 2001, Murray was named one of the fifty most significant players and coaches in Minnesota hockey history. He's one of the people who make Minnesota the State of Hockey.

The game is different now than it was when Murray was coaching half a century ago. These days, almost 30 percent of the NHL's roster spots are filled by American players. In January 2021, Team USA beat Canada 2–0 to win the IIHF World Junior Championship for the second time in five years. A big reason for both of those things is the strength of our developmental leagues.

In Murray's characteristically humble way, this book makes the case that he and his contemporaries put US hockey on "the road to respectability." Given everything we've accomplished in the past fifty years, I think we've done much better than that.

INTRODUCTION

Even the most casual sports fan who barely knows a thing about hockey knows the name *Herb Brooks*, coach of the 1980 US Olympic team that stunned the Soviets 4–3 in the so-called "Miracle on Ice."

More dedicated fans—especially those who cheered for the Minnesota North Stars back in the day or spend the first weekend in March watching the Minnesota State High School Hockey Tournament on TV—are familiar with Lou Nanne, Gophers hockey star, co-captain of the 1968 US Olympic team and one of only two defensemen in Western Collegiate Hockey Association (WCHA) history to win the league scoring title.

Ardent supporters who live in the State of Hockey or follow the Gopher men from wherever they are, know the team plays its home games at Mariucci Arena, named for the almost mythic Big Ten-star John Mariucci, equally well known for his punishing hits on the football field *and* the hockey rink. After a decade spent in the pros, including four seasons with the Chicago Blackhawks, the "Godfather of Minnesota Hockey" returned home to coach the Gophers hockey team for thirteen years and led the 1956 US Olympic team to a silver medal in Cortina d'Ampezzo, Italy.

Located right next door, Ridder Arena—the first facility built in the United States specifically for women's college hockey—is where the Gophers women's team played and it's named in honor of yet another distinguished leader and champion of the sport, Bob Ridder. He not only helped to organize and co-found the Minnesota Amateur Hockey Association (MAHA), he served as general manager of the 1952 and 1956 US Olympic men's teams and became one of eight original co-owners of the Minnesota North Stars franchise.

Going back a little further, Golden Gophers enthusiasts who've followed the team for years all know the name *Doug Woog*, South St. Paul High School star, NCAA All-American, member of the 1967 US national team, and head coach of his alma mater from 1985 to 1999.

Minnesota hockey fanatics who weren't even born until long after the man retired can tell you all about the legendary John Mayasich: three-time All-American, silver medalist and leading scorer for the 1956 US Olympic team, gold medal winner at the 1960 Olympics, and the number one all-time player in Minnesota high school hockey history, according to the *Star Tribune*.

Speaking of 1960 and the "Forgotten Miracle" gold medal win, don't forget the often overlooked, underappreciated Jack McCartan. He earned All-American honors in goal with the Gophers in 1959 ... only to top that off by earning an All-World distinction while helping to win the gold medal at the 1960 Olympics.

Not only are all of these men rightfully enshrined in the US Hockey Hall of Fame—along with hockey administrators Walter Bush, Tom Lockhart, Thayer Tutt, and Hal Trumble, and star players Henry Boucha, Keith "Huffer" Christiansen, John Cunniff, Mike "Lefty" Curran, Robbie Ftorek, Gary Gambucci, Mark Howe, Bob Paradise, Tim Sheehy, and Ken Yackel—they also share another equally important common bond. Each of them either played *with*, played *for*, or worked *in concert* with All-American forward, general manager, and coach Murray Williamson.

Or, in the rare case of Herb Brooks, all three.

Williamson would never claim to be anything other than Brooks's teammate, coach, friend, and colleague—much less a mentor figure. Herbie did everything his way, or he didn't do it at all. He was a student of the game but sure as hell no one's apprentice.

This book is not an attempt to give Williamson, or anyone else for that matter, an outsize role in the rise and rebirth of US amateur hockey in the two decades between the 1960 and 1980 gold medals. Those who might want yet another *story behind the story* that painstakingly reexamines how a bunch of college kids caught lightning in a bottle, dethroned the Soviet juggernaut, and shocked the world will surely be disappointed. There are entire library shelves purporting to tell that story. The world doesn't need one more.

This book turns over its fair share of rocks and digs below the surface to reveal plenty of lesser-known details and surprising anecdotes; but in the end, it's less about crushing checks, unbelievable passes, and game-winning goals than it is about enduring the trials and tribulations of building a championship program that brought home silver and gold.

The often-intertwined career paths of Brooks and Williamson began at the same place and time: playing together as Gophers freshmen under rookie coach Glen Sonmor. Brooks was fresh out of high school, still living at home with his parents, while Williamson had already been through the Canadian Junior A circuit and had enrolled the previous spring as a transfer student.

Despite their differences in life experience and nationality, they spent the next three years together in cold, cramped locker rooms, jammed together on the bench, trying to get some sleep on overnight busses and midnight trains, and swinging by the Blue Note in Chicago to see Count Basie.

After graduation, Brooks and Williamson soon found themselves as teammates again, playing for the St. Paul Steers; Williamson also served as general manager and coach. In 1967, Brooks was already on the roster of the US national team when Williamson was forced to relieve John Mariucci as coach and right the ship himself. Unsurprisingly, when Williamson went on to coach the 1968 US Olympic team, Brooks was on that roster too. As he was in 1970 and 1971.

In fact, the only national team coached by Williamson that *didn't* have Brooks on the roster was the 1972 US Olympic team, and Brooks only missed out on that because he was in the midst of becoming head coach for the Gophers. Even then, in what had clearly become a pattern of crossing and recrossing paths, Brooks and Williamson teamed up to protect the amateur status of players in the newly formed Midwest Junior Hockey League when the NCAA threatened to pull its support for college hockey entirely.

Much of the reason you may not know the details of some of these stories goes back to the beating heart of Williamson's philosophy: "It's amazing what you can do once you decide not to focus on who's going to get the credit." Even that pearl of wisdom, he attributes to his colleague and longtime friend Bob Fleming.

"It's amazing what you can do once you decide not to focus on who's going to get the credit."

Along with the other greats alluded to earlier, Murray Williamson was inducted into the US Hockey Hall of Fame—as well as three other separate hockey halls of fame—though you'd likely never hear it from the man himself. He'd rather talk about all the great players he coached on the notorious St. Paul Steers, a team so good it beat the Swedish national team, tied the Soviet B team, and went on to became the core nucleus of the US national team. Or maybe he'll tell you about the legends he skated with at Williams Arena as a freshman when the 1956 US Olympic team split its training time between Minneapolis and Duluth.

He can tell you all about his US national team's must-win gold medal game in Bucharest, Romania, in 1970, where any other result would have knocked the US team from Olympic contention, or the subsequent silver medal the US earned in Japan, or the time he spent talking hockey with renowned Soviet coach Anatoly Tarasov in the bleachers of Moscow's CSKA Ice Palace while the "Father of Russian Hockey" barked instructions to his players through a megaphone . . .

Lucky for you, the book you now hold in your hands tells all of those stories and more.

Drawn from personal journals, contemporaneous writings, and dozens of interviews, *The Road to Respectability* is more than a mere boilerplate recap of one coach's storied career. Williamson's time spent behind the bench with two US Olympic teams—as well as five other US national teams—gives rare, unfiltered access to many of US amateur hockey's key turning points and momentous decisions, not to mention a window on the numerous, largely unheralded men who shared a mutual passion for hockey and vision for excellence. Together, they painstakingly laid the foundation and built the systems that helped unseat one of the most formidable sports dynasties of the twentieth century.

Incredible? Absolutely. But not exactly a miracle.

This is the story of collective vision and passion, dedication, and seemingly endless grunt work. Without question, many others deserve their fair share of the credit too; and yet, one man's work can be found threading through it all. He's the last person to seek accolades, much less attention and praise, but he sure as hell got the job done.

For that, we are all grateful.

CHAPTER ONE

TRIALS AND TRIBULATIONS:
THE FIRST THREE DECADES OF US NATIONAL AND OLYMPIC TEAMS

Prior to 1952, an alphabet soup of governing bodies fought to control the process of selecting and managing the United States men's Olympic hockey team. The first US Olympic team was organized in 1920 by William Haddock, who was then-vice chairman of the ISHU (International Skating and Hockey Union).

Deemed an "all-star lineup" of the country's top amateur talent, the vast majority of players came from just three hockey clubs: the St. Paul Athletic Club, Pittsburgh Athletic Association, and Boston Athletic Association. Beyond North America, ice hockey was still in its infancy. As a result, the United States outscored their opponents by a whopping 52–2 margin, while the Canadians boasted a point differential of 31–1. Unfortunately, the Canadians also downed the United States by a score of 2–0 in the semifinal round on their way to winning the gold medal. The United States, of course, claimed silver.

After the first Olympics, the ISHU ceded control to the United States Amateur Hockey Association (USAHA) with the approval of the Amateur Athletic Union (AAU), which at the time controlled virtually every aspect of amateur sports in the United States. Throughout the 1930s and 40s, the Amateur Hockey Association of the United States (AHAUS, now known as USA Hockey) and the AAU continued to jockey for position and curry favor with the IOC (International Olympic Committee) and the USOC (United States Olympic Committee), not to mention the *Ligue Internationale de Hockey sur Glace* (LIHG), which organized, managed, and governed international ice hockey tournaments in non-Olympic years.

With no clear chain of command at the national level, everything came to a head in St. Moritz, Switzerland, at the 1948 Olympics, when two separate teams insisted they were the *true* US National team. One squad was led by then-IOC vice president Avery Brundage, a fierce, unapologetic defender of "sports for the sake of sports."

The other team, by contrast, had been organized and was led by second-generation entrepreneur Walter Brown. Like his father, George V. Brown, Walter saw organized sports as a money-making venture whether the athletes were deemed *amateurs* or *pros*. Walter had cut his teeth as coach of the Boston Olympics, a farm team for the Boston Bruins. He'd also founded the Ice Capades, owned the Boston Celtics, and managed Boston Garden.

Importantly, Brundage's team of "true amateurs" had been endorsed by the USOC and was sponsored by the AAU. Brandishing his team's recognition by those key organizations, Brundage discounted Brown's Olympic squad as a bunch of "shamateurs"—athletes who normally played for professional clubs but were conveniently granted amateur status within the international context. Nevertheless, Brown's Olympic team was sponsored by AHAUS and approved by the LIHG. With those two heavyweights on his side, Brown argued that Brundage and the Olympic committee "only cared about ice hockey once every four years."

With no clear resolution in sight, the IOC refused to certify either team and Brundage threatened to pull the entire US Olympic delegation. Finally, after twenty-four hours of rancorous negotiation, Brundage backed down—much to the relief of the Swiss organizing committee, since the gate receipts from ice hockey were projected to be the most profitable of all the Olympics' events. Walter Brown's team was allowed to play with the understanding they'd be barred from winning a medal. With a record of 5–3–0, they were not officially ranked in the Olympic tournament but officially finished fourth in the LIHG World Championship.

Three years later, in an ill-fated attempt to avoid similar controversy, US officials followed the well-established Canadian model and sent the winner of the 1950 US Senior Amateur Championship to the world tournament the following year. Thus, the Bates Manufacturing Hockey Club of Lewiston, Maine, represented the United States at the 1951 World Championships. They managed to beat Finland 5–4 and tie Great Britain 6–6 but went winless in their other four games, finishing tied for fifth place out of seven teams.

For the 1952 Olympics, the AAU and AHAUS finally came together, forming a selection committee chaired by Princeton athletic director Asa Bushnell. In the words of the *USA Hockey Results Book*, published in 1986, "This independent committee, completely outside the framework of either organization, was formed of four members from each group and was called the US Ice Hockey Committee."

Among the AHAUS delegates was Bob Ridder, one of the founding members of the MAHA and its president at the time. "The committee was given full power to organize and select a team to represent the United States in the '52 Olympics," states the *USA Hockey Results Book*, also noting they chose Bob Ridder to manage the team and John "Connie" Pleban to coach.

"Under the dynamic leadership of Ridder," the authors continue, "the team was successfully organized and financed." In fact, behind the scenes, Walter Brown had been working with Ridder for years to create a sustainable system for "successfully organizing and financing" a true national team. Slowly, their shared vision was starting to become a reality.

Slowly, their shared vision was starting to become a reality.

In fall 1951, in what would ultimately become common practice for most coaches and managers charged with organizing the US national team, tryouts were held in both Boston and Minneapolis. The final roster included eight players from Minnesota, six from

Massachusetts, and one from Rhode Island. The team then assembled in Boston on January 1 and managed to squeeze in thirteen exhibition games before they left for London on January 20. Overseas, "a number of pre-Olympic games were played in England, France, Switzerland, [West] Germany, and Belgium."

Once the Olympics began, the United States came out strong, beating Norway, Germany, Finland, and Switzerland by a combined score of 27–8. In fact, they posted their first and only loss in game five, falling to Sweden 4–2 in a tightly contested match. The United States rebounded quickly, however, notching a pair of decisive wins over Poland and Czechoslovakia. Heading into their final contest, the US team was still very much in contention for its first Olympic gold medal.

Unfortunately, despite a furious third-period comeback, the US skaters fell short, tying Canada 3–3 to leave them with a near-perfect record. "It looked at the start as though the Canadians were going to sweep to their eighth straight victory without a tie or defeat," said the Associated Press. "The champions were so aggressive American goalie Dick Desmond of Medford, Mass., had to make 21 [saves] while the Americans got only four shots at the enemy nets."

With a mark of 7–0–1, the Canadians finished with 15 points for the tournament, besting the second-place Americans, who finished at 6–1–1 for 13 points. "The United States Olympic team comes home with glory," said Minneapolis *Tribune* sports columnist Dick Cullum. "Although it had to settle for second place because of a previous defeat, it finished magnificently by tying the championship Canadian team in the last game."

Head coach Connie Pleban was also gratified by his team's effort. "I am more than satisfied with the results," he said. "The boys played great hockey; so did the Canadians. And I think our Dick Desmond proved to be the best goalie in the tournament."

Exhibition contests included, the US team's overall record was 14–8–5 versus the best teams in Europe. Needless to say, winning Olympic silver just four years after the St. Moritz debacle was a remarkable turnaround. There was still plenty of room for improvement, but

US hockey was on the rise and seemingly well positioned for future success.

In the non-Olympic year of 1953, only Sweden, Switzerland, and West Germany managed to muster national teams. Sweden won all four of its games—played in Basel and Zurich, Switzerland—for a decisive 4–0–0 sweep to claim the rather pitiful "world" championship title.

The United States also failed to muster a team for the 1954 World Championship in Stockholm, Sweden, when the Soviets made their debut, stunning Canada 7–2 in the series finale to win the gold medal. Unsurprisingly, the Canadians reacted to their shocking upset with a mixture of disbelief, anger, and embarrassment. It was also a wake-up call for the US hockey program.

Six months later, Walter Brown was officially named president of the LIHG, which also formally changed its name to the International Ice Hockey Federation (IIHF). In his two years away from international competition, Brown's perspective evolved. Ridder also shared much of his thinking. They knew European countries like Sweden and Czechoslovakia had been taking a more holistic view of their hockey programs since the end of World War II, building their national teams around players and coaches who stayed together for years. With the Soviets now in the mix, Brown and Ridder sensed the balance of power was shifting. If they, too, didn't focus on sustaining a long-term program, the United States might be doomed to perennial mediocrity. With the Olympics still two years away—and no committees or politics to stifle and slow things down—they knew it was time to act.

In a sly but ingenious move, rather than simply form a one-off squad to compete in the next world tournament, Brown and Ridder decided to recruit a core group of players to serve as the nucleus for 1955 and beyond. Many years after the fact, Ridder explained the surprisingly informal process. "Walter and I would get on the telephone and make all the decisions," he said. "It wasn't a problem. There wasn't anybody else."

In short order, the duo agreed to name former Boston Olympics player Al Yurkewicz as head coach and St. Paul Saints skipper Al Blatzheim as general manager. All four men then acted as their own selection committee, recruiting seven players from top amateur teams in the East and eight from the Midwest.

The Minnesota contingent included several area standouts who'd spent time in Walter Bush's newly formed United States Hockey League (USHL), home to the Rochester Mustangs, Minneapolis Bungalows, and Minneapolis Culbertsons—three of the best senior teams in the country. Among them were Wendell Richard "Wendy" Anderson, Gordon Christian, Richard Leo "Dick" Dougherty, John Matchefts, Dan McKinnon, and Richard Peter "Dick" Rodenhiser, all of whom carried over to the 1956 US Olympic team too. Rodenhiser went on to play for the 1960 gold medal team. Yurkewicz's two top picks turned out to be goalie Don Rigazio, from Cambridge, Massachusetts, and former Harvard Crimson captain Walt Greeley.

Whether by luck or design, insight or intuition, by the mid-1950s, Walter Brown and Bob Ridder had created a winning formula. For the next quarter century, virtually every US team that competed on the world stage would feature a core group of players and recent alumni from top collegiate programs throughout the East Coast and Upper Midwest, particularly those who'd played youth hockey in New England and Minnesota. Ironically, this blueprint would be discarded and rediscovered multiple times over the next two and a half decades before it was used to wondrous effect in 1980—when Herb Brooks used it to pull off a miracle.

> *Whether by luck or design, insight or intuition, by the mid-1950s, Walter Brown and Bob Ridder had created a winning formula.*

CHAPTER TWO

DON'T EXPECT ANY MIRACLES: MARIUCCI WINS SILVER AT THE 1956 WINTER OLYMPIC GAMES

In a brief but memorable scene from the movie *Miracle*, defenseman Jack O'Callahan and goalie Jim Craig stare at the preliminary roster for the 1980 US Olympic team on a bulletin board on the day of final cuts.

"How's it looking?" O'Callahan asks.

"Lotta guys from Minnesota and Boston," Craig responds.

"Yeah," O'Callahan quips, "that's gonna work."

Unsurprisingly, Hollywood's version of the East–West collegiate rivalry was amplified for effect, but the roots of this regional quarrel were deep and strong. It's no coincidence that the tryouts for US national and Olympic teams were most often held in Minneapolis and Boston. When an East Coast coach led the team, the majority of his players came from eastern teams, especially Boston College and Boston University. When a Midwesterner was in charge, the bulk of the players came from Minnesota. For decades, both regions felt they were woefully underrepresented and always seemed to get the short shrift.

Of course, as a Minnesota native and former Gopher, nobody knew more about the state's top hockey prospects than John Mariucci, then in his third year coaching at his alma mater. Mariucci and Ridder had met four years earlier, when Mariucci played for the St.

Paul Saints. On paper, the rough-hewn bruiser from the Iron Range and the Harvard-educated media mogul were complete opposites. Nonetheless, they bonded over their love for the game and drive to succeed. Even more importantly, each understood and respected the other's talents.

Back in his first year as a college coach, patrolling the Gophers bench in a smart double-breasted suit, bow tie, and fedora, Mariucci took the 13–13 team he'd inherited from Elwin "Doc" Romnes all the way to the NCAA National Tournament at the Broadmoor. Unfortunately, after a 3–2 win over the Rensselaer Polytechnic Institute (RPI) Engineers in the semifinal, Vic Heyliger's Wolverines easily outpaced the Gophers, thumping them 7–3 to win their third consecutive championship title.

Equally determined the following season, Minnesota reached the finals again, swamping Boston College by a score of 14–1 in the semifinal game. Two nights later, however, the high-flying Gophers crashed, falling to RPI in an overtime heartbreaker. With a 5–4 loss in the books, the Gophers settled for runner-up for the second year in a row. Nonetheless, Mariucci had quickly built a stellar reputation as a great recruiter with a keen eye for talent, who intuitively understood the fine art of motivation.

Mariucci also tended to fly by the seat of his pants. "Even as a sophomore, I ran practice half of the time," says Williamson. "Maroosh was either late or off on the luncheon circuit somewhere, running his Abbott and Costello routine with his buddy Johnny Kundla" (then-coach of the Minneapolis Lakers who went on to coach the Gophers).

Ridder, on the other hand, was the consummate professional: highly organized, detail-oriented, and thorough. He also appreciated the fundamental economics of financing a hockey team. Reflecting on how he raised money for Olympic and national teams, years later, Ridder said, "We made a deal to play the western colleges, sold the radio and television rights and made a lot of money. We played to standing-room only crowds in Duluth, Warroad, Grand Forks, Minneapolis, and St. Paul. Everybody gave us half the gate. It was wonderful. It had never happened before because nobody had ever organized it."

As a veteran manager of the 1952 US Olympic team, Bob Ridder was confident in his own ability to organize and manage the 1956 team. All he needed was a great coach. By spring 1954, Ridder was convinced Mariucci was the best NCAA coach in the country—and Maroosh had the hardware to prove it. After compiling an overall record of 23–6–0 his rookie season behind the bench, Mariucci won the Penrose Memorial Cup for college coach of the year. Doubling his win total to 46 the following year, Mariucci tallied nearly as many victories in two seasons as Doc Romnes had posted in his entire five years with the Gophers.

Ridder and Mariucci seemed to complement each other perfectly. There was just one small problem. In the words of Seamus O'Coughlin, author of *Squaw Valley Gold: American Hockey's Olympic Odyssey*, "Mariucci was not genteel enough for Eastern tastes."

O'Coughlin's assessment is an understatement. Before May 1952, when Mariucci became head coach for the Gophers, he was known for his brawn, not his brains. A gifted natural athlete, he'd been a two-sport star in high school, equally well-known for his punishing hits on the football field and the ice rink, despite not playing organized hockey until eleventh grade when he was cut from the basketball team.

After transferring to the University of Minnesota from Eveleth Junior College, Mariucci went on to earn All-Big Ten honors in football in 1939—playing offensive and defensive end under College Football Hall of Fame Coach Bernie Bierman—and All-American honors in hockey the following spring, leading the Gophers to a perfect 18–0 season.

Even after Mariucci guided the Gophers to the national title his senior year, Minnesota sportswriters were skeptical he could make the jump to the National Hockey League (NHL). "We were a little doubtful about Mariucci's chances of making the grade in professional hockey because of his attitude on the ice," explained *The Minneapolis Star* shortly after the college standout won a spot on the Chicago Blackhawks' roster. "At times, as a Gopher, he was pretty much a showoff." Even worse, the paper noted, "He also got a little rough."

"A little rough" in college, perhaps, but merciless in his role as an NHL enforcer. "Anybody who tried to intimidate us had to have some pretty big balls," recalled Chicago Blackhawks teammate Max Bentley, "because as soon as they went after us, they'd have to turn around and get ready for Big John, who'd come flying off the bench in a hurry. And there wasn't any doubt as to why he was coming, either, because he left his stick and gloves on the bench!" Thanks to Mariucci's fists of iron, the speedy but diminutive Bentley won the NHL scoring title in 1946 and again the following year.

In one legendary battle, Mariucci was already bleeding from an opponent's high stick to the face when he launched into an epic slugfest with Detroit's John "Black Jack" Stewart, considered by many to be the hardest-hitting player in the NHL at the time.

After a brief but furious skirmish on the ice, the two pugilists found themselves in a clench, tightly grasping each other's jerseys. Soon, the referees intervened, pried the pair apart, and escorted them to their respective penalty boxes as they traded unprintable insults. Moments later, the battle erupted again, prompting officials to scatter lest they find themselves on the receiving end of an errant blow.

"They started in the penalty box; then they were all over the damn place," recounted fellow Eveleth native John Karakas years later in *Squaw Valley Gold*. "In the stands. In the dressing room. Lasted 20 to 30 minutes." Others claim the battle raged for 45 minutes or more. Either way, the two combatants set the record for the longest fight in NHL history—a mark that still stands to this day—relentlessly trading blows as a crowd of 13,900 watched in amazement.

A social chameleon with a knack for knowing how to work a crowd, Mariucci loved to tell anyone who'd listen that his face had been cut over 150 times. "He looked like a blocked punt," quipped goalie Willard Ikola, who played for Mariucci at the 1956 Olympics.

"His face looked like it was used for target practice at the local ice rink," echoed Murray Williamson.

"Just looking at John's face probably helped inspire the rule requiring face masks in modern day youth hockey," added Herb Brooks.

"I didn't get this from playing hockey," Mariucci insisted, with a self-deprecating grin. "I was born this way."

As much as Mariucci embraced and even cultivated his image as an iron-jawed bruiser, however, his players saw a different side. Behind his almost cartoonish public *goombah* image was a proud college graduate who could speak four languages and loved art and history.

"Somewhere in Europe," remembered Jack McCartan, who played for Mariucci at Minnesota and on the US national team, "we were riding on the team bus and he was lecturing us on the history of the area, just like he was a teacher."

One hawkeyed sportswriter for the *Brooklyn Daily Eagle* profiled Mariucci's wit in a piece about the visiting Blackhawks. The year was 1941, Mariucci's rookie season.

"Literary light on the Hawk outfit is Johnny Mariucci," wrote Harold Parrott in the *Brooklyn Daily Eagle*. "He does the book reviews for the rest of the team, this big bruising defenseman, and he has steered them all off Hemingway's *For Whom the Bell Tolls*. 'Got sick of the hero being called Robert Jordan every minute,' he explains. 'It was never Bob, or Jordan. And if it was mentioned once that Robert Jordan wore rope-soled shoes, it was in there a hundred times. I just couldn't wade through the thing. It was dull.'"

Though Mariucci's critique may not have been deserving of space in the *New York Times Book Review*, he was much smarter than he often pretended to be. He saw the game differently from many of his contemporaries, especially those in the Western Intercollegiate Hockey League (WIHL).

"John never liked rough play," says Williamson, "and he absolutely *hated* taking dumb penalties." Mariucci prized speed, skill, and conditioning. Seven decades later, that may sound simplistic and trite, but at a time when "dump and chase" was the order of the day for North American teams at every level, it was pretty innovative, if not downright radical.

> "Skate hard both ways, play defense, and stay away from penalties," O'Coughlin writes in a brief summary of Mariucci's philosophy.

"Skate hard both ways, play defense, and stay away from penalties," O'Coughlin writes in a brief summary of Mariucci's philosophy. If it sounds familiar, it's also the same foundation on which future Olympic coaches Williamson and Brooks built their medal-winning teams.

"Everything starts with defense," echoes Williamson. "You can always find a few guys to bang the puck in the net, but if you don't have good defenders, none of it matters."

When John Mariucci was named coach of the 1956 US Olympic team, public outcry on the East Coast was fast and furious. Generally, those who protested cited two interrelated factors. First, after having spent nearly three hundred games behind the bench for Boston College, several area newspapers felt John "Snooks" Kelley deserved the job. Second, Mariucci had been an NCAA head coach for only three years. He needed to pay his dues.

Further, the rumor mill noted, Mariucci's name was presented at the December USOC meeting only to be voted down by the thirteen-member committee. Instead of coaching the US Olympic team, he would be sent to Duluth to lead the Western Selection Committee tryouts. He would still have a role, but he was out of the running as coach.

Under consideration were Vic Heyliger of Michigan, Eddie Jeremiah of Dartmouth, Wes Moulton of Brown, Connie Pleban of the Minnesota-Duluth branch, and Snooks Kelley, who'd been a college hockey coach since 1932. By the next USOC meeting on January 15, however, Jeremiah and Moulton had withdrawn their names and Kelley was considered a lock.

Meanwhile, unknown to the eastern contingent of the USOC, Pleban also withdrew his name and agreed to swap places with Mariucci. Now, Pleban would head the Western Selection Committee while Mariucci joined Heyliger and Kelley as a coaching candidate.

"The contention of the objectors," wrote the *Boston Globe* at the time, declining to name a source, ". . . was that certain members of the Olympic Committee had acted illegally to railroad the Minnesota mentor into the job."

The former NHL defenseman and Gopher coach for the past three years "is a personable, humorous character with a reputation for coaching clean, effective college hockey," the *Boston Globe* conceded, "but some Eastern members of the committee are resentful of manipulations which now find the United States Olympic hockey team with both a coach and manager from Minnesota and with the final selection site for the squad at Duluth, Minn., next winter."

Kelley, for his part, was gracious, swiftly tamping down the budding controversy. "I'm honestly delighted with their choice," he told Boston press the day of the public announcement. "My feelings, my heart rest with my BC team. I don't want to leave them for a second, let alone the two months required by the Olympic games."

In Mariucci's home state, the reaction was very different.

"Indications are that Gopher players will carry the big load," wrote Minneapolis *Tribune* sports columnist Sid Hartman. "Mariucci's great Minnesota line of Gene Campbell, Dick Dougherty, and John Mayasich may be reunited when practice starts in Duluth Dec. 15," mused Hartman giddily, inadvertently highlighting the East Coast faction's charges of favoritism. "Other former Gophers are also candidates, if the makeup of the present US team now touring Europe is any indication," Hartman concluded.

Over in West Germany's Ruhr valley, Brown and Ridder's plan was unfolding beautifully. The United States finished fourth at the 1955 World Championship with a record of 4–2–2. Meanwhile, Canada got their revenge over the Soviet Union, shutting them out 5–0 to win the gold medal. The Soviets won silver, and Czechoslovakia took the bronze, finishing one point higher than the Americans despite a 4–4 tie in their head-to-head matchup. Future Olympian Dick Dougherty emerged as the second leading scorer while Don Rigazio was named the tournament's top goalie.

By November 1, in accordance with Brown and Ridder's plan, a core group of players had gathered to practice at Williams Arena. Among them were Minnesotans John Mayasich and his former Gopher linemates—exactly as Hartman predicted—as well as Eveleth natives and former Michigan Wolverines John Matchefts and Willard Ikola. Representing the East were Harvard captain Bill Cleary, who'd won the NCAA scoring title his senior season, and goalie Don Rigazio.

Looking back on his freshman year, Murray Williamson remembers seeing some of the Olympians practice. Occasionally, the Olympic hopefuls even scrimmaged the Gophers or all of them practiced together.

Williamson was impressed by the Olympians' speed and their individual skills. Beyond that, he was captivated by the way they played the game. "Watching them on attack, breaking into the offensive zone, everything I'd learned up in Canada during juniors seemed so primitive. It was all zones and lanes and staying in your position no matter what. If you were one of the wings and roamed more than ten feet away from your side boards, there'd be hell to pay. Do it again, you're benched. Skate like hell and back-check, but most of all, skate your lane."

Mayasich, in particular, was fluid and intuitive, creating time and space for himself and his wings. "What set him apart was that he was the smartest hockey player I've been around," Herb Brooks told *Sports Illustrated* in 1999. "He was subtle, like a great chess master, and he made players around him better. It was like he saw the game in slow motion." It was still a far cry from the interweaving Soviet style that Brooks himself later adapted, but these were the inklings of a new style.

> "He was subtle, like a great chess master, and he made players around him better. It was like he saw the game in slow motion."

Technically, the 1956 US Olympic team held open tryouts in both Boston and Minnesota, but much of the roster was set well before those tryouts. Mariucci admitted as much before the first cuts were made. "It's an easy job to pick the first twelve," he told the Minneapolis *Star*, "but the big problem is the next five. We have fifteen guys who could fill the bill for the last five."

In the end, Mariucci rostered nine players from his home state—including three from his hometown—six from Massachusetts, one from Michigan, and one from North Dakota. Unsurprisingly, when Bob Ridder announced the Minnesota-heavy roster shortly before Christmas break, the Boston press erupted again, villainizing the Gophers coach for his regional bias.

A few days before the team left for Italy, the Olympians did their best to silence the critics for good. In an exhibition that took the form of three separate periods against three separate opponents in a single session, the Olympic team drubbed Boston College 8–0 and Northeastern 9–1 before easing up on Harvard for a 1–0 victory.

Whatever sportswriter John Ahern might have thought before the game, the lopsided result left him spellbound. Describing the US team in the *Boston Globe*, he wrote, "It has nearly everything any amateur hockey team needs. It has wonderful skaters, wonderful stick handlers, wonderful scorers. It is extremely strong up the middle. It is extremely strong in-goal. It is well coached, well-conditioned." Only one question remained: "Can it win the Olympics?"

Quoted further down in the same article, Snooks Kelley described the players in glowing terms but perhaps avoided complimenting Mariucci. "They're all Fancy Dans," he said. "They play positions perfectly, and they're in wonderful condition. People are waiting to see what happens when hard-checking defensemen get at them. I say no one will get a good piece of these kids. That's the way they play. They're excellent."

Mariucci was quick to tamp down expectations and keep his players grounded. He reminded everyone that the Canadians were still the odds-on favorite, with the Soviets and Czechs close behind. "We have a good squad," he conceded, "one of the best that has ever represented America, but I'm told by the experts not to expect any miracles."

Undefeated in fifteen US exhibitions, with six more wins abroad, Mariucci remained worried about his team's chances when they arrived in Cortina d'Ampezzo, Italy. He called the wins against European competitors "empty victories" because the teams weren't very good. Previously, he'd said that "spirit and determination" were his players' biggest assets, "but now we're even failing to hustle." Of course, he may have been playing mind games with his top two forwards—as Brooks sometimes would in the future—but he made it clear to the press that he was displeased with everyone's performance other than the third line.

Once the tournament started, the United States dropped a tight game to Czechoslovakia 4–3 but came roaring back 4–0 against Poland to advance to the medal round. There, the team took care of business against West Germany 7–2, then pulled off the biggest upset in team history with a decisive 4–1 win over Canada.

"I watched that game with Glen Sonmor," Murray Williamson says. "We were Canadians and wanted to watch it together. Both of us had mixed feelings. National pride, I suppose, but we wanted Maroosh to win too. We were cheering for both teams. Of course, it was pretty special to watch your coach win a game like that."

Up on the Iron Range, people were practically shouting from the rooftops. "It's the biggest thing to hit Eveleth since the discovery of iron ore!" said one unnamed resident.

> Up on the Iron Range, people were practically shouting from the rooftops. "It's the biggest thing to hit Eveleth since the discovery of iron ore!"

"John Mayasich of Eveleth, Minn., pulled the 'hat trick' to fire the American victory—which must rank as one of the greatest upsets ever in Olympic hockey," wrote the *Jacksonville Daily Journal* from Cortina.

"Eveleth finally is getting world-wide recognition as the cradle of American hockey," said a jubilant Cliff Thompson, who'd coached both John Mayasich *and* John Mariucci in his legendary career.

"Canada was an overwhelming favorite to capture its seventh Olympic hockey championship," the Associated Press noted, "but its hopes sagged badly with the American victory." With losses to both the United States and USSR, Canada was forced to settle for bronze, their lowest finish at an international tournament to date.

The United States went on to thump Sweden 6–1 and beat Czechoslovakia 9–4 in a shocking upset, posting nearly double digits against one of the world's toughest defenses. Arguably, that victory was more impressive than their win over Canada. Between these two victories, however, the younger, less experienced Americans faced the powerhouse Soviets. On the score sheet, they lost 4–0, but the American players agree the outcome was never in doubt.

"Most of those guys were in their upper twenties, some guys in their early thirties," said goalie Willard Ikola decades after the game, still wowed by the Soviet squad. "They were the so-called Red Army team, because all of them were in the service, and their primary job was to play hockey, so they were well-drilled."

"We thought they'd be like the Germans or the Swedes, but we were stymied," echoed Dick Dougherty in *USA Hockey Magazine* years later. "We'd never seen anything like that before in North America."

"To this day, I can draw on a board exactly what they did to score their first goal," John Matchefts said. "It's amazing how clever they were. They just passed and passed and passed, then tipped the puck in. That was the game, right there."

"They can outpass anything in the National Hockey League," Mariucci told reporters after losing to the Soviets. "It's their legs and instincts that get the job done . . . You never saw such fierce interest in condition. The morning after they won the Olympics, the Russians were out on the ice, practicing . . . The only thing they lack right now is ingenuity. Sometimes they can't seem to come up with that finishing punch. But give them time, they'll get it."

When asked why the Americans don't simply copy the Russian style, Mariucci said, "Our boys just wouldn't spend the time 10 months a year, 14 hours a day, to perfect that style. Hockey isn't 99 percent of our life here, and our kids won't make the sacrifices needed to develop that technique. Give our boys a stick and a puck, and they want to do two things most: Shoot the puck and knock someone down."

Home in the United States two weeks later, Maroosh described his team's unexpected silver medal performance with one of his classic one-liners. "Everybody played as well as they possibly could," he said, "and some played even better."

Bob Ridder, by contrast, gave the lion's share of credit to his controversial coach. "They didn't think he could represent the United

States properly," he said, "which shows they didn't understand [John] at all."

In the Hollywood version of the United States' unlikely gold medal win in 1980, Herb Brooks hands his assistant coach Craig Patrick a list of names. Surprised, Patrick responds, "You're missing some of the best players." Barely glancing up from the piles of paperwork scattered all over the table, Brooks says, "I'm not looking for the best players, Craig; I'm looking for the right ones."

The US national team would continue its wondrous ascent from silver in 1956 to gold in 1960 before floundering for over a decade. In a politically charged environment imbued with infighting and favoritism, a parade of managers and coaches would wipe the slate clean and start from scratch, only to learn the same lessons over and over again.

CHAPTER THREE

A BARBER'S SON WITH A DREAM: WINNIPEG YOUTH STANDOUT AND MONTRÉAL CANADIENS PROSPECT

Like most kids in his neighborhood, from the very moment he'd first laced up a pair of skates to play shinny with his friends, Murray Williamson had dreamt of wearing *le chandail bleu, blanc, rouge* of the Montréal Canadiens. Whatever it took, however he got there, he wanted nothing more than to wear the same iconic sweater donned by hockey legends like Howie Morenz, Jacques Plante, Joseph Bernard "Boom Boom" Geoffrion, and Maurice "Rocket" Richard.

Unlike the vast majority of kids on youth hockey teams across Canada, however, for almost three solid years, Williamson was on pace to achieve his lifelong dream. In fact, when he was just fifteen, Williamson was recruited and signed by Montréal scout Lawrence "Spud" Russell to play for the St. Boniface Canadiens, arguably the crown jewel in a vast network of junior and juvenile teams sponsored by Montréal throughout Western Canada.

Notably, prior to the first NHL amateur draft in 1963, there was no official system for signing amateur players and legally securing their rights. Instead, each of the Original Six relied on an ad hoc system of subsidy agreements, which gave the sponsoring NHL team rights to all of its players, even if this "sponsorship" consisted of little more than a pile of brand-new jerseys, an armload of sticks, and a bucket of pucks.

Despite Montréal's remarkable success with the sponsorship system later, the Toronto Maple Leafs were actually the first to conceive and perfect it in the first place. It was acting general manager Frank Selke who devised and rolled out the system while Maple Leafs General Manager Conn Smythe—one of the team's first owners and its foremost founding father—was away in Europe, commanding an antiaircraft battalion for the Royal Canadian Artillery during World War II.

With Smythe conspicuously absent for the first half of the 1940s, the Leafs began to sponsor and even purchase an array of junior teams throughout the country. It wasn't simply a madcap buying spree. It was the opposite, in fact. Relying on a battalion of professional scouts, local tipsters, and notorious rink rats, Selke and his team of bird dogs beat the bushes to track down the most promising prospects and make sure they got onto a Maple Leaf affiliate team. As Selke later recalled in his autobiography, *Behind the Cheering*, "Before the other NHL clubs caught on, we had signed most of the good lads in Canada."

By the time WWII ended, Selke's popularity within the Maple Leafs organization was at an all-time high. In fact, many of the team's directors wanted Selke to stay in the GM role even after Smythe had returned from Europe. Meanwhile, Smythe had found himself in the midst of a bitter power struggle over the presidency of Maple Leaf Gardens Ltd., the holding company that owned both the arena and the NHL team who competed there. When Selke publicly waffled and failed to support Smythe's bid to run the parent organization, the friction between them sparked into an all-out conflagration, burning both their working relationship and longtime friendship to the ground.

In May 1946, Frank Selke resigned from the Toronto Maple Leafs, definitively ending his tenure with the team he'd helped manage for the previous seventeen years. Two months later, however, he was hired by Montréal, becoming GM for the team that had just won two Stanley Cups in the preceding three seasons. Selke quickly replicated the sponsorship system he'd devised in Toronto, striking deals with teams from Saskatchewan to Manitoba, soon creating one of the most extensive feeder systems in all of professional sports.

Certainly, Selke fed the egos and pumped the players in every region where the Canadiens had a presence; but at the same time, he seemed to have a particular passion for Winnipeg's junior teams. In the December 14, 1946, issue of the *Winnipeg Tribune*, for example, Selke announced he'd be happy to send one of his junior teams to play in Winnipeg if local fans and players wanted to see how their boys might fare against one of the top junior teams in the whole country. In what must have been a bit of good-natured flexing, Selke even suggested it didn't matter to him whether he sent his undefeated, all French-Canadian Nationales or his runner-up junior Canadiens.

In the very same issue, Selke announced that well-known local coach Russell "Spud" Murray—in the midst of a season with the juvenile Winnipeg Monarchs at the time—had accepted the position of scout with the Canadiens for the Winnipeg region. The message from Selke was clear: if you want to skate with the best, you need to be part of the Canadiens system.

Ironically, the recruiting Selke had done for his previous NHL club in recent years had been far too successful. The sponsorship system he'd used with the Toronto Maple Leafs had yielded a core team of players that went on to power the Leafs to four Stanley Cups in five years, between 1945 and 1949.

The message from Selke was clear: if you want to skate with the best, you need to be part of the Canadiens system.

Stanley Cup wins notwithstanding, Selke and Russell publicly extolled both the virtues of playing within the Montréal farm system and the ever-increasing opportunities to play hockey professionally.

"There is a great future for any boy who wants to make a career out of hockey," Russell told Saskatchewan's Regina *Leader-Post* in December 1949. "With the game expanding all the time, especially in the United States, it's impossible to meet the demand for new players... Take our own Montréal setup. We've got to find players for our many pro farm teams and the senior Royals. Replacements are needed, too, for the parent Canadiens who are gradually becoming a bunch of old men. Let me tell you, it's tough getting enough good puckmen to go around."

No wonder youth hockey standout Murray Williamson had leapt at the chance to sign on the dotted line and join the St. Boniface Canadiens when recruiter Spud Russell came calling earlier that year. Undoubtedly, Williamson saw himself as part of the youth movement that was about to conquer the ranks of professional hockey at every level.

> *Williamson was the definition of that tireless, passionate kid who "eats, breathes, and sleeps hockey."*

Plucked straight from the roster of a bantam team in south Winnipeg before he'd even turned sixteen, Williamson was the definition of that tireless, passionate kid who "eats, breathes, and sleeps hockey." To say that he *worked hard* is a gross understatement. Over the next three seasons, whenever Williamson wasn't playing or practicing with his official team, he played shinny hockey on the outdoor rink at the Lord Roberts Community Centre—in reality, two decommissioned Candian National Railway boxcars cobbled together into a makeshift warming house—and, incredibly, even found time to lead the Riverview bantam A team to a city championship.

Decades after the fact, when asked how he found the time to coach a bunch of teenagers nearly as old as he was, Williamson responds with his typical deadpan wit: "In those days, it's not like there was a bunch of guys lined up outside the door, champing at the bit to coach youth hockey. It might be a big deal now, but back then, nobody wanted the job." Maybe so, and yet it seems likely that Williamson was already starting to hone his natural ability to recruit and motivate players, even if he didn't understand that yet himself.

By the middle of the 1952–53 season, young Murray Williamson had every reason to keep buying what Selke and Russell were selling. Since signing with Montréal and joining their feeder system, Williamson had moved from the juvenile squad to the junior A team right on schedule, without so much as a hitch. From his own perspective, he was truly "living the dream." He belonged to an NHL franchise, with all the prestige that entailed, and knew he looked damn good in his leather team jacket emblazoned with the iconic Canadiens insignia.

Unfortunately, that season in particular, the St. Boniface roster was stacked, built around Ab McDonald, who went on to join the NHL in 1958 and proceeded to win four straight Stanley Cups: three with Montréal and a fourth with the Chicago Blackhawks. Unbeknownst to Williamson, as the four-team Manitoba Junior Hockey League (MJHL) headed toward the playoffs, higher-ups within the Montréal organization judged him to be too small to fit their long-range plans. With a postseason showdown looming between St. Boniface and their archrival, the Monarchs, Williamson was dangled as "trade bait" to any Winnipeg junior team that stepped up with a decent offer.

For those who follow hockey closely, it's an all too familiar refrain: *playoff hockey is different.* Throughout the regular season, smaller, faster players can get the job done, leading their team to the top of the standings with finesse and agility. Once the postseason hits, however, a different brand of hockey emerges. The games get more physical, rougher and harder hitting. Raw talent and skill don't necessarily hold the same advantages they did earlier in the season. Suddenly, hockey seems all about big bodies colliding in spectacular fashion, literally fighting for puck possession as though the game were a street brawl. This time of year, as they say, you don't get points for style. It's an all-out battle, and a team's postseason success often depends on its size and ability to knock people down.

With a height of five feet, seven inches and a weight of 165 pounds, Murray Williamson was deemed too much of a hindrance to get a spot on the Canadiens playoff roster. Shortly after Christmas, with no viable trade in the works, Williamson was loaned to the last-place Winnipeg Barons for the remainder of the season.

He was crushed. Even worse, when the Barons predictably failed to advance past the Brandon Wheat Kings in the first round of the playoffs, Williamson found himself alone in the stands at his home arena, watching his teammates demolish the Wheat Kings in four straight games to win their first ever Turnbull Cup. Having already swept the once-feared Winnipeg Monarchs by the same 4–0 margin in the semifinals, the local hockey press buzzed, wondering just how far the undefeated "St. Boniface Six" might ultimately go.

Soon, there was even more reason for Winnipeg hockey fans to think the sky was the limit. In the Abbott Cup semifinals, the Canadiens Junior A squad from the Manitoba league handily defeated their namesake from Fort William, notching four more wins against their only postseason loss. Disillusioned and deflated, Williamson struggled to enjoy the ride. Even as the wins piled higher and St. Boniface steadily marched toward the Memorial Cup—the Holy Grail of Canadian Junior A hockey—Williamson's once-coveted Canadiens team jacket hung disused in the closet.

Deep down, Williamson knew it was time to start reassessing his hockey career and seriously consider getting an education. His father, who worked as a barber, had been after him for years to keep up with his schooling and think about his future after he finally hung up his skates. With the Barons long out of the playoffs and no meaningful way to contribute to the success of his Canadiens squad, Williamson had plenty of free time to sit and work out a plan.

Meanwhile, St. Boniface went on to win their next playoff series, too, downing the Lethbridge Native Sons by a mark of 4–2–1 in seven games. They'd won the Abbott Cup and the right to represent Western Canada in the National Junior A Championship. Ultimately, the St. Boniface Canadiens ran out of steam and fell well short in their bid to win the Memorial Cup. They dropped three of the four games that were played in Winnipeg to the visiting Barrie Flyers, as well as one game played in Brandon.

St. Boniface had entered the final round of the tournament playing well and riding high but only managed to win the first game of the series. They were overmatched from the start and never quite found their rhythm. Even so, the team is remembered fondly and enshrined in the Manitoba Hockey Hall of Fame. Small consolation, no doubt, for Murray Williamson. His name is listed with his St. Boniface teammates, but most of them actually played for the coveted Memorial Cup.

Never one to bemoan his fate or fixate on things beyond his control, Williamson knew one thing for certain: he didn't want to be a barber. Nor did he want to be a manual laborer or a truck driver for a local brewery like so many of his neighborhood friends. Somehow, he'd make it work. He'd play hockey as long as he could while taking pains to make sure he'd have a decent career when his playing days were over.

Williamson ended up back on the St. Boniface roster for the 1953–54 season, and the idea of not playing junior hockey was inconceivable. Sure, he knew he should probably think about college someday, but there was still plenty of time for that. Sometimes dreams die hard, and though he'd been devastated to not take part in his team's magical playoff run, somehow he wasn't bitter. In fact, he was ecstatic to be back in the Canadiens system.

Throughout the first half of the season, Williamson's passion showed, especially on the scoreboard, where he averaged one point per game. He'd never been the top dog, but with double-digit goals and assists by early December, he was reliably productive and a tenacious two-way player who was exciting to watch.

As the whole team was hitting its stride on the way to a stunning regular season mark of 31–3–2, St. Boniface headed south to play a two-game weekend series against the University of Minnesota Golden Gophers, the team who'd finished second only to Michigan in the NCAA Division I Championship the previous season. With two great second-place teams in their respective leagues on a collision course, pundits and fans alike had sky-high expectations.

Without question, the teams delivered.

In what turned out to be the peak experience of Williamson's Junior A tenure—if not his entire playing career—St. Boniface swept the Gophers, dropping them by scores of 5–4 and 6–3. More importantly, perhaps, Williamson was enthralled by the big-time atmosphere, knowledgeable fan base, and incredible hockey program. Decades after the fact, Williamson still fondly recalls his immediate thought the first time he stepped onto the ice at Williams Arena: *My God, you could put a lot of hay in this barn.*

Rather than hay, however, more than 4,800 fans packed the stands for Friday night's game, with 5,136 taking in the Saturday session. The building was electric, and the hockey was as good as it gets. Williamson left impressed with head coach John Mariucci as well as star players Ken Yackel, Wendy Anderson, and John Mayasich, who went on to win two Western League scoring titles in 1954 and 1955 while simultaneously collecting All-American honors three years in a row.

> *Williamson still fondly recalls his immediate thought the first time he stepped onto the ice at Williams Arena: My God, you could put a lot of hay in this barn.*

As for Mariucci's impression of the boys from north of the border, he had nothing but good things to say. "We want to play them every year," he told the *Star Tribune* after the series. "St. Boniface has the best junior hockey team I have ever seen."

On the long bus ride home, with sights and sounds from the games replaying over and over in his head, a seed was planted somewhere in Murray Williamson's mind. As his father repeatedly noted, there were several Winnipeg players—some of whom grew up right in their neighborhood—who'd received full scholarships from big-name universities in the United States. These young men were able to play the sport they loved while getting an education and building for their future. Perhaps it was time to admit (if only to himself) that his father's words made a lot of sense. Hockey versus hitting the books . . . Maybe he could do both.

Less than two months later, the St. Boniface top brass gave Williamson the jolt of inspiration he needed. With the Canadiens riding high and cruising their way to a second consecutive MJHL championship, the indefatigable winder was officially traded to the ill-fated Winnipeg Barons for three unspecified midget players.

Williamson likes to joke that he was swapped for "two broken sticks, a barrel of used pucks, and half a case of beer." Either way, as in the previous season, he found himself sitting alone in the stands, half-heartedly cheering his former teammates once the playoffs began. This year, however, they only managed three wins in eight postseason games. Clearly, the ride was over for St. Boniface and the kid who'd dreamt of playing at the Montréal Forum.

In his second stint with the Winnipeg Barons, Williamson played briefly with a winger named Bill Reichert. The two only skated together for a handful of practices and games because Reichert had just accepted a scholarship offer from the University of North Dakota and soon left for Grand Forks. Notably, Reichert had been one of Winnipeg's best junior players, racking up eleven goals and thirteen assists in twenty-three games before pulling the plug on his season with the Barons. With the Winnipeg Blackhawks the year before, Reichert had tallied an even more impressive twenty goals and twenty assists on his way to being named a Second Team MJHL All-Star. Most intriguingly, Reichert was also five feet, seven inches tall: another compact, speedy forward in the mold of Williamson himself.

Though Williamson was then unfamiliar with the University of North Dakota, Reichert had been impressed when the Barons played there. Everything seemed to be pointing in the same direction. Some of Williamson's other friends had recently accepted college hockey scholarships. Next year, a pair of them would be playing for Michigan State in East Lansing. Two others were set to attend the University of Michigan in Ann Arbor.

With only so many prospects to choose from, virtually every Junior A player who got his name in the paper received the occasional phone call from a so-called "scout" or "assistant coach" from a D1 college. Much of the time, these calls were actually made by freshman players trying to get on the coach's good side or even the occasional booster who fancied himself a vital part of the management team. Either way, it was little more than hot air—a no-cost way to promote the school and maybe cash in on a long shot.

With his team atop the standings and his name frequently on the scoresheet, Williamson was fielding a steady stream of calls. Maybe it was time to start paying attention to what some of these "coaches" actually had to say.

The more Williamson thought about it, the more Vic Heyliger's powerhouse Wolverines seemed like the perfect fit. After winning their first NCAA National Championship in 1948, the Wolverines had added a string of three consecutive national titles between 1951 and 1953. Heyliger's rosters were packed with Canadian hockey players, including some Junior A standouts Williamson knew by name. The next time the Wolverines called, Murray was going to listen.

The days got longer and warmer, neighborhood parks turned green, and thoughts of hockey melted away. Williamson hung up his skates and dug out his baseball glove. He'd listened patiently to numerous vague overtures, but none of them had panned out. That's when he caught wind of an opportunity that piqued his interest.

A promoter from Duluth by the name of Len Naymark was trying to organize a Senior A hockey team to play in the newly formed Thunder Bay–Arrowhead League. Two core teams played out of Thunder Bay: the Port Arthur Bearcats and the Fort William Beavers. The third Canadian team, the Fort Frances Canadians, was about four hours west, on the Minnesota–Ontario border. The two American teams—the Hibbing Flyers and Naymark's newly christened Eveleth–Virginia Rangers—were located in the heart of Minnesota's Mesabi Iron Range, historically one of the state's most prolific hockey hotbeds.

Like most of the other teams, Naymark was trying to build his roster around a line of good Junior A players who'd recently aged out of the system. He'd supplement them with veterans who'd played semipro and still had something left in the tank. To sweeten the deal for his younger prospects, Naymark offered full tuition at Eveleth Junior College, a stipend to cover expenses, and so-called "money for books"—thinly veiled code for "spending money."

It was exactly the kind of deal Williamson was after. With a full-blown fifty-game schedule and all of the teams within a half-day's bus ride, it was hard to pass up.

Williamson packed his bags for Eveleth. As for any complications regarding NCAA eligibility rules, insiders assured the young skater that if he went to Michigan, Vic Heyliger could fix anything. Meanwhile, Williamson would gain great experience competing with other young standouts and wily veterans who'd been around the block a time or two already.

Before the season even began, Williamson was forced to start growing up quickly. Few of his teammates went to school or seemed to care about much of anything other than hockey. When they weren't at the rink, they just bummed around, shooting pool and drinking beer.

Before long, Murray befriended Elio Gambucci, a local shopkeeper with his finger on the pulse of pretty much everything that happened anywhere on the Iron Range. He also happened to be older brother to Andre Gambucci, one of Murray's Ranger teammates and a hockey old-timer. A few short months later, Papa Gambucci's friendship would prove invaluable. In the beginning, though, Elio mainly gave the kid somebody to talk to and a reason to stay out of trouble.

When the hockey season finally began, people turned out in droves. Attendance exceeded three thousand for two separate Rangers contests, with one game played in Virginia topping out at thirty-five hundred. Local fans and boosters were buzzing, optimistic about their team's future and the new senior league. As the Rangers stumbled to start the season, however—slogging their way through a stretch of nine losses in their first thirteen games—enthusiasm rapidly waned. In a matter of weeks, average sales dropped to about five hundred tickets per game, nowhere near enough to keep the team afloat.

Naymark frantically published unabashed pleas for Canadian reinforcements in newspapers throughout southern Manitoba and Minnesota's Arrowhead region. Even more dramatically, he parted ways with Rangers coach and local celebrity Connie Pleban. As a former star player at Eveleth High School and Eveleth Junior College, Pleban was well known and well liked across the Iron Range. He'd garnered international attention as the coach of the US national team that won the silver medal at the 1950 Ice Hockey World Championships in London, England, and a second silver at the 1952 Olympics in

Oslo, Norway.

Though many fans were outraged by Naymark's sudden ouster of their hometown hero, Canadian player-coach Albert "App" Dorohoy managed to briefly right the ship. Dorohoy—a veteran player who'd recently spent two years with the Medicine Hat Tigers of the Western Canada Junior Hockey League—led the Rangers to a stellar mark of nine wins and two losses in the early weeks of December, including a six-game win streak.

Even so, with the league's Canadian teams well ahead in standings and frequently mopping the floor with their US rivals, the Rangers never rose higher than third place. Increasingly bored and frustrated by games that seemed to follow the same old tired script, home game attendance fell off a cliff. One Sunday afternoon, after the Rangers had been whipped 10–0 by league-leading Fort William the night before, a paltry seventy-eight fans paid to see the follow-up matinee against second-place Port Arthur.

Fans surely knew they'd be treated to a rough, entertaining brand of hockey; but with a virtually guaranteed chance they'd see yet another loss, it simply wasn't worth it. Even up on the Iron Range, where hockey and life are inextricably intertwined, there were better places to be and better things to do.

A dyed-in-the-wool promoter like Lenny Naymark wasn't prepared to carry a team that was losing money. Neither was Frank Riggio, owner of the Hibbing Flyers. Shortly after Christmas, with his team down 7–2 against the visiting Rangers, Riggio got on the mic during the second intermission to announce his team was withdrawing from the Thunder Bay–Arrowhead League. This would be Hibbing's final game. Each team added a goal in the anemic final frame; the Rangers won 8–2; and that was that.

> The Rangers players were stranded with no income and nowhere to go.

Before league officials could even decide how to reshuffle the schedule, Naymark told the local papers his team was folding too. In less than a week, the league went from five teams to three, with all remaining teams stationed north of the border. In a flash, the international Senior A league that had begun with such fanfare a few short months ago was decimated. The Rangers players were stranded with no income and nowhere to go.

Earlier that fall, Williamson had sincerely believed he'd made the right decision—instead, he'd hit a dead end. Thankfully, in the few short months he'd been there, Williamson had befriended Elio Gambucci, and Elio Gambucci knew *everyone* . . . including the "Godfather of Minnesota Hockey," who'd been born and raised right there in Eveleth.

CHAPTER FOUR

WILLIAMSON MEETS MARIUCCI IN AN EVELETH POOL HALL

The first widely publicized ice hockey game in Minnesota was played in 1895, when the University of Minnesota hosted the Winnipeg Victorias at Athletic Park in Minneapolis. By 1903, hockey teams in Eveleth were playing on an enclosed sheet of natural ice that measured an impressive 75 by 150 feet. In January 1919, after three years of planning and construction, city officials christened the Eveleth Recreation Building, which featured two separate sheets of ice: a curling rink on the ground floor and a skating rink above. In 1921, the Eveleth Reds joined the United States Amateur Hockey Association, winning the Group 3 title their first season with a nearly unblemished record of 13–1.

And things were just getting started.

In 1926, former Minneapolis Central High School star and University of Minnesota standout Cliff Thompson began coaching the Eveleth High School team. Two years later, he also became the coach of Eveleth Junior College. Simultaneously coaching both teams, Thompson led the junior college to the country's number-one ranking, according to a system devised by Professor Theodore Tonnele at Princeton University. Outpacing powerhouse programs like Yale, Minnesota, and Clarkson, one of Eveleth Junior College's toughest opponents was the other team Thompson coached—his Eveleth High School squad.

Between 1928 and 1940, Eveleth Junior College posted a record of 171 wins, 28 losses, and 7 ties. Incredibly, Thompson's record with the high school team was even more impressive.

In 1945, the Eveleth Golden Bears won the first Minnesota State High School Championship. Between 1948 and 1951, they added four more state titles. All told, by the time Thompson finished his 32-year high school coaching career, he'd amassed 534 wins and 9 ties against a mere 26 losses.

In three-plus decades of coaching youth hockey, Thompson developed ten players who went on to play for NHL and US Olympic teams. Among them were Stanley Cup winners Frank Brimsek and Mike Karakas, Olympic silver medalists John Matchefts and Willard Ikola, and superstar forward John Mayasich, who led the US Olympic team to its first men's hockey gold medal in 1960.

Perhaps even more impressive, the vast majority of Thompson's players returned to the Iron Range once they'd finally finished competing at the sport's highest levels. Coach Cliff Thompson didn't merely produce individual players—he helped create intergenerational family hockey dynasties.

Up on the Iron Range and across Minnesota—if not everywhere ice hockey reigned supreme—these were some of US hockey's most well-known founding families.

By the mid-1950s, some of Eveleth's most well-known surnames included Palazzari, Karakas, and Gambucci, all of whom went on to have at least one family member inducted into the US Hockey Hall of Fame. Up on the Iron Range and across Minnesota—if not everywhere ice hockey reigned supreme—these were some of US hockey's most well-known founding families. And their de facto ringleader, ambassador, and *godfather* was the gregarious, larger-than-life John Mariucci.

Elio Gambucci had become something of a father figure to Murray Williamson since the kid arrived. So when the Rangers suddenly folded and marooned one of their youngest players in northern Minnesota, Gambucci activated his network to help his young Canadian friend. First, he got Williamson a job tending bar at the American Legion. Then he turned his attention toward getting the youngster's hockey career back on track.

During their brief existence, Elio's younger brother Andre had also played for the ill-fated Rangers. Andre was a former three-sport superstar at Colorado College who'd earned All-American honors twice. He led the Tigers to their first NCAA Ice Hockey Championship in 1950 and followed that up by winning silver with the 1952 US Olympic team. Elio was convinced that any young player who skated stride for stride with his brother was destined to do great things.

Unbeknownst to Williamson, the elder Gambucci had reached out to his pal John Mariucci, who'd been coaching the Gophers hockey team for the past seven years. Gambucci wanted Maroosh to know there was a young Canadian prospect living in Eveleth, itching for the chance to play for a top college program.

Meanwhile, Williamson's boss at the Legion learned that his new bartender was still underage. Not willing to risk the loss of his liquor license, he let Williamson go, leaving the teen out-of-towner exactly where he'd been a few short weeks earlier. With the pressure steadily mounting and time running out, Williamson found himself at a crossroads: One path led back to a tedious job at home in Winnipeg and maybe a roster spot on a decent Senior A team. The more promising but difficult path led to a US college that could offer a spring scholarship.

It wouldn't be easy, but Williamson was determined to try, repeatedly calling long distance to leave messages for Vic Heyliger or *anyone* connected to the Michigan Wolverines. In the interim, with no job and no daily practice (though still enrolled at Eveleth Junior College), Williamson began to frequent Karakas's pool hall. Managed by John Karakas—the fourth brother of six and the only one to play forward rather than goalie—this Iron Range institution was the epicenter of the latest hockey news and inside information.

"It was a dingy, smoke-filled place that looked like the set of a Martin Scorsese movie," recalled Gary Gambucci, Elio's son. It was also the perfect venue for the old-timers to hold court, like John's brother Mike

Karakas, the first prominent NHL goalie who'd been born and played within the US system. With Mike and other local legends swapping stories and telling tales almost every night, there wasn't a better place for a young hockey player to contemplate his future.

By then, of course, Elio Gambucci and John Mariucci had spoken. The coach had done his homework and knew Williamson had been on the St. Boniface team that beat his Gophers *twice* at Williams Arena two years prior. He likely even remembered what the Minneapolis *Star Tribune* called "nifty combination play by Bruce Carmichael and Murray Williamson"—the slick pinpoint passing that tormented his defense throughout the two-game series. Certainly, it also stung that a visiting Junior A squad had posted the first series sweep in Mariucci's first two seasons as a head coach.

Likewise, after a weekend trip to Minneapolis to play the University of Minnesota—who'd advanced all the way to the NCAA Division I championship game to cap their 23-win season—Williamson knew firsthand about the Gophers' star-studded program and its colorful coach, John Mariucci.

The part we may never know is whether John Mariucci knew exactly where to find Murray Williamson the night they met or if their first encounter truly came down to luck. For decades, the way Williamson told the story, it was all a matter of chance. If the young Winnipeg native hadn't happened to run into John Mariucci in an Eveleth pool hall, almost certainly, Murray Williamson would have played for the Michigan Wolverines.

So the story goes, Williamson was shooting pool, half-listening to the old-timers spin yarns about their glory days as he pondered his future. At some point, Mariucci arrived, greeting his hometown pals, cracking jokes, and catching up on the latest buzz. If Williamson noticed the coach and recognized who he was, he was careful not to betray that piece of information too soon. Instead, he was purely focused on winning his game of eight-ball.

As Williamson continued to work his way around the table, he found himself needing to sink one last routine bank shot. At this point, Mariucci was standing with his back against the wall, silently watching the game as the conversation hit a lull. Williamson lined up his shot, pulled back his cue . . . and struck Mariucci square in the stomach.

The coach let out a groan, exaggerated for effect, acting as though he'd been sucker punched. Williamson instinctively whirled, staring directly into the eyes of the former NHL tough guy. Williamson had been ousted from two separate games for fighting in his brief career with the Eveleth Rangers (including a "near riot" in Fort Frances), but he wasn't foolish enough to even *pretend* to tangle with Maroosh.

Thankfully, peacemaker Luke Karakas—one of the middle brothers and the third consecutive goalie in the clan—darted between the two men and proceeded to make introductions. Mariucci smiled, Williamson relaxed, and the two men shook hands. Mariucci then asked why Williamson was shooting pool in the first place, when clearly he should be home, reading and studying. Williamson responded that he fully intended to do so as soon as he won some money to buy the textbooks.

Mariucci quickly countered that any *legitimate* program would pay for tuition and books as well as room and board, and maybe even give him a little pocket money for "expenses." Having commandeered the teen prospect's attention, Mariucci chided Williamson for pursuing a roster spot with league rival (and longtime friend) Vic Heyliger. "How could you even *consider* putting on a Wolverines jersey?" Mariucci wondered.

Not bothering to wait for an answer, the coach invited Williamson to the Gophers' home season finale against Michigan in mid-February. Then, Mariucci suggested, Williamson could see for himself how the Gophers program stacked up against one of the best teams in the NCAA.

From Williamson's perspective, Mariucci's offer came out of the blue. Since becoming the Gophers' coach in 1952, Mariucci had been a staunch supporter of homegrown talent. "This is a state institution," he said, "and should be represented by Minnesota boys. If they're not quite as good as some Canadians, we'll just have to work a little harder, that's all."

Williamson was intrigued and flattered by Mariucci's attention. After all, this ten-minute conversation had been more detailed—and felt more concrete—than the noncommittal discussions he'd been having with both Michigan and Michigan State for months. Why not check it out? What did he have to lose? If nothing else, it was a chance to see two-time All-American and Western League scoring leader John Mayasich play his final home game as a Gopher.

Williamson happily accepted the coach's offer. He would attend the Saturday night game of the Gophers–Michigan series next month. Who knew? Maybe he *would* end up in a Gophers jersey. Playing for anyone as colorful as Maroosh sure seemed like a lot of fun. The young Winnipegger was cautiously optimistic his fortunes were about to change.

CHAPTER FIVE

WILLIAMSON BECOMES A GOPHER

By the time the Minnesota–Michigan game rolled around, Mariucci's mood—and circumstances—had changed in several material ways. After beginning the season with a 5–1 record in league play, Colorado College had never looked back, effectively locking up one of two play-off bids given to western league teams every year. Meanwhile, with Michigan Tech disqualified from postseason play for using freshmen, Minnesota, Denver, and Michigan were all within a half-game of each other, vying for the final spot.

To further complicate matters, earlier that same week, the University of Minnesota had formally granted Mariucci's leave to coach the 1956 US Olympic team in Cortina d'Ampezzo, Italy. Knowing Mariucci would miss most of the next college season, some sports-writers claimed the coach was too distracted to finish the current campaign. A decisive 5–2 loss to the Wolverines in Friday night's contest underscored the media's concerns. According to the Minneapolis *Star*, "Not only were they outhustled and outplayed by Michigan," but it was one of the team's "poorest exhibitions of the season."

Mariucci couldn't argue with the newspaper's blunt assessment. "We really played poorly and looked disorganized," he said glumly after the game. Mathematically, the Gophers were still alive going into game two of the weekend series . . . but a beleaguered team desperately fighting to stave off elimination is not what either man had pictured that night in Karakas's pool hall.

Even so, Williamson boarded the bus for Minneapolis excited to see a game between two Big Ten rivals in front of six thousand rowdy fans. The campus atmosphere had fired his imagination when he'd visited as a St. Boniface player. He was looking forward to returning to Williams Arena to experience a game from a whole new perspective, amongst the screaming student fans.

Three and a half hours later, the bus pulled into the downtown station and Williamson proceeded straight to the Andrews Hotel, hoofing eight icy blocks down Nicollet Avenue. He checked into his room, dropped off his bag, and began to wait in the lobby for Coach Mariucci, who'd said he'd meet him there at 6:30, two hours before the opening face-off. After waiting for over an hour, there was still no sign of the coach. So Williamson took a taxi to the rink and slipped in through one of the team doors in the back.

Inside, the atmosphere was electric. Williamson was impressed and entranced by the spectacle. He couldn't help but picture himself in maroon and gold, playing for a built-in fan base that consistently turned out in the thousands. The contrast between his recent experience with the Eveleth–Virginia Rangers—where owner and promoter Len Naymark practically had to beg fans to pay attention—and a big-time university program was stark and palpable. Some of the Rangers games were so empty and quiet, you could practically hear the popcorn popping at the concession stand. Here, you could feel the roar in your chest when the fans got excited. This, in Williamson's mind, was what hockey should be.

Here, you could feel the roar in your chest when the fans got excited. This, in Williamson's mind, was what hockey should be.

It didn't take long for the rambunctious crowd to explode. Less than three minutes into the game, Ken Yackel blasted a shoetop high shot from the blue line that found the back of the net. The hometown fans erupted, cheering and jeering wildly, but the Gophers' only lead of the series lasted a mere nine minutes. Finding himself with the puck and only one man to beat deep in the Minnesota zone, sophomore sensation Tom Rendall deked the lone defender and flipped a quick shot past Gophers goalie Jim Mattson.

Ironically, Tom Rendall was one of Murray Williamson's childhood pals and a major reason why the Wolverines had been so high on Williamson's list. The two had not only grown up together in the same hockey-obsessed neighborhood as teenagers; they'd competed on rival Winnipeg teams in the Manitoba Junior Hockey League. In fact, before accepting an offer from Michigan in 1953, Rendall had won two consecutive MJHL championships with the Winnipeg Monarchs.

In many ways, Rendall represented the kind of college recruit John Mariucci decried—a full-time hockey player who'd traded his high school education for a shot at the pros. Scoring an unassisted goal in the Gophers' final home game must have further cemented the coach's convictions.

Seven minutes later, the Wolverines scored again and the outcome seemed no longer in doubt. In the end, the Gophers outshot the visitors by a margin of 34–23, but that statistic belies Michigan's dominance—and crisp pinpoint passing—around the Gopher net. Even worse, for only the ninth time in his entire college career, John Mayasich failed to register a point. Instead, he took two penalties in the third period to post his only marks on the scoresheet. Regardless, Mariucci left the Gophers superstar on the ice the last four minutes and thirty seconds to close out the game, with the crowd roaring their approval.

Without question, a two-game sweep concluding the Gophers' home season is far from the storybook ending Mariucci had hoped to showcase for his young recruit from north of the border. Even so, from the fans' unflagging support in the face of difficult odds to the team's relentless never-say-die attitude, Williamson liked what he saw. He'd already imagined it must be a lot of fun to play for any coach as colorful and charismatic as Mariucci—the way his team carried itself and the vibrant campus atmosphere merely sealed the deal. Williamson headed downstairs to tell larger-than-life Maroosh he wanted to be a Gopher.

After waiting several minutes outside the locker room, Williamson started to worry it might not be a great time to announce his decision. Luckily, before he could change his mind and make a break for the exit, the coach finally emerged. At first, he seemed dejected; but seeing Williamson, Mariucci smacked his palm against his forehead dramatically and apologized for his mistake. With everything else on his mind, the coach had forgotten about the plans they'd made in Eveleth.

Seeing the coach's mood lighten, Williamson was relieved. He told Mariucci how much he wanted to be a Golden Gopher, particularly if he could be enrolled in time for the spring term. Mariucci smiled and said, "You're smarter than you look." They agreed to hammer out the details the following morning at the Andrews Hotel.

This time, Mariucci didn't forget about his meeting with Williamson. The two men quickly got down to business. Seated across from each other at a small, wobbly table by the door of the hotel bar, Mariucci literally outlined his offer on the back of an envelope, itemizing everything from the cost of tuition and books plus room and board, to promised extra income from miscellaneous side jobs the coach would arrange.

In terms of ice time and training, Mariucci reminded his prospect that he'd have to spend a year on the freshman team before he'd be eligible to play in league games. That said, the coach also noted there were plenty of strong senior leagues throughout the Twin Cities, with numerous teams who played at a very high level. There, Williamson could get some extra ice time without affecting his NCAA eligibility—just one of the advantages that made playing in Minnesota a unique opportunity.

The two men shook hands, and Murray Williamson boarded the bus back to Eveleth, completely unaware that by altering his own track, he was also changing the future course of amateur hockey throughout the United States. Williamson wasn't only signing up to be a Golden Gopher—he was starting down a path that would lead to incredible friendships, world travel, and a head coaching position with the US Olympic team.

CHAPTER SIX

ST. PAUL JOHNSON WINS THE 1955 STATE TOURNAMENT

Two weeks after the Gophers finale, across the river in St. Paul, the St. Paul Johnson Governors came soaring into the eleventh annual Minnesota State High School League (MSHSL) Tournament. After posting a nearly perfect regular season record of 22–1–1, the Governors were a presumptive favorite for the second year in a row. "Johnson has another big team with good speed," said the *Minneapolis Star*. "Stu Anderson is their top goal scorer, and Herbie Brooks is their chief playmaker."

Brooks and Anderson each centered St. Paul Johnson's top two lines, but they were linemates on power plays and penalty kills. "Nothing was as electrifying to a high school crowd at the St. Paul Auditorium as when the line of Herb Brooks, Pete Kelly, and Stu Anderson were on the attack," mused one fan in the wake of Brooks's untimely death in 2003. "The crowd knew that they were on the attack just from the sound."

Despite losing the semifinal to Eveleth the previous year, there was no doubt they'd be back. Unfortunately, the Governors' opening game got off to a weird and unpredictable start. The marquee matchup featured Minneapolis South against the defending state champions, Thief River Falls.

Begun at 7:30 p.m., the quarterfinal contest was still knotted at two goals apiece more than three hours later. By then, the two teams had played a full regulation game and nine overtime periods. In the St. Paul auditorium's back hallways and locker rooms, the St. Paul Johnson Governors and Roseau Rams restlessly waited for their own game to start.

Eventually, high school league officials temporarily suspended play to give the players some rest. In the interim, Johnson and Roseau took to the ice, with the opening face-off at 10:52 p.m. Inevitably, in the midst of the seemingly endless battle between Minneapolis South and Thief River Falls, the Johnson–Roseau game felt like a letdown, especially since the two teams combined for a single goal.

After the first period, South and Thief River Falls played their tenth overtime installment. After neither team scored, Johnson and Roseau returned to play their second period, also scoreless.

Finally, at 12:20 a.m., in the eleventh and final overtime period, Jimmy Westby lit the lamp for Minneapolis South, sending his team to the semifinals. All told, the marquee event consumed a whopping 87:50 of game time—a state tournament record that stood until 1996—and was instantly deemed the centerpiece of "one of the greatest days of sports entertainment the state has ever known," according to the *Minneapolis Star*. Ironically, describing the game-winning goal, which he'd launched from beyond the blue line, Westby admitted, "I just shot. I didn't aim."

With fans still buzzing about "the most thrilling game in state hockey tournament history," Johnson and Roseau played an uneventful third period, with no points and no penalties. In the end, Stu Anderson assisted on what proved to be the game winner, an efficient, workmanlike goal midway through the first period, tallied nearly two hours prior.

The Governors' next game pitted them against the suddenly ascendant Tigers from Minneapolis South. Literally overnight, the Tigers had become the emotional favorite to win it all. Nine minutes into the game, however, Brooks swooped in to score an unassisted goal and the Tigers were on their heels. The ice seemed tilted against them.

South later tied it up, but late in the third period, the Governors

DETROIT RED WINGS - CHICAGO BLACK HAWKS

Chicago Stadium

1947

#19 Doug Jackson
(Chicago)

#10 W. Mosienko
(Chicago)

#5 Max Bentley
(Chicago)

(Hatless)
E. Froleick
(Chicago Trainer)

Harry Lumley
Rt. Goalie
(Detroit)

#2 Jack Stewart
(Detroit)

John Mariucci
(Chicago)

John Mariucci fighting Black Jack Stewart of the Red Wings in a historic 1947
brawl that lasted twenty minutes.

THIS IS SITE, BUT WHO'LL PLAY?

Contenders' Marks

West

North Dakota 14-4.
Colorado College 11-7.
Denver 11-9.

East

Harvard 16-3-1.
Boston College 16-5-1.
Clarkson 10-2.

Two teams will represent East and West in three-day NCAA hockey meet here next week. That's John Marucci, Gopher coach, pointing to the Williams arena tournament site.

St. Boniface Rips Gophers 6-3 to Sweep Ice Series

By DICK GORDON
Sunday Tribune Staff Writer

The St. Boniface hockey team operated Saturday night on the theory there's safety in numbers. That is number of goals and number of men on the ice.

The Canadians thus wound up pasting Minnesota's comeback kids 6-3 at Williams arena largely on the strength of three first-period goals rung up when the Gophers had a man in the penalty box.

Then after Minnesota's bread and butter line of John Mayasich, Dick Dougherty and Gene Campbell gave the snow-defying crowd of 5,136 a chance to cheer with a three-goal rally that left the Gophers trailing only 4-3 midway in the final period, the Canadians utilized the "numbers game" again.

TWICE THEY caught the pressing Gophers with all their men down ice and broke a player loose with only goalie Jim Mattson to beat.

Each time the opportunist Bonis capitalized for the two insurance markers to complete the first series sweep against Minnesota since John Mariucci became coach.

So deft was the Canadian passing and so able was the blocking and checking of their defense that the Gophers were well on their way to their first whitewashing in two seasons until the third period surge. And it was Gordon Dibley in his debut game as goalie that almost turned the trick, too.

Some nifty combination play by Bruce Carmichael and Murray Williamson and deadly long shooting by Bob Jasson and Barry Beatty got the Canadians ahead by 4-0 after two periods even though the rather ragged playing Gophers missed at least three open nets in the second session.

THEY CONTINUED muffing good opportunities in the last period until Mayasich sent Dougherty a forward pass in front of the pack and Dick con-

nected at 4:17. Ken Yackel and Dougherty again made it a thriller with two more goals in six minutes before Leo Konyck and Ab McDonald counted with St. Boniface's clinching goals.

Two of the Boni missing regulars from the Friday night victory, Ed Dudych and Al Johnson were on hand last night, but curiously it was their third line and reserve defense which fashioned all their goals.

But as a disappointed Mariucci said afterwards: "All the Canadians looked equally good."

Minnesota (3)— Pos. St. Boniface (6)—
Mattson .... G .... Dibley
Yackel .... LD .... Holiday
Anderson .... RD .... Akers
Mayasich .... C .... Wyant
Campbell .... LW .... Konyk
Dougherty .... RW .... McDonald

SPARES. Minnesota—Petranek, Jetty, Schutz, Malmey, Meredosh, McKenzie, Meredith, Johnson, St. Boniface—A. Johnson, Thoenderwerth, Dudych, Williamson, Finnson, Carmichael, Jason, Beatty.

FIRST PERIOD. Scoring—St. Boniface, Carmichael (Williamson, Akers), 3:54; Williamson (Carmichael, Jason), 11:07; Jason (unassisted) 17:35. Penalties—Monahan, Dougherty, Jetty, Thoendwerath, Wilson, A. Johnson.

SECOND PERIOD SCORING: St. Boniface —Beatty (Jason) 13:20. Penalties—Monahan, Carmichael.

THIRD PERIOD SCORING: Minnesota—Dougherty (Mayasich-Yackel) 4:17; Minnesota—Yackel (Mayasich-Dougherty), 8:36; Dougherty (Mayasich) 12:24. St. Boniface—Konyk (McDonald) 16:51; McDonald (unassisted) 17:17.

STOPS:
Dibley, St. Boniface .... 7 8 13—28
Mattson, Minnesota .... ? ? ?

OFFICIALS: Bill McCline, Arnie Bauer.

SCORES

FOOTBALL

COLLEGES

Notre Dame 40, Southern Methodist 14.
Florida State 41, Tampa 6.
Prairie View 33, Florida A&M 27.
Houston 29, Tennessee 19.
Allen 33, Paul Quinn 6 (Iodine Bowl).
St. George 28, Austin 12.
Southern U. 41, Xavier (La.) 13.

PROFESSIONAL

Murray Williamson's first exposure to Gophers hockey when his junior team ventured to Minneapolis to play them.

1957 U of M Gophers. Front row: Jack McCartan, Bill Swanson, Dick Burg, Bob Schmidt, Jack Petrosky, John Newkirk, Bob Turk, Murray Williamson, Don Vaia. Back row: John Mariucci, Terry Bartholome, Herb Brooks, Marv Jorde, Tom Riley, Mike Pearson, Gary Alm, Ken Whelen, Unknown, Marsh Ryman.

At Chicago's Blue Note Jazz Club in 1958: Jerry Melnychuk (Williamson's Gopher roommate for two years), Joe Williams, Joe Lucania, Williamson, Jim Rantz, and Count Basie in the background.

Gophers post game with Michigan University, 1958: Tom Rendall, Gary Starr, Murray Williamson, John Rendall.

1958 U of M Gophers. Front row: Jerry Melnychuk, Marv Jorde, John Newkirk, Mike Pearson, Jack McCartan, Bob Turk, Dick Burg, Tom Riley, Murray Williamson. Back row: John Mariucci, Herb Brooks, Jim Rantz, Bill Pederson, Gary Alm, Larry Alm, Jim Westby, Myron Grafstrom, Bill Schlafke, Marsh Ryman.

1959 All-American Murray Williamson, left wing, University of Minnesota.

1959 U of M Gophers. Top row: John Mariucci, Roger Rovik, Rick Alm, Tom Simpson, Larry Smith, Stu Anderson, Jerry Katz. Middle row: Dick Gaudette, Roger Benson, Jerry Norman, Elmer Walls, Dave Rovik, Wayne Meredith, John Hall, Mike Doyle. Bottom row: Jerry Melnychuk, Murray Williamson, Herb Brooks, Larry Alm, Tom Riley, Gary Alm, Myron Graftstrom, Jim Rantz.

1960 Olympic Hockey Team. Front row: Larry Palmer, Jack Kirrane (Captain), Bill Cleary, Bob Owen (Alternate Captain), Bill Christian, Jack McCartan. Middle row: Jim Claypool (Manager), Bob Cleary, Bob McVey, Rod Paavola, Roger Christian, Gene Grazia, Tom Williams, Jack Riley (Coach). Back row: John Mayasich, Paul Johnson, Weldy Olson (Alternate Captain), Dick Rodenhiser, Dick Meredith, Ben Bertini (Trainer).

Original St. Paul Steers Hockey Team, 1962-1963. Top row: Gordan Genz, John Herzog, Larry Alm, Dick Paradise, Murray Williamson, Art Miller. Bottom row: Marv Jorde, Jerry Melnychuk, Bob Currie, Gus Rheaume, Marcel Rochon, John Rendall. Not pictured: Lynne Davis, Dick Burg, Dick Meredith, Wayne Meredith, Terry Bartholome, Bob Turk, Myron Grafstrom.

A Steers game with the Waterloo, Iowa, Blackhawks before a full capacity crowd.

First Steers practice at Wakota Arena with owner/manager Walter Bush, 1963-64.

1965 US Nationals with Jake Milford, Ken Yackel, Murray Williamson, and Bob Ridder.

During a 1967 practice session Herb Brooks, center, talks with Coach Murray Williamson, left, and the late Bill Masterton, who later died in a tragic accident while playing for the Minnesota North Stars.

Front row: Bill Halbrehder, Herb Brooks, Ken Williamson, Bill Masterton, Murray Williamson, Jim Ridley, Gerry Edman, Rod Blackburn.
Back row: Dave Metzen, Jerry Melnychuk, Marsh Tschida, Bob Currie, Larry Alm, Marv Jorde, Myron Grafstrom, Art Miller, Jim Arndt, Dave Brooks, Dick Rose (Trainer), Don Niederkorn (Equipment Manager).

World Championships, Vienna, 1967. Front row: Rod Blackburn, Don Ross, Marty Howe, Bill Masterton, Murray Williamson, Bob Currie, Herb Brooks, Carl Wetzel. Middle row: Don Niederkorn, Doc Nagobads, Dick Rose, Lou Nanne, Ron Naslund, Craig Falkman, Dave Metzen, Marsh Tschida. Back row: John Rendall, Terry Casey, Tom Hurley, John Cunniff, Art Miller, Len Lilyholm, Jerry Melnychuk, Doug Woog. Masterton and Nanne were part of the team but could not compete because the Act of Congress was pending.

Practicing in Vienna are from left, in white uniforms, Don Ross, Terry Casey, Tom Haugh, and Jerry Melnychuk. From left, in dark jerseys, are Craig Falkman, Marty Howe, Coach Murray Williamson, Bob Currie, and Carl Wetzel.

Carl Wetzel against the Russians during the 1967 World Championships.

Chatting with Russian coaches Anatoly Tarasov and Arkady Chernyshev.

Pausing in an airport while heading home from Vienna are, from left, Bob Currie, Art Miller, Marty Howe, Ron Naslund, Terry Casey, and John Cunniff.

WILLIAM JOHN MASTERTON, GEORGE SAMUEL KONIK, AND LOUIS VINCENT NANNE

MARCH 6, 1967.—Committed to the Committee of the Whole House and ordered to be printed

Mr. FEIGHAN, from the Committee on the Judiciary, submitted the following

REPORT

[To accompany H.R. 2048]

The Committee on the Judiciary, to whom was referred the bill (H.R. 2048) for the relief of William John Masterton, George Samuel Konik, and Louis Vincent Nanne, having considered the same, report favorably thereon with amendments and recommend that the bill do pass.

The amendments are as follows:

On page 1, line 4, strike out the name ", George Samuel Konik,".

Amend the title so as to read:

A bill for the relief of William John Masterton and Louis Vincent Nanne.

PURPOSE OF THE BILL

The purpose of this bill, as amended, is to provide that William John Masterton and Louis Vincent Nanne shall be held and considered to have been lawfully admitted to the United States for permanent residence as of September 24, 1959.

The bill has been amended to delete the name of George Samuel Konik who was one of the beneficiaries of the bill as introduced.

GENERAL INFORMATION

The beneficiaries, William John Masterton and Louis Vincent Nanne are 28 and 25 years of age, respectively. Both are natives and citizens of Canada who were admitted to the United States as students and have since been admitted for permanent residence. They were members of their respective varsity hockey teams and were named on the all-American hockey team during their senior year. They require

65–007

Act of Congress to waive the waiting period for Bill Masterton and Lou Nanne to become American citizens, signed by President Lyndon Johnson.

pumped in two goals in a 32-second span to win it going away.

In the tournament finale between St. Paul Johnson and Minneapolis Southwest the following night—the first ever championship game between two Twin Cities teams—a record-setting crowd of 7,825 fans poured into St. Paul Auditorium. With fierce partisans on both sides, many fans wondered if the Governors would live up to the hype or wilt before the surging Southwest.

Two and a half minutes in, the Governors scored the first of three unanswered first period goals. On their fourth shot of the game, the Governors "cracked through" in dramatic fashion when Brooks took Wigen's feed from behind the Southwest net and "lifted the puck over fallen goalie George Noble." Seven minutes later, "dazzling, incredibly strong Stu Anderson made it 2–0 . . . batting in a rebound from a tangle in front of the net." Lastly, Brooks tallied his second goal after a game of "cat and mouse" with Southwest's defense, exchanging passes with Rod Anderson until finally banging it home.

Incredibly, in two separate sequences, St. Paul Johnson ended up with two men in the penalty box. "But on each occasion, Stu Anderson took charge at mid-ice, dancing and weaving, eating up time" to kill off Southwest's 5-on-3 advantage and keep them off the scoreboard. In fact, Southwest's only goal came at even strength with less than eight minutes left in the game, too late to have much impact, much less stem the tide of the Governors' opening onslaught. Ultimately, in the words of *Star Tribune* staff writer Bob Harris, "Poised, powerful St. Paul Johnson exploded for three first period goals, and that was enough to turn back hustling Minneapolis Southwest . . ."

The following Monday morning, two days after the championship game, the Minneapolis *Tribune* concluded, "Johnson was big and fast, and it was well prepared." The team knew "what to do around the net—its own net and its opponent's . . . Its passing was sharp and true . . . and it shot to kill." They'd overcome "the best balanced field the tournament has ever had" to

> The team knew "what to do around the net—its own net and its opponent's . . . Its passing was sharp and true . . . and it shot to kill."

emerge as "one of the strongest champions" since tournament play began in 1945.

In little more than a decade, the Minnesota State High School League had built what was likely the premier state high school hockey tournament in the country, a designation retained to this day. More importantly, perhaps, they'd created an infrastructure for recruiting and developing great hockey players—talent that would form the nucleus of US National and Olympic teams for decades to come.

CHAPTER SEVEN

MARIUCCI LAYS OUT HIS VISION FOR MINNESOTA HOCKEY

Despite the overabundance of superlatives used at the time, the 1955 MSHSL Tournament remains a watershed moment. In its eleventh year, the Thursday-through-Sunday event drew a record twenty-eight thousand fans, a feat that took the state basketball tourney almost three full decades to accomplish. On top of that, there was a major geographic shift, with four metro area schools unexpectedly earning a trip to the semifinal round in place of perennial northern powerhouse teams like Eveleth, Roseau, and Thief River Falls.

For Gophers coach John Mariucci—a fierce advocate for Minnesota high school hockey ever since he played for the Eveleth Golden Bears—the fact that the strongest champions came from a well-balanced field was precisely the point. Stiff competition helped grow the sport and raised everyone's level of play.

Mariucci saw MSHSL hockey and its role as a feeder system for top US college programs as a "much more solid," sustainable model for player development than the Canadian junior leagues.

"Up in Canada, they make hockey the life of a kid when he is ten or twelve years old," he told the Minneapolis *Tribune*. "They shoot these youngsters into organized play that is virtually professional. Hockey becomes their lone interest. They are trained for nothing else. Sure, great ones come out of such a program; but for every one that makes it, ten fall by the wayside." Underscoring the point, he added,

"When I was with the Blackhawks, I bet the average education level of the other fellows on the team was the tenth grade. I was the only player on the squad with a college education. Maybe I was the only one in the league who had graduated from college."

Mariucci had been the proverbial Big Man on Campus in his time as a student athlete at the University of Minnesota. As a naturally gifted two-sport varsity star, he'd embodied the NCAA's original purist notion that college athletes should play competitive sports "only for the pleasure and the physical, mental, moral, and social benefits directly derived therefrom." In the twelve years since Mariucci had played for the Gophers, however, the nature of college sports had changed dramatically.

By the end of WWII, US collegiate hockey had dwindled to a mere twenty-one programs. The NHL contracted, too, shrinking from ten teams in two divisions at the end of the 1930–31 season to the misnamed "Original Six" by 1942.

In the nine years since WWII ended, however, college hockey had returned with a vengeance. By 1954, the number of programs had doubled and showed no signs of slowing down. Confoundingly, even as hockey exploded across US college campuses, the NHL plateaued at six teams. Soon, the result was apparent to anybody with a basic grasp of free market economics: With dozens of top Canadian prospects aging out of the Junior A system each year, the ever-increasing *supply* of talented young players soon overwhelmed *demand*. There simply weren't enough open roster spots on professional teams to meet the growing surplus.

Western league coaches like Michigan's Vic Heyliger, Michigan State's Amo Bessone, Colorado College's Tom Bedecki, and Denver's Murray Armstrong began to cherry-pick top players from powerhouse Junior A clubs. Not that eastern coaches were entirely immune to the idea of trading a free education for on-ice prowess. RPI's Ned Harkness, Boston University's Jack Kelley, and St. Lawrence University's Olav "Ole" Kollevoll were all known to court their fair share of Canadian players. In fact, of the thirty-one Canadian students enrolled at St. Lawrence in 1955, eight played varsity hockey—clearly undercutting the notion that these former top amateur prospects happened to choose St. Lawrence purely for academic reasons.

Without question, these coaches knew that by landing even a handful of top-tier recruits, they could vault their programs into national title contention almost immediately. Accordingly, Princeton coach Dick Vaughn suggested that college teams should be barred from competing in the national tournament two years in a row.

Without question, these coaches knew that by landing even a handful of top-tier recruits, they could vault their programs into national title contention almost immediately.

"There is nothing wrong with having Canadian boys playing US college hockey," he said. "They are fine boys, good students, and loyal graduates." The real problem, Vaughn insisted, was the single-minded pursuit of national titles. Driven by nothing more than "the urge to be an NCAA champion every year, whatever the cost," some coaches had lost their perspective, clearly forgetting that "colleges exist for educational purposes."

Dartmouth's Eddie Jeremiah didn't bother to sugarcoat his blunt assessment, telling *Sports Illustrated* that "the wholesale importation" of Canadian players was "making a farce" out of the NCAA playoffs.

Not to be outdone, Harvard's Cooney Weiland noted that the influx of Canadian athletes was "ruining US college hockey."

Presumably moved by the fact that three of his team's six starters were Canadian nationals, St. Lawrence University coach Ole Kollevoll completely disagreed. "People who criticize US colleges for using Canadian hockey players are really on the wrong track," he said. "They ought to be thankful that Canadians are helping to make the game more popular in this country. Their players are improving all the time, and much of the credit should go to the Canadians for setting such good examples of how hockey should be played."

Despite the fact that he'd blasted the Canadian development model back when he was a player, as rookie head coach of the Gophers, John Mariucci espoused a more nuanced view. "I used to be resentful against the number of Canadian players on US hockey teams," he told the Minneapolis *Tribune's* Sid Hartman in autumn 1953. "Now, I've changed my mind. I'm convinced that Canadians have made college hockey a top sport."

Rather than villainize Canadian players, Mariucci laid the blame squarely at the feet of an ad hoc system that left college coaches few choices. Outside of Minnesota and a handful of East Coast prep teams, he noted, "other states don't have fully developed high school programs, [and] some have none at all." Without a sustainable player development program in place, US college coaches were effectively forced to use Canadians to fill their rosters.

> Without a sustainable player development program in place, US college coaches were effectively forced to use Canadians to fill their rosters.

If the Gophers hoped to compete with the other freewheeling teams of the Western Intercollegiate Hockey League, Minnesota's best prospects needed to play for the hometown team. "Not every player," Mariucci told the assembled crowd at a pre-state tournament luncheon in the glamorous art deco ballroom of the Lowry Hotel. "We just want the top 5 percent."

Ironically, mere days after this bold pronouncement, the second Canadian prospect signed by Mariucci in as many years was unpacking his bags at Centennial Hall on the University of Minnesota's East Bank campus. Incongruous as it may have seemed to an outside observer, however, the move was actually part of Mariucci's overall plan.

"One good Canadian player is worth ten American coaches," he said. "The players can learn much more watching the good Canadians than they can by listening to their coaches."

As a veteran Junior A prospect who'd spent his teen years in the Montréal Canadiens farm system, Murray Williamson typified the so-called "Canadian player problem" that sparked intense debate among hockey insiders and the sporting press. As luck would have it, a mere two weeks after moving into his dorm room, several factors converged to give the Canadian teen a golden opportunity to prove why he was there in the first place. With Minnesota out of the playoffs for the first time in three years, Mariucci had shifted his focus to the US Olympic team, which he would coach at the 1956 Winter Games in Cortina d'Ampezzo, Italy.

Bob Ridder, Olympic team manager, and Walter Bush, founder and manager of the Minnesota senior league team known as Culbertsons, had begun to schedule games between Mariucci's core group of Olympic hopefuls and other top amateur squads. Bush had also begun to intensify his search for cities beyond Minnesota capable of supporting a new minor league franchise in his fledgling semipro Central League. Logically, with a beautiful new 15,000-seat arena set to open in Des Moines, Iowa's capital city jumped to the top of the list.

Two months prior, Murray Williamson had watched John Mayasich from the stands of Williams Arena as a recruit. Now, the young Canadian import was about to square off against the Minnesota legend in Iowa's first-ever indoor hockey game.

CHAPTER EIGHT

MARIUCCI, RIDDER, AND BUSH BRING HOCKEY TO IOWA

Minnesota's first indoor ice hockey game was played in 1901; by the mid-1950s, its neighboring state to the south had yet to embrace the sport. Iowa's newly unveiled state-of-the-art arena, featuring "plush opera-type seats" and a full-size sheet of artificial ice, was about to make history, however, and everyone involved wanted to make the most of the once-in-a-lifetime opportunity.

Des Moines city leaders, feeling that they lacked the kind of expertise to stage such a grand opening, reached out to their hockey-obsessed Minnesota peers for assistance. Coincidentally, media mogul Bob Ridder, Don Clark, and Everett James "Buck" Riley had recently coalesced around a shared commitment to supporting and growing high-level amateur hockey throughout the United States, especially the Upper Midwest. The three men recruited Minnesota sports icon John Mariucci, along with rising star Walter Bush, and eagerly agreed to help organize and plan a memorable event.

True to form, despite sharing several objectives, each one also pursued a personal agenda. For TV-, radio- and newspaper executive Bob Ridder—then in his second stint as general manager of the US Olympic hockey team—it was the perfect way to raise a sizable chunk of the $25,000 needed for training and travel expenses. For Central League President Walter Bush, it was a golden opportunity to educate and grow a previously untapped fan base and gauge community interest in a potential new team. And for Coach John Mariucci, it was a rare chance to give his Olympic players some much-needed ice time while also mimicking the conditions of having to play on the road.

Despite these seemingly disparate, incongruent objectives, the group soon devised an intuitive, mutually beneficial solution: an exhibition game featuring Culbertsons vs. the simply named All-Stars. One side would highlight the often-eclectic nature of Minnesota's best senior league teams, with former Dartmouth star and 1952 Olympic silver medalist Arnie Oss splitting ice time with incoming freshman Murray Williamson, who'd yet to even be fitted for his Golden Gophers jersey. The other side, by contrast, would showcase a core group of well-known ex-Gophers stars, like John Mayasich, Dick Dougherty, Dick Meredith, Gene Campbell, and Wendy Anderson, all of whom were sure to be on the 1956 US Olympic team roster.

Ideally, this one-off contest between recent college grads playing at their peak and one of the most well-known senior teams in the Upper Midwest would pack the arena, producing a boisterous playoff-type atmosphere. Game time was set for eight o'clock on April 12, with reserved tickets going on sale two weeks ahead of time. In the interim, the Minnesota contingent turned their attention toward marketing and promotion.

On Tuesday, April 5—exactly one week before the ceremonial puck drop—"youthful Harvard graduate" Bob Ridder and John Mariucci traveled to Des Moines to finalize plans for the game and "give press and radio people of this city an idea what to expect," according to *The Des Moines Register* the following day. Ridder also promoted "a 30-minute clinic to explain the techniques, rules, and penalties of hockey" to be held before the game. During the game itself, a referee would also "man the public address system during" to describe and interpret play as it happened.

Mariucci, for his part, began by heartily praising Des Moines' new "ideal facilities for collegiate ice hockey," enthusiastically noting, "Drake shouldn't be afraid to have a hockey team, because amateur hockey is booming in the middlewest." Not only that, "Drake would fit right in" with the Golden Gophers and the other western league teams, all but guaranteed to make money with "collegiate style hockey."

As for the upcoming Olympics, Mariucci predicted a third-place finish for the US team, conceding the gold medal to the Canadians and the silver to Russia, who'd been coming on strong. Nonetheless, Mariucci observed, "If hockey continues to boom in the United States, the day may not be too far away when we might challenge Canada's claim to the throne."

> Nonetheless, Mariucci observed, "If hockey continues to boom in the United States, the day may not be too far away when we might challenge Canada's claim to the throne."

Before the US Olympic team could ever hope to compete on the world stage, however, it first needed to prove dominance over teams like Culbertsons. At showtime, "it took the All-Stars over a third of a game to get rolling." But once they finally got up to speed, the All-Stars "slammed home six second-period goals and went on to win 10–7," as reported by Maury White in *The Des Moines Register* on April 13, 1955.

As for the level of play, the same reporter wryly noted "the game was never dull" and featured "some terrific brawls over that little black puck." Elsewhere in his account, White also detailed some of his favorite scoring plays, including Rube Bjorkman's "solo, swivel-hipped drive" that resulted in an unassisted goal.

"It looked like modified mayhem," the author concluded, even though it was merely "a nominally rough game according to folks who know."

Perhaps most intriguingly, in what must be a rare case—if not one-of-a-kind event—three-time All-American John Mayasich and future All-American Murray Williamson were the top scoring stars, with each man posting three goals to accomplish "a feat called a 'hat trick.'"

Without question, from sports reporters to everyday fans, hockey in Des Moines was a hit. The game's paid attendance of about 3,100 netted the US Olympic Committee over $2,000 after covering their expenses and splitting the gate receipts. Intentional or not, Ridder, Mariucci, and Bush had created a template to be used in the future. In the late 1960s and early '70s, Coach Murray Williamson took his St. Paul Steers on seasonal barnstorming tours with the dual purpose of raising money for the national team and giving his players a taste of the international tournament grind.

In fact, later that same year, Walter Bush and the Central Hockey League took their show on the road, scheduling multiple games on neutral ice at "The Vet"—as Des Moines' arena was known. Some weekend games attracted as many as two thousand fans, especially when the Rochester Mustangs took on Culbertsons or the Minneapolis Bungalows played crosstown rival St. Paul.

Over the next several years, with Minneapolis–St. Paul, Rochester, and Des Moines as regional bases, Bush steadily grew his fledgling league, turning it into a springboard for his own career and an unofficial feeder system for the US national team. In 1959, he managed the US national team at the world championships in Brno, Czechoslovakia, getting his first taste of international competition.

"It's an awful lot of work," he said, "but hockey is a game I like very much. It's meant a lot to me, and I feel that whatever I can do for it in return, I owe to it."

CHAPTER NINE

VIC HEYLIGER LAUNCHES THE NCAA NATIONAL CHAMPIONSHIP TOURNAMENT

Whether Des Moines' city fathers envisioned themselves on the cutting edge of urban planning or knew they were simply jumping on a popular postwar trend, indoor heated rinks with artificial ice were popping up in cities—and on college campuses—from Maine to California.

"In recent months, rinks have gone up at Amherst, Williams, MIT, Middlebury, and Penn State," wrote journalist Whitney Tower in the February 21, 1955 edition of *Sports Illustrated*. "Still more are planned for Nebraska, Colgate, and elsewhere where hockey has captured the imagination of sports-loving college officials and alumni."

This sudden emergence of college hockey seemed completely out of the blue. Prior to WWII, the most popular spectator sports in the United States had been major league baseball, college football, boxing, and horse racing. Hockey and basketball were still relatively new, struggling for attention from media outlets and sports fans, not to mention consumer dollars.

To further complicate matters, once the United States officially entered the war and mobilized its resources on behalf of the Allies, college and professional sports became a mere afterthought. Hockey, in particular, was nearly decimated. With well over sixteen million active service members in the US armed forces—not to mention travel restrictions and food- and fuel-rationing programs—the number of college hockey teams sharply fell from twenty-seven at the end of John Mariucci's senior season in 1940 to less than ten by spring 1945.

In the wake of the war, however, an astonishing 2.2 million returning veterans enrolled in post-secondary education thanks to the Servicemen's Readjustment Act of 1944, otherwise known as the GI Bill. With this sudden influx of bodies and a giddy sense of post-war optimism, college sports came roaring back. Hockey exploded—especially in northern states—quickly becoming a fan favorite on campuses everywhere.

"Artificial ice is being installed wherever hockey-minded students are enrolled," wrote Tower, causing "the fifty-odd colleges which play varsity hockey" to compete in front of "their biggest crowds in history."

To be clear, the first mechanically frozen ice rink had opened in London, England, in 1876. By the 1940s, however, a series of significant technical improvements and lower equipment costs allowed rink managers to create consistently smooth, solid ice immediately adjacent to warmer, more comfortable spectator seating. Gone were the days of bundling up in thick layers of clothes only to shiver through gameplay before hastily retreating to a separate warming room—accessible only to those who'd paid a premium—during brief period breaks while the ice was cleaned and resurfaced. Though far from the only factor, better climate control no doubt made the whole experience better for everyone involved, coaches and players included.

Remarkably, despite significant outflows for technology and infrastructure, college hockey quickly became something of a cash cow for athletic departments and booster clubs throughout the Upper Midwest. The track and baseball programs at Michigan lost a combined $12,000 in 1954, for example, while the hockey program netted over $22,000.

"The haul was $25,000 at North Dakota and $70,000 at Minnesota," marveled *Sports Illustrated*. "When North Dakota plays Minnesota," writer Whitney Tower continued, "special trains take [five hundred] loyal rooters into Gopher Land from Grand Forks to cheer for victory."

Plush "opera-type" seating aside, perhaps the most important factor in college hockey's meteoric rise was the creation of a true NCAA National Championship, a long-enduring dream—if not outright *obsession*—of legendary coach Vic Heyliger.

"Ice hockey has all the requisites for a popular intercollegiate sport," Heyliger told the press in spring 1944, predicting boom times ahead. "It's fast, colorful, and pleases crowds. Once we educate college audiences to the sport and teach students to enjoy the game . . . ice hockey should take its place along with college football and basketball."

With a tangible sense of excitement and track record to back it up, the newly appointed Michigan coach was uniquely positioned to make such an audacious claim. Even as the number of college hockey teams dwindled throughout the first half of the 1940s, Heyliger had worked wonders at the University of Illinois.

When he took the helm of the university's fledgling ice hockey program in 1939, it's said there were only eighteen hockey players on campus—barely enough to fill the varsity roster. Long before his first practice as the Fighting Illini coach, however, Heyliger had recruited a whopping thirty-two freshmen.

Heyliger's off-season efforts soon paid huge dividends. After posting a meager three wins for the 1939–40 season, Illinois racked up a stunning 17–3–1 record to win the Big Ten title the following year. They were also named unofficial "national champions," a title they retained for the next two seasons.

In his four years of coaching at Champaign-Urbana, Heyliger compiled an overall record of 40–20–3 (impressive in light of the fact that eleven of those losses came in his rookie season). At the same time, he developed three standout American players who jumped directly from college to professional clubs: Aldo Palazzari, who played with the New York Rangers and Boston Bruins; Lieutenant Norbert Sterle, known simply as "Norb," who played for the Chicago Blackhawks before he was killed while serving in Italy; and Amo Bessone, who later went on to coach Michigan State for twenty-eight years.

Unfortunately, Heyliger's stellar run as a first-time collegiate coach was abruptly cut short when the US Army Specialized Training Program requisitioned the Champaign-Urbana campus. Mere weeks after completing the 1942–43 season, the ice rink and student union were converted into mess halls and the university's hockey program was suspended indefinitely. In November 1944—after a year spent languishing with no rink, no team, and no hockey—Heyliger resigned and accepted an offer to coach at his alma mater.

"At the time the Army took over," wrote columnist Glenn Roberts in the campus newspaper *The Daily Illini*, "Illinois had a very successful hockey program, a fine coach, and a conference championship team, but no rink. After the war, when they got the rink back, they had neither a coach nor a team."

Once Heyliger returned to Ann Arbor, however, the former Wolverines star was newly energized and bursting with optimism. Chomping on his ever-present unlit cigar, Heyliger began to envision a comprehensive plan for college hockey expansion. It was built around three core concepts: a formal agreement to play by a unified set of rules; a cooperative and inclusive national coaches association; and an annual league-wide playoff to determine the national collegiate title.

> Chomping on his ever-present unlit cigar, Heyliger began to envision a comprehensive plan for college hockey expansion.

"Champions from Eastern, Midwestern, Rocky Mountain, and West Coast sections could meet," he told the Associated Press in January 1947, "and a national champion could be determined in an elimination playoff."

Granted, since Michigan went on to win the first NCAA National Championship in 1948—as well as an incredible six of the first ten titles—the coach's motivation may have been *more than a little self-serving*. Nonetheless, in the absence of a true national championship playoff, Heyliger strongly felt that fans, players, coaches, and boosters would never be fully invested in their team's long-term success.

A geographically centralized annual championship, by contrast, would put every club in contention at the start of each new season.

More than anything else, this tangible "Holy Grail" would get everyone on the same page, governed by the same set of guidelines with respect to eligibility, season schedules, and recruitment—not to mention the basic rules of the game.

"Canadian amateur rules, similar to the National Hockey League's code, permit body checking in any zone and forward passing up to the center red line," the Associated Press explained in an article describing Heyliger's vision. "American collegiate regulations allow body checking only in the defensive zones and passing up to the offensive blue line. Face-off provisions also differ. In American hockey, the puck must lie on the ice, while in Canadian hockey, the referee drops the puck in play."

Underscoring the endless potential for confusion and controversy, Heyliger pointed out that with thousands of rowdy fans cheering at the top of their lungs, "nobody can hear the whistle . . . and an anxious player is bound to swipe at the puck too soon."

To a player like Heyliger, who'd spent parts of two different seasons in the NHL with the Chicago Blackhawks, some of the discrepancies between collegiate and professional rules were downright embarrassing. "When we play several Canadian clubs, they laugh at us when we ask them to play by our rules," said Heyliger, in an interview with the Minneapolis *Tribune* in February 1947, prior to a Gophers–Wolverines game. "They tell us to get in line with modern hockey, and they are right."

Unspoken but clearly implied in Heyliger's comment was the disdain he shared with his Canadian counterparts for the "rinky-dink" aspects of amateur hockey as it was played below the 49th parallel.

No particular rule fully embodied the sometimes-substantial difference between US college hockey and the more "modern" game played by the NHL and its related leagues. But in aggregate, the contrast was stark. Contemporary hockey was faster, harder hitting, and more dynamic than its predecessors. College hockey rules committees had frozen the game in time, even as it grew and changed everywhere else.

Heyliger understood that a unified set of rules was just a means to an end. The promise of a bona fide national championship would be the real driving force. Heyliger sat down and wrote a letter to every college coach in the country, "whether it was a major varsity college team or a club team," and suggested they all have a meeting.

The vast majority responded favorably. Heyliger set a date for the first weekend in May, and hockey coaches from across the country descended on the Hotel Lincoln in New York City.

"Almost all the New England coaches were there," Heyliger said. Also in attendance were coaches from points further west, namely Minnesota, Michigan Tech, Colorado College, and even the University of California at Berkeley.

Just as Heyliger had predicted, once the meeting began, most of the other coaches were particularly excited about the prospect of a national championship tourney. Before they could even begin to hammer out the details, however, everyone knew they needed a governing body to oversee logistics and finances. Thus, by emulating the framework of the recently established American Baseball Coaches Association—which had similarly convened twenty-seven college baseball coaches in June 1945—the attendees drafted and ratified a constitution and bylaws and proceeded to choose its inaugural board of directors.

Murray Murdoch from Yale was elected president; UC-Berkeley's Julius Schroeder was named vice president; and Vic Heyliger became secretary-treasurer. Harry Cleverly (Boston University), John Howard "Howie" Starr (Colgate), Cyril L. "Cheddy" Thompson (Colorado College), and Richard Vaughan (Princeton) rounded out the rest of the group's administrators.

With a governing structure in place, the newly created American Hockey Coaches Association (AHCA) returned its attention to the creation of an officially sanctioned NCAA hockey tournament. Soon, consensus built around the idea of a four-team tournament with one representative from each of the following sections: the Ivy League, New England, the Midwest, and the Far West. Meanwhile, former Hamilton College standout Ed Stanley—who also managed and coached the senior amateur Clinton Hockey Club—was tasked with creating a league to house the various teams from Upstate New York and Pennsylvania, including Clarkson, Colgate, Cornell, Hamilton, Lehigh, and Penn State.

By unanimous vote, the AHCA decided to work with the NCAA to choose a centralized, neutral site to host the first tournament. Initially, many of the coaches favored a Midwestern "hockey town," like Chicago or Detroit. Heyliger, on the other hand, preferred the Greater Boston area for its "greatest concentration of hockey colleges." The biggest concern was financial. Without a decent percentage of the gate receipts, they'd never be able to bring four teams from across the country to a three-day tournament.

"Cheddy Thompson and I were on the site committee," said Heyliger twenty years later in a personal interview with former assistant Wisconsin Badgers Coach Bill Rothwell. "So we called places like Boston Garden and Madison Square Garden . . . to see if they would have any interest in sponsoring a national intercollegiate hockey tournament." Instead, they hit a dead end. "Hell, we didn't get anywhere. They said they would do it on a percentage basis, but not on a guarantee basis, which we felt we needed to insure that expenses were met."

Discouraged but not defeated, Heyliger and Thompson had an idea. "So, as a last resort, we called Thayer Tutt at the Broadmoor Hotel and told him about our predicament." Almost immediately, Tutt was intrigued.

"If I can sell it to the El Pomar board, which controls everything at the Broadmoor, I will sponsor the tournament," he said.

The call was a stroke of genius. Aside from an eighteen-hole championship golf course, manicured walking paths, and outdoor cafes, the five-star Broadmoor Resort also featured an 1,800-seat indoor ice arena. With a stunning arched interior, exposed wooden beams, comfortable seats, carpeted aisles, and an Olympic-size ice sheet, the Broadmoor World Arena was designed to host not only hockey but world-class figure skating events as well.

By 1947, however, the rink still hadn't yet hosted a major hockey tournament. So when Heyliger called out of the blue to propose a national collegiate playoff to be held at the Broadmoor, the stars aligned. "Two weeks later," Heyliger later explained, "Thayer Tutt got back to us and told me that they would pick up all the expenses . . . transportation, meals, housing, hotel, and any other general expenses the teams incurred—even the cost of the hockey officials."

Incredibly, not only did the Broadmoor foot the bill for the first tournament, they did so for a full decade. As Heyliger later noted, back in the early days, "the tournament wasn't run for the money involved. It was more of a social event, an experience for the players."

> As Heyliger later noted, back in the early days, "the tournament wasn't run for the money involved. It was more of a social event, an experience for the players.

With a parade, a ball, a banquet, and door-to-door service in Cadillac limousines, Boston College coach John "Snooks" Kelley heartily agreed. "They showed a bunch of kids what western hospitality was all about," he said. "Thayer Tutt did everything possible to see that the hockey players enjoyed their visits. I don't think any member of the team will ever forget . . . It was just, well, heaven on earth. That's what we called it. Heaven."

CHAPTER TEN

WILLIAMSON AND BROOKS:
GOPHER FRESHMAN TEAMMATES

After spending a hot, dirty summer working on the back of a garbage truck in Winnipeg's Fort Garry district, Murray Williamson moved into historic Pioneer Hall on the University of Minnesota campus in fall 1955. Having transferred the previous spring, Williamson had already completed his first college term. He couldn't help but feel awkward and visibly out of sync with the rest of his freshmen peers. The fact that he was the lone Canadian recruit on the Gophers freshman roster certainly didn't help.

Despite being one of the most vocal proponents for US player development at the collegiate level, John Mariucci had recruited his first Canadian prospect the previous year. Fort Frances, Ontario, native Mike Pearson caught Mariucci's attention and earned a spot on the Gophers freshman team. Mariucci liked the fact that Pearson was more interested in academics than athletics, having previously turned down offers from the Pittsburgh Hornets and Toronto Maple Leafs to pursue a college degree.

Also, unlike many Canadian players on rival Western Intercollegiate Hockey League (WIHL) teams who entered the league already well into their twenties, Pearson was only nineteen, essentially the same age as his US-born teammates. For Mariucci, this distinction was vital. A quality guy like Mike Pearson didn't perceive college hockey as a lowly alternative to thrashing around in the minors while awaiting his chance to join one of six NHL teams. Rather, finding a roster spot in a top US college program was his first choice, giving him the chance to play the sport he loved while building for his future.

Murray Williamson, by contrast, had never been a particularly strong student, despite his recent attempts to get an education at Eveleth Junior College while playing for the ill-fated Rangers—a dream his father had long envisioned. Williamson wouldn't *object* to getting a free education, but after enduring several years in the Junior A meat grinder, he was first and foremost a hockey player. He was used to enduring marathon seasons that spanned forty to sixty games rather than the mere twenty allowed by NCAA rules.

"Up in Canada, they have the advantage of a longer season," Williamson told a local newspaper reporter in the fall of his freshman year, unable or unwilling to mask his frustration. "I used to haul out my skates in September and wouldn't put them away until April." Perhaps speaking a bit too freely in public, Williamson's perspective underscored the fact he was one of very few non-Minnesotans in Mariucci's program.

Maroosh had freely admitted it would be a "mighty task" to replace graduating seniors Dick Meredith, Jim Mattson, and superstar John Mayasich. Nonetheless, he'd publicly pinned his hopes on an ambitious two-year plan. He would build his team around his eleven returning sophomores. Then, he'd add a freshman class of stellar high school recruits whose names sounded like they were cribbed directly from a stack of 1955 MSHSL Tournament scoresheets.

"We must get the state's best every year to meet the challenge of the Canadian-dominated teams," Mariucci had proclaimed earlier that year at the Lowry Hotel. A mere six months later, in the wake of an epic postseason that "went down in the record books as the greatest in history," the coach had gotten his wish. No fewer than twelve players who'd competed in the MSHSL Tournament had enrolled at Minnesota.

Among the incoming freshmen were Jack Almquist, Jack Delmore, and John Larson from Roseau; Joey Poole and Loren "Sid" Vraa from Thief River Falls; Larry Alm and Jim Westby from Minneapolis

South; and Merv Meredith, George Noble, and Roger Rovick from second-place Minneapolis Southwest.

Despite the accomplishments and potential of those players, however, Gopher hockey insiders were most intrigued by two recruits from St. Paul: the flashy but muscular Stu Anderson and the speedy, more cerebral Herb Brooks. In 1954, the electrifying duo had led the Governors to a third-place finish. The next year, they won it all, an accomplishment that stuck with Brooks for the rest of his life.

"Winning the 1955 State Tournament with my best friends was the single most successful moment in my life," he reportedly said, reflecting on the championship game years later, "even more than winning the 1980 Olympics."

It's the kind of statement you make in the heat of the moment. You're hoisting the State Championship banner and you feel like the King of the World. Those who knew Brooks, however, insist he truly meant it. Either way, Herb Brooks and the "Miracle" have become so intertwined over the past four decades, it's easy to forget he had a life beyond the one we saw on the silver screen. Twenty-five years *before* he coached Team USA, Herb Brooks was known as a savvy, fluid skater with great instinct for making big plays.

Murray Williamson, on the other hand, was nearly twenty-one years and three months old when the *Star Tribune* quietly noted, in April 1955, "one of Winnipeg's standout players" had officially transferred from Eveleth Junior College to the Gophers. Understandably, with an estimated 170 games already behind him—not to mention six months away from playing organized hockey—Williamson was eager to hit the ice and begin his college career, even if that only meant a seemingly endless string of routine practices occasionally interrupted by a rare intrasquad scrimmage.

If anyone understood Williamson's aggravation with lack of ice time, it was freshman coach Glen Sonmor, a twenty-six-year-old former pro and fellow Canadian who'd grown up in Hamilton, Ontario. Sonmor had recently suffered a career-ending eye injury, hit by an errant slap shot from his Cleveland Barons teammate Steve Kraftcheck.

Coincidentally, five years earlier, Sonmor and John Mariucci had been teammates when they played for the Minneapolis Millers. After a season skating together, the seasoned NHL pro took the youngster under his wing.

"We were in the playoffs in Omaha," Sonmor recalled, quoted by John Gilbert in his book *Herb Brooks: The Inside Story of a Hockey Mastermind*, "and John said, 'Kid, all my teammates have always been Canadians, and you're the first one who ever finished high school. You're going to college.' So every summer, I'd come back from pro hockey and go to the University of Minnesota."

True to form, once Mariucci heard the heartrending news, he graciously arranged for Sonmor to fill in for Marsh Ryman as coach of the freshman team. Ironically, the opening had been created by Mariucci himself. He was taking a leave of absence to coach the 1956 US Olympic team, so Ryman was subbing for him.

Sonmor had been a star for the Brandon Wheat Kings when they won the Abbott Cup in 1949. He'd also scored twenty goals in back-to-back seasons with the Barons. Unfortunately, he'd never quite hit his stride in the NHL. In thirty games with the New York Rangers, he only scored twice. Still, he knew good hockey when he saw it and had nothing but praise for his fellow Canadian.

"Murray has real hockey sense," he said. "He shoots quick and is extremely clever around the opponent's net." Predicting a bright future, he said, "Williamson should help the varsity plenty next year," before adding cheekily, "he's got that Canadian touch."

Once Gophers hockey fans finally got a look at the much-hyped class of rookies, they heartily agreed with Sonmor's assessment. "Hockey followers marvel at the Northerner's skill in stick handling and passing," raved one local paper, while the *Minneapolis Star* simply concluded that the second Canadian prospect to join the Gophers in two years "looks as if he will also help the varsity plenty next year."

> Predicting a bright future, he said, "Williamson should help the varsity plenty next year," before adding cheekily, "he's got that Canadian touch."

In the traditional varsity freshman scrimmage, however, the flashy Williamson incongruously stayed off the scoresheet while Minnesotans Roger Rovick, Merv Meredith, and Herb Brooks all tallied first-period goals to stun their elders. Eventually, the upperclassmen exploded, pumping in three goals in two minutes as they cruised to a 7–4 win, keeping the pecking order intact.

That goal by Brooks may well have been the first time teammate Murray Williamson really took notice of the quiet, analytical kid from St. Paul who still lived at home with his parents. Though all the other freshmen—especially those who'd competed against Herb Brooks and Stu Anderson—were clearly familiar with the pair's recent state tournament exploits, Williamson had remained largely oblivious to the championship mystique that seemed to follow them everywhere they went.

"Somebody told me two guys who'd played on the State Championship team were coming to the U," Williamson says. "I guess it sounded impressive. I just didn't know why." Williamson couldn't shake the perspective he'd had since he was a kid. "If you played hockey in the Prairie Provinces there were only three cups," he explains. "The Abbott Cup, the Memorial Cup, and the Stanley Cup. If it wasn't one of those three, we couldn't care less."

Since the first time he'd laced up skates to play a game of shinny at the neighborhood rink, Williamson had understood the step-by-step progression. The first task was to land a spot on one of the top Junior A teams sponsored by an NHL club. There, you went on to win your league championship and compete for the Abbott Cup, the yearly prize awarded to the top Junior A team in Western Canada. After that, you moved up to play the top team from the East in a best-of-seven series for the Memorial Cup, awarded to the top Junior A team in the whole country. Finally, after your stellar career in juniors, you played for your NHL team and competed for the Stanley Cup—which you won in the third period of the seventh game after scoring the go-ahead goal on a breakaway.

For young Canadian players, there was no such thing as high school hockey. Any player worth his salt was swept into the sponsorship system, his professional rights acquired by an NHL club who then assigned him to one of their feeder teams. "In those days," says Williamson with a self-deprecating chuckle, "they bought us for the cost of a $100 team jacket. Mine had a big red C for the Canadiens. I thought I was a really big deal. Every one of us did. The system worked like a charm."

Precollegiate resumes notwithstanding, Brooks and Williamson had seen each other dozens of times by early December. With Brooks living off campus, however, commuting back and forth to practice every day, the two rarely interacted away from the rink. Eventually, the two future Olympic coaches became lifelong friends and colleagues; but for most of their freshman year, neither one of them seemed to much notice the other at all.

Of course, as is often the case with a mythical figure like Brooks, there are those who never met him yet feel like they know him well . . . and those who spent years by his side yet still don't understand what actually made him tick.

"I had Herb for six years," says stalwart defenseman Bill Baker from the 1980 team, "in college at Minnesota, on the Olympic team, and in the NHL. I'm not sure I *ever* knew him."

Mariucci, by contrast, wore his heart on his sleeve. He was probably incapable of playing mind games with his players. Instead, he cut to the chase and let you know where you stood, often with one of his classic, quotable one-liners. "Williamson!" he would say—or Brooks or whoever it was—"every day you're playing worse than the day before, and today you're playing like tomorrow."

Anyone who ever suited up for Maroosh knew he had a good heart. He was the definition of *a players' coach*. He would do anything for his players, and they loved him for it. Some of those whom he competed against, however, never got to see his kinder, gentler side. Some of his fellow coaches, particularly on the East Coast, all too willingly bought into the tough guy act, painting him as little more than a hooligan on or off the ice.

CHAPTER ELEVEN

THE PAPER SALESMAN WHO BROUGHT DOWN THE WIHL

When John Mariucci coached the 1956 US Olympic team, sportswriters, fellow coaches, and fans commended his players for their hard, clean brand of hockey and ability to adapt to "the European style." Harvard coach Ralph "Cooney" Weiland, by contrast, thought Mariucci's collegiate players were uncontrolled goons.

After dropping a two-game series against Minnesota at Williams Arena in December 1957, the former Boston Bruins star famously unleashed an infamous tirade several old-timers can still quote. "The style of hockey Minnesota played against us Saturday would not be tolerated in the East," Weiland complained to the press. "You might as well use *picks and shovels* instead of hockey sticks."

While it's true that Harvard defenseman John Copeland suffered a broken wrist in a collision with Williamson along the boards, Minnesota was only called for three penalties on the night (two less than Harvard's five).

"No hockey player worth the name will complain about a legitimate body check in the open," Weiland continued, "but when they charge a guy into the fence, put elbows and sticks in his face, use threatening gestures and molest a player when he doesn't even have the puck, it's time to call a halt."

Hearing Weiland's comments later, Mariucci was mystified. "I'm embarrassed and a little disgusted," he said the following Monday. "I thought Friday's game was the rougher of the two, but both seemed exceptionally clean . . . I can't understand Cooney. I saw him for quite a while after the game Saturday, and he never said a word about dirty play."

If Mariucci's reputation for hospitality is any indication, the two coaches likely met for a drink shortly after the game, laughing and swapping stories for hours. No doubt referee Arnie Bauer was also along for the ride. "It was about the cleanest game I ever worked," he told reporters. "Actually, Mariucci doesn't coach his team to body check much. The Gophers rely on the poke check, and Harvard seemed to me to try much more body checking."

By the mid-1950s, *where* body checks could be thrown was the subject of an increasingly fractious debate. Since 1928, collegiate rules specified a two-minute penalty for any body check thrown *outside* the defensive zone. In the 1930s, however, the NHL began to allow body checks *anywhere* on the ice. Since then, two contrasting styles of play had emerged that generally broke down along geographic lines.

As the product of elite boarding schools and Ivy League universities, hockey on the East Coast tended to favor speed, skill, and teamwork while also discouraging "unnecessary rough play." Coaches and pundits embraced a "scientific" vision of hockey, where passing and tactics were prized.

In the Midwest, by contrast, players and coaches mimicked hockey as it was played by their Canadian neighbors. In northern working-class cities like Eveleth, Hibbing, Duluth, Marquette, and Fargo, the game was much rougher and more individualistic. On the municipal rinks and ponds of immigrant neighborhoods, you skated hard into the corners and battled for the puck. It was a game of keep-away, even from your own teammates.

As recently as 2015, a senior forward from North Dakota broke down the contrasting styles that generally persist to this day. "In the West, it's more of a grinding, physical game," he told reporters. "On the East Coast, it's more wide open and offensive. It'll be interesting to see how the styles clash." It's a statement that could have been made at virtually any point in the past eight decades.

As for John Copeland's broken wrist, Williamson is blunt. "He had his head down and turned into me. Yeah, I guess I hit him, but you've got to keep your head up. That's just basic hockey."

Within the Western League, the rhetoric was overheated, with constant accusations of biased refs and inconsistent calls. After North Dakota lost to the Gophers 4–3 at Williams Arena, visiting coach Al Renfrew blasted the officiating as "the worst I have ever seen." Since both officials were from Minneapolis, Renfrew suggested one Canadian official should have worked the game.

"Why stop there?" Mariucci retorted sarcastically. "Why don't we just move the game to Canada? That way, the players can go home for the weekend."

In a calmer, more reflective moment several weeks later, Mariucci added, "The trouble with North Dakota and other teams in the league is that they want to play by Canadian rules. This is a league of American colleges, run under NCAA rules. Why should we submit to Canadian rules just because most of the players in the league come from Canada?"

Over the years, Mariucci could sound maddeningly inconsistent when addressing the "Canadian player problem." Sometimes, he saw Canadian players as a boon to the league, raising the level of play and pushing US-born players to develop and keep improving. Other times, he openly criticized his fellow coaches—as he did with Renfrew— accusing them of importing way too many Canadians, quashing state high school leagues by ignoring US-born players.

> "Everybody in hockey knew he was 100% for the American player and 110% for Minnesotan."

Either way, he knew he was in a privileged position. With arguably the best state high school league in the country, his home state was a gold mine, and his mission never wavered. In the words of Dan McKinnon, captain of the 1956 US Olympic team, "Everybody in hockey knew he was 100% for the American player and 110% for Minnesotan."

On the same day he was named Gophers hockey coach, Mariucci proclaimed, "I took this job with the idea of winning with Minnesota boys, and I'm sure we can do it." Echoing the coach's commitment and enthusiasm the following day, the Minneapolis *Star* wryly noted, "The ink was hardly dry on Maroosh's contract before he left this afternoon for the hockey hotbed of Eveleth, hopeful of lining up as many of the Range's prospects as possible."

No question, Canadian skaters raised the caliber of US college hockey in the 1950s and '60s. Whether or not they also lifted the skill of American players or simply gobbled up roster spots is an entirely separate question. Either way, at the time, even if a Canadian player had signed a formal agreement that bound his services to a specific professional team—complete with disbursements for room, board, and other expenses— *technically*, he maintained his amateur status. At least, he did in the eyes of the Canadian Amateur Hockey Association (CAHA).

Despite the clear language contained in the NCAA's supposed "amateur code," plenty of US college hockey programs happily accepted CAHA's assessment, ignoring the clause that read "one who takes or has taken pay, or has accepted the promise of pay, in any form . . . or has directly or indirectly used his athletic skill for pay in any form, shall not be eligible for intercollegiate athletics." With virtually no enforcement throughout the postwar boom years, there were essentially no restrictions on recruiting top "amateurs" from Canadian Junior A teams. Coaches like Michigan's Vic Heyliger, Michigan State's Amo Bessone, Colorado College's Tom Bedecki, and Denver's Murray Armstrong readily exploited every loophole to pack their rosters with ringers in the relentless pursuit of the coveted national title.

In fact, during the Wolverines' 1955–56 season, their exclusively Canadian roster included Wally Maxwell, a twenty-two-year-old left wing who'd actually played two games with the Toronto Maple Leafs *prior* to enrolling at Michigan. After he'd already posted seven goals and four assists en route to a season record of 20–2–1, however, NCAA officials declared Maxwell ineligible and he was banned from postseason play. Prolific sophomore center John Rendell and stalwart defenseman Neill Buchanan were also disqualified. Even so, the Wolverines topped Michigan Tech by a score of 7–5 to capture their sixth NCAA national title in nine years.

One year later, Colorado College had four different players between the ages of twenty-four and twenty-seven on their official roster. (Denver's oldest player, by contrast, was a sprightly twenty-four years of age.) Among CC's elder statesmen were future Chicago Blackhawk Bill "Red" Hay and notorious bruiser Cy Whiteside, a 190-pound, six-foot-two-inch defenseman whose *pre*collegiate career included stints with numerous Junior A teams and Scotland's Ayr Raiders of the British National League.

In defense of his recruiting tactics, CC's Canadian-born coach Tom Bedecki told *Sports Illustrated*, "Canadians are better hockey players than Americans, not because they are better athletes, but because they are better trained . . . Canadian boys start playing as young as seven or eight. There are a number of different divisions for youngsters, and they play five years of competitive hockey at the rate of about forty games per year. When they come to us, they've got about [two hundred] games under their belts. They know how to play hockey."

Unsurprisingly, Bedecki failed to mention Mariucci's major complaint: many of these Canadian players were upwards of twenty years old by the time they entered college. It was precisely this gap in age and experience that frustrated Mariucci to no end. If the playing field wasn't level, how could American players ever hope to catch up?

In the decade since WWII ended, according to *Sports Illustrated*, "the annual invasion by hundreds of Canadian students, a good many of whom, by some fortuitous chance, also happen to be crackerjack hockey players" had pushed aside all but a minute percentage of the top American skaters. In the 1956–57 season alone, Colorado College rostered eighteen Canadians and one American skater; the University of Denver lineup featured seventeen Canadians and one US-born player; and North Dakota played with thirteen Canadians and three Americans. Minnesota's roster, by contrast, had "but three Canadians and nineteen Americans"—the exact opposite of the three other teams.

The Western League had been an unstable alliance right from the start. Without enough Big Ten teams to form a purely Big Ten league, Vic Heyliger had cobbled together a makeshift confederation composed of seven teams from five different conferences.

"The league has always been an unwieldy, synthetic affair," said Heyliger, "racked by distrust and dissatisfaction since it was born in 1951." By the time the Gophers' annual Christmas break trip rolled around in December 1957, the writing was on the wall.

In previous years, the Colorado trip had been a highlight of the Gophers' season. Nothing else quite compared to staying at the Broadmoor Hotel and playing in Denver Arena—a former WWII navy drill hall that had been torn down and reassembled to house the fledgling Pioneers.

This year, things felt different.

Before the first game even started, the younger, less experienced Gophers were on edge. "Marv Jorde was so nervous, he somehow ended up with two contact lenses in the same eye," says Murray Williamson, a junior at the time. "We spent ten minutes crawling around, looking all over the place for the one he thought was missing before he finally figured it out."

Minnesota had good reason to worry. "In the first period of the first game of our road trip, Colorado College came out and literally beat up our squad," Williamson continues. "Mariucci was having trouble actually keeping guys on the ice." To make matters even worse, a group of boisterous CC students behind the Gophers bench had been heckling Mariucci since the opening face-off. At one point, the coach spun around and growled, "You guys better go find a Canadian league to play in, because we're not coming back!"

After a frenetic first frame, the Gophers trailed the Tigers 3–2. Even that slim one-goal lead felt insurmountable. Despite plenty of crushing hits and high elbows at both ends of the rink, the two local referees had only called one lousy penalty.

"And it was on Marv Jorde!" Williamson exclaims, shaking his head in disbelief all these decades later. "Two minutes for high-sticking.

1968 Pre-Olympic tournament podium: Lou Nanne, Vitali Davidov, Terry O'Malley (Canada), unknown Czech player.

Murray Williamson's official Olympic photo, 1968.

1968 Olympic team. Front row: Jack Ferrera, Jerry Melnychuk, John Cunniff, Lou Nanne, Herb Brooks, Len Lilyholm, Pat Rupp. Second row (standing): Dick Rose, Don Niederkorn, Bob Paradise, Jack Morrison, Larry Stordahl, Doug Volmar, Bruce Riutta, Larry Pleau, Paul Hurley, Doc Nagobads, Murray Williamson. Top row: Marsh Tschida, Tom Hurley, Jim Logue (replaced Ferrera), Bob Gaudreau, Craig Falkman.

1968 Olympic team heading to Grenoble, France.

Warm-up session in Grenoble. Left to right are Len Lilyholm, Jerry York,
Bob Gaudreau, Don Ross, Larry Pleau, and others.

Murray Williamson with Lou Nanne during practice session in Grenoble.

Herb Brooks and Don Ross at the gold medal ceremony for the World B
Championships in Bucharest, Romania.

1970 US national team.

1971 US national team.

Russian hockey coach Anatoly Tarasov, left, chats with Murray, center, during the 1971 World Championships in Berne, Switzerland. At right is a Russian interpreter.

US Goalie Carl Wetzel grimaces playing against the Russians in Berne.

Carl Wetzel against the Russians in Switzerland, 1971.

1971 national team members Murray Williamson, Carl Wetzel, Hal Trumble (manager).

Mingling with the super-team Russians, 1971.

Displaying Minnesota hospitality to Anatoly Tarasov, left, and a Russian interpreter, seated right, are Williamson and his three sons during Christmas 1971. Seated in Tarasov's lap is Randy Williamson. With him are brothers Dean, center, and Kevin.

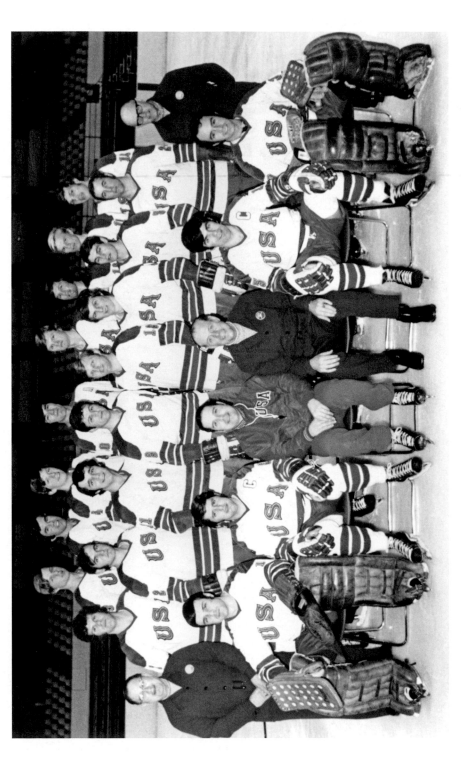

1972 Olympic team. Front row: Pete Sears, Keith "Huffer" Christiansen, Murray Williamson (Coach), Hal Trumble (Manager), Tim Sheehy, Mike "Lefty" Curran. Middle row: Bud Kessel (Equipment Manager), Bruce McIntosh, Jim McElmury, Larry Bader, Frank Sanders, Ron Naslund, Wally Olds, Charlie Brown, Tim Regan, Doc Nagobads. Top row: Mark Howe, Craig Sarner, Tom Mellor, Henry Boucha, Dick McGlynn, Kevin Ahearn, Robbie Ftorek, Stu Irving.

Robbie Ftorek scoring against Poland in the 1972 Olympic Games.

Playing against Sweden in the '72 Olympics.

1972 Olympic game action with Huffer Christiansen and Henry Boucha scoring against the Russians.

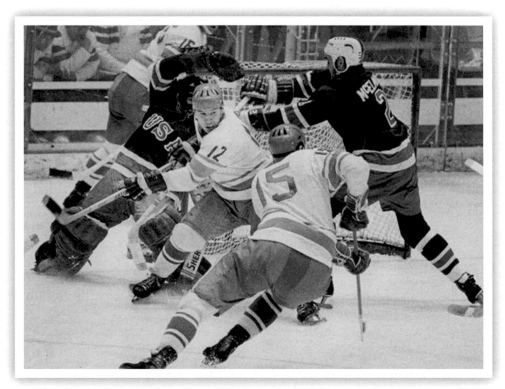

Lefty Curran and Jim McElmury doing handstands versus the Russians at the 1972 Olympic Games.

Snowball fight in the Olympic Village.

Post-game celebration in the Olympic Village with Kevin Ahearn,
Hal Trumble, unnamed Russian star, and Frank Sanders.

Silver medal ceremony in Sapporo, Japan, February 1972.

1972 Russian national team with Tarasov.

Silver medal ceremony in Sapporo, Japan.

The most placid guy on the team! Explain that one to me. He was protecting himself so he wouldn't get steamrolled."

"Turning loose a bruising, body-checking style of play" in the middle period, the Tigers exploded for four unanswered goals. Then the fists started flying. In the final minute of the second period, Gophers brothers Larry and Gary Alm were both ejected for fighting, along with the Tigers' Murray Dea and Jack Smith.

Back in the locker room for the second intermission, Herb Brooks wondered aloud why a bunch of scrawny kids barely out of high school were playing a team of much bigger, stronger Canadians. Williamson quietly noted that maybe they should be careful not to make too much of a fuss since the Gophers also had three Canadians on their roster. Mariucci whirled and said, "That can change if you're not careful."

Minnesota held its own in the third period, but by then, it didn't matter. "It was a team victory for the Tigers, who outskated and outfought the visitors all the way," said the Denver *Free Press.* "The smaller Gophers were hardly in the contest after the first twenty minutes."

"You can't give one coach a machine gun and the other a bow and arrow," Mariucci vented. "What are they trying to do? The Big Ten can't use players like that. Is it fair for us to use one set of rules and them another?"

His frustration boiling over, Mariucci took a swipe at Murray Armstrong, whose Pioneers Minnesota would face the following evening. "You can't tell me that some of these DU players haven't been to professional tryout camps and received expense money," he said, referencing the resumes of certain former Junior A players in the Denver lineup.

Canadian-born Armstrong—himself a product of the Saskatchewan Junior League—was widely known for unapologetically recruiting former Junior A players. His inaugural "freshman" class included former Regina Pats players Conrad Collie, Wayne Klinck, and Murray Massier, all of whom had followed their coach to Colorado College. Detractors soon branded the Tigers as the "Regina Ex-Pats."

With this "war of words" still echoing down the hallways and into the locker rooms, it didn't take very long for the teams to find themselves in the midst of a "free-for-all." In a contentious first period, Minnesota forward Mike Pearson intercepted an ill-advised pass in front of the Denver net and banged it home to give the Gophers a 2–1 lead. Moments later, with the first frame about to expire, Gopher defenseman Larry Alm ran into a Pioneer winger behind the Gophers net. Moments later, sticks and gloves littered the ice and both benches had emptied as the game quickly descended into "the full rhubarb."

Eventually, the referees got control and cleared the ice for five minutes. Things simmered down after that; but with no more scoring the rest of the game, both teams seemed more interested in racking up the number of hits than putting the puck in the net.

Despite the Gophers' 2–1 upset of the vaunted Pioneers, the following afternoon Mariucci insinuated things had already passed the point of no return. "Next season, we'll probably play an independent schedule," he said, noting that CC and Denver would not be among the Gophers' opponents. "We'd like to play Duluth branch and Big Ten schools—Michigan, Michigan State—and perhaps we can interest other Big Ten schools to compete."

Back in the Midwest, even as Denver was downing Minnesota 4–2 in their rematch, Michigan and Michigan State were filing letters of withdrawal from the WIHL. The two schools cited major discrepancies in eligibility standards and recruiting practices as their primary reason, but Murray Armstrong remained defiant.

"The usual reason for an age rule is to protect younger boys from more mature players," he said, "but in this case, the Big Ten wants to protect players only from mature *foreign* students. If an American student is older, that's quite all right . . . Western League hockey is top-grade hockey because we do have Canadian players . . . They're good students, and they're not here just to play hockey."

By then, it didn't matter. With Michigan and Michigan State dropping out of the league, Minnesota's withdrawal was inevitable. "There's open defiance of the rules," said Mariucci. "Things have reached a ridiculous stage. Aren't we interested in developing

American hockey players?"

In the series finale, the Gophers came out flying, pumping in three first-period goals and adding two more in the second to take a 5–0 lead before Colorado College even got on the board. At the same time, Jack McCartan turned away 47 of 50 shots for a dominant 8–3 win. By then, newspapers were far more interested in sensationalizing the coaches' feud, however, than simply recapping the game.

Asked to comment about the escalating feud, Armstrong said, "Show me one player on my team who has attended a pro tryout camp. There isn't one. Yet everybody believes we're full of professionals. Why don't they get the facts?" Armstrong concluded his rant by saying Mariucci was nothing more than "a paper salesman from Minnesota trying to explain away a bad loss," referring to the fact that Mariucci ran a wholesale paper business on the side.

> "Show me one player on my team who has attended a pro tryout camp. There isn't one. Yet everybody believes we're full of professionals. Why don't they get the facts?"

"When John read those remarks in the paper Sunday morning, he switched his wrath from the CC *team* to Murray Armstrong the *person*," Williamson says. "Over the years, the two coaches had been friends, but they couldn't be more opposite people. John was an Iron Ranger who liked his martinis after the game. Armstrong never drank and looked like a Lutheran minister."

A few days later, local reporters asked him to comment on Armstrong's outburst. Mariucci insisted it was time to stop bickering and get back to playing hockey. Before dropping the subject, however, Mariucci took one last shot, slyly underscoring his team's success against the Pioneers. "I wish my overall record was as good as my record against Armstrong and Denver," he deadpanned.

On January 8, 1958, the University of Minnesota sent its official letter of withdrawal to professor W. A. Longacre, secretary of the WIHL. The letter read, in part, "In the opinion of our Senate Committee on Intercollegiate Athletics and our hockey coaches, the WIHL has been unable to achieve [eligibility standards] that are compatible with the obligations of this university as a member of the Big Ten Conference. We therefore find no alternative but to withdraw from the league."

Leaving their options open, they added, "Our withdrawal does not necessarily mean we will no longer compete in hockey with other league institutions; merely that we do not deem it desirable to continue under league obligations as to scheduling."

With the three Big Ten teams out of the picture, Michigan Tech also withdrew shortly thereafter and the league effectively imploded, leaving the teams to play an independent schedule. For the 1959–60 season, all seven of the former WIHL member programs came back together to form the Western Collegiate Hockey Association (WCHA). With the option to set their own schedules and no league obligation to play every member team, Denver and Minnesota would not play each other in the regular season for over a decade.

Meanwhile, the Gophers had been mathematically eliminated from postseason contention by the time they faced Colorado College for the second time. Nonetheless, they provided an ironic finale for the ill-fated WIHL. By sweeping the Tigers in their final two games, they knocked CC out of the playoffs and put in Denver. After a thrilling 2–1 overtime win on Saturday night at Williams Arena, Minneapolis *Star* columnist Charles Johnson wrote, "What a finish the Minnesota hockey team made against Colorado! That was hockey at its best in recent years for the Gophers. More power to those scrappers."

Exactly one week later—also at Williams Arena—the Denver "Regina Ex-Pats" beat North Dakota 6–2 to win the NCAA National Championship. Wayne Klinck and Conrad Collie were instrumental in the lopsided win, and Murray Massier was named MVP.

It had been a tumultuous season, but Mariucci had won the battle and made his point. As a fierce advocate for homegrown talent, he practiced what he preached, building his rosters around a core group of high school stars from his home state. Throughout his career with the Gophers, he remained deeply committed to recruiting and developing US-born players.

During his fourteen years at the University of Minnesota, Mariucci coached eleven All-Americans and numerous other skaters who went on to play for and coach US Olympic teams and pro clubs. He was instrumental in the careers of Herb Brooks, Bob Johnson, John Mayasich, Lou Nanne, Doug Woog, Ken Yackel, and a diminutive fireplug from Winnipeg by the name of Murray Williamson.

With a silver medal of his own, a silver from Williamson, and both silver and gold from Brooks, no hockey coach did more to help bring home Olympic medals than Maroosh. He is merely one of the numerous coaches, builders, and visionaries who helped pave the road to Lake Placid, but his contributions were second to none.

CHAPTER TWELVE

WALTER BUSH LAYS THE FOUNDATION
OF THE USHL

US Hockey Hall of Fame inductee Walter Bush started playing hockey at age seven. If there was anything even vaguely resembling a sheet of ice, Bush and his friends would trundle off to Lynnhurst Field at 48th and Fremont in southwest Minneapolis to play a game of shinny.

"But there weren't really any teams quite yet," Bush said in 2013 interview with the Minneapolis Storm Youth Hockey Association. "It was all pickup hockey with whatever kids happened to show up."

In ninth grade, Bush enrolled at Breck. At the time, it was an all-boys military academy. It was there Bush made his first foray into organized sport, playing tennis, football, and hockey for the school's varsity teams. He loved hockey most of all but didn't get a lot of ice time, so he also played at nearby Lake of the Isles whenever he could.

As a member of the Kenwood Huskies in a newly created outdoor league, Bush skated alongside some of Minneapolis's best youth hockey players and future stars. Teammate Arnie Oss later won a silver medal with the 1952 US Olympic team. Dickie Meredith also won silver, in 1956, and later added gold at the 1960 Olympics.

After an unremarkable high school hockey career, Bush spent four years in the Ivy League under legendary coach Eddie Jeremiah. He graduated from Dartmouth in 1951 and moved back to the Twin Cities to pursue a law degree.

Somehow, despite the intense demands of studying for the state bar exam, Bush managed to "keep his skates sharp" by forming, playing for, and coaching the legendary senior league team sponsored by Culbertson's Cafe.

As part of Minnesota's far-flung, ever-changing collection of senior amateur leagues, the Culbertsons played their home games on the sleek artificial ice of the new 5,400-seat Minneapolis Arena at 29th and Dupont—a mere two-and-a-half miles from where Bush grew up. They were paid $25 for every home game, "but two percent of our gate receipts went to something called AHAUS," Bush recalled. "We had no idea what that was or why we paid them, and since I was the only lawyer on the team, I sort of got 'volunteered' to go to the next AHAUS meeting in Duluth."

It was a decision that would forever change the course of amateur hockey in the United States. Bush not only got a detailed behind-the-scenes look at amateur hockey economics, he hit it off with the men who were slowly turning a disparate collection of local teams, players, and leagues into a unified national association. These were the pioneers, visionaries, and builders of amateur hockey in the United States: men like Walter Brown, Bob Ridder, Connie Pleban, Cal Marvin, and Thayer Tutt. Over the next thirty-five years—"by pure accident," as he liked to say—Bush would become one of the most recognized and respected leaders in hockey.

Bush made his first mark in spring 1955, a watershed moment for senior league hockey in Minnesota and the Upper Midwest. Over the previous decade, a head-spinning eighteen different hockey clubs, from seven different cities in three different states, had competed in an ever-shifting array of leagues. Bush knew this chaotic arrangement was not sustainable. He had a vision for consolidating and streamlining league operations and steadfastly started working to make it a reality.

Built on the scaffolding of the former American Amateur Hockey League (AAHL), the subsequent Central Hockey League (CHL), and the short-lived Minnesota Hockey League (MHL), the newly reinvented United States Central Hockey League sought to build and sustain franchises by recruiting and retaining top-tier talent. The players would not be paid; but by anchoring teams in cities with a heartfelt connection to hockey, plenty of job opportunities, supportive employers, and a healthy dose of local pride, Bush hoped he could make it work.

For the inaugural season, Minneapolis was home to two of the league's four teams, Bungalows and Culbertsons. St. Paul featured a team sponsored by Peter's Meats. And Rochester reinvented the Mustangs. In any case—whether despite or because of its small geographical footprint—right from its inception, the league was a prime destination for top-caliber graduates from the University of Minnesota, North Dakota, Dartmouth, and other major US college teams. A handful of players had even formerly played in the NHL.

"Our teams are composed mostly of former college and pro stars," Walter Bush told Bill Bryson of the *Des Moines Register* in the November 9, 1955, edition. "Hockey is different from most sports," he said, explaining the mixture of players that ranged from those in the twilight of their careers to those who'd yet to play an official NCAA contest. "A pro can stay out for two years and regain his amateur status ... Our amateur hockey compares favorably with the best played anywhere in the [United States]."

John Mariucci, for one, had finished his pro career on unaffiliated minor pro teams in each of the two Twin Cities, suiting up for the Minneapolis Millers in 1949–50—and again in his final season of 1951–52—while playing in St. Paul for the season in between. In 1953, when Mariucci became head coach of the Gophers, he saw the budding league he'd recently left as the perfect place to develop young players. They could get some much-needed ice time and maybe learn a few tricks from wily veterans who'd been knocking around for years on various minor pro teams.

By 1959, Bush had become the director of AHAUS and general manager of the US national team. That year, Bush and Marsh Ryman—the head coach who'd previously coached the Gophers' freshman team—implemented an ambitious fifty-five-game exhibition schedule against Senior A and D1 college teams. The additional ice time against top competition worked wonders, yielding impressive wins over Finland, Sweden, and Czechoslovakia at the world tournament. The team finished with a respectable 3–2 record to finish in fourth place.

The following year, Bush served as a director on the United States Olympic Committee for the 1960 Winter Games and was tangentially involved in helping to organize the first gold-medal-winning US hockey team. After that stunning success, Bush stepped away to serve as president of the Minnesota Amateur Hockey Association. He held that position until 1963, overseeing significant growth in the number of teams and players.

After the collapse of Canada's Eastern Professional Hockey League, Bush organized a group of investors and bought the newly defunct Kingston Frontenacs. Led by a young player-coach by the name of Harry Sinden, the Frontenacs relocated to Minnesota and became the Minneapolis Bruins. Bush had become a pro franchise owner and begun his ascent to NHL team president.

In the meantime, Bob Fleming and Connie Pleban led the US national team to an impressive third-place finish at the 1962 World Championships in Colorado Springs. With just two weeks of practice and two exhibition games behind them, the United States posted a solid record of 5–2–0. Of course, with the Soviets, Czechoslovaks, and Canadians all absent due to political tensions, the Americans never faced three of the world's top teams. Whether despite or because of that, the following year, everything came crashing down.

Depending which headline you read in your local newspaper, the US team was either ripped, routed, crushed, pummeled, pulverized, or whipped 17–2 by Sweden.

After losing their first three games at the 1963 World Championships in Stockholm by a combined score of 31–8, the United States faced the hometown Swedes. Depending which headline you read in your local newspaper, the US team was either ripped, routed, crushed, pummeled, pulverized, or whipped 17–2 by Sweden. It was the single most humiliating defeat in US hockey history.

Despite a five-week European tour prior to the championships, the US players never once found their legs on foreign ice. "I am afraid the [United States] will finish last," said Swedish coach Arne Strömberg. "They should do better than this, but you can't blame the kids. It is the system which allows a team like this to tour Europe that is to blame."

The Associated Press was less forgiving, calling the United States' loss "the worst defeat yet for Uncle Sam's third-rate sextet, [plunging] the Yanks even deeper into the cellar without a win or a point." Three different Swedish players had each tallied a hat trick, "pouring in on US goalie Ron Chisholm time and time again with the US defense spread all over the ice."

The following morning, President John F. Kennedy called David Hackett, special assistant to the attorney general.

"Dave," Kennedy began, "I noticed in the paper this morning where the Swedish team beat the American hockey team 17–2."

"Yeah, I saw that," said Hackett.

"Christ, who we sending over there? Girls?"

"I know. They haven't won a game."

"God, we've got some pretty good hockey players, haven't we?" asked Kennedy a few moments later. "I suppose they're all playing on their college teams, are they, or something? I'd like to find out . . . who sort of sponsors it and the kind of players they've got . . . 'cause I think it's a disgrace . . ."

"And they've been beaten by everybody," Hackett chimed in.

"Yeah. So, obviously, they shouldn't send a team unless they can send a good one," said Kennedy. "Will you find out about it, let me know?"

"I'll find out and let you know," said Hackett.

Later that afternoon, Hackett called Harvard hockey coach Cooney Weiland, who gladly gave his two cents. The morning after that, Hackett sent a surprisingly insightful memo to President Kennedy, outlining four key reasons for the US team's poor performance:

1. It is difficult to attract the talent available in an off Olympic year.

2. Most of the good players who are out of college (like the Cleary brothers of the 1960 Olympics) cannot afford to go.

3. Most of the good players in college cannot afford to take the time.

4. Organization and management this year were not as good as in an Olympic year and past world championships.

Hackett went on to assure Kennedy that the 1964 US Olympic team, to be coached by Eddie Jeremiah of Dartmouth, "will be a good team and be representative of this country." That said, he reminded the president, "We have never done as badly in off years as we did this year; and unless we can generate more interest, support, and, most important of all, financial backing, there is every possibility we will do as badly in 1965."

President Kennedy had rightly surmised one of the biggest problems the US Ice Hockey Committee faced: many of the country's best prospects were unwilling or *unable* to commit to spending three months or more with the US national team at the peak of their college careers.

After graduation, all but a handful of the very best players quickly ran out of options. Historically, there were very few amateur teams—much less amateur leagues—where players could keep getting ice time, compete against other top prospects, and keep developing once their college careers were over.

Walter Bush had not set out *specifically* to create a development league for senior amateur players. By creating seventy-five roster spots on five different franchises throughout the Upper Midwest, however, that's exactly what he'd done. After building the United States Hockey League from scratch and bringing the Boston Bruins farm club to Minneapolis—using exactly the same traits the US Olympic Committee sought—it was time for Bush to reprise his general manager role in time for the 1964 Winter Olympic games in Innsbruck, Austria.

There was just one minor problem: even the indefatigable Walter

Bush couldn't practice law, run a minor pro franchise, commission a senior amateur league, and manage the US Olympic team. Something had to give. He could hand control of the Bruins over to one of his partners. He could also find someone to manage the USHL. He needed someone to buy the Steers. Before long, he'd thought of the perfect candidate: a fiery young player-coach with good leadership skills and inexhaustible passion. Bush just needed to get the kid back from Canada.

CHAPTER THIRTEEN

FROM THE ST. PAUL STEERS TO THE US NATIONAL TEAM

After graduating from the University of Minnesota with a degree in business, Murray Williamson got a job with International Milling, the second-largest flour milling company in the world. With mills and offices scattered from New York to Texas in the United States and Alberta to Ontario in Canada, IM was a sprawling international operation that sold its products under multiple brand names.

By the late 1950s, its subsidiary Robin Hood Flour was steadily diversifying its products. Since Williamson was a Canadian citizen, he was attached to the Robin Hood brand and sent to Port Colborne, Ontario, for corporate training. There, he nabbed a roster spot on the Port Colborne Sailors, a Senior A team in the Ontario Hockey Association.

"It was damn good hockey," Williamson says, "but it wasn't my cup of tea." Most of the players were those who'd aged out of Junior A, maybe knocked around on a minor pro team or two, and then transitioned to a senior league to avoid all the travel. "It was rough, which I could handle, but it wasn't really my people."

Before long, Walter Bush called and said, "Why don't you come back?" Bush told Williamson he had a spot for him on the St. Paul Steers, which was also quality hockey, but much more in line with what Williamson was after. There were a few ex-pros, but about half the players were former Gophers or guys who'd played on other

D1 teams.

Williamson headed south, got a job with Honeywell, and eventually became player-coach-manager for the Steers. On the eve of the 1963–64 season, Bush thought it was time for Williamson to take the next step. He called Williamson and suggested they meet for lunch at Jax Cafe, the unofficial clubhouse of northeast Minneapolis, about three miles north of Williams Arena.

After ordering the lunch special (open-faced roast beef sandwiches), Bush pitched Williamson his idea. For $3,000, the player-coach could own the St. Paul Steers. Exactly as Bush had predicted, Williamson was all for it. Soon, they'd worked out the details, shaken hands, and the deal was done.

> After ordering the lunch special (open-faced roast beef sandwiches), Bush pitched Williamson his idea. For $3,000, the player-coach could own the St. Paul Steers.

"To be honest," says Williamson, "I'm not sure I ever paid Walter the full three thousand. I didn't write him a check right then; I know that for sure. He said he would take the money out of future gate receipts, but I'm not sure that ever happened. I think he just gave me the Steers. That's the kind of thing Walter did."

In Williamson's first year as owner, the Steers went on to win the USHL championship and post an impressive record against several WCHA teams. With a keen eye for talent and unyielding focus on skating and conditioning, Williamson was quietly building an elite amateur team.

Over the next three years the Steers steadily improved, with three signature games that caught the attention of high-level AHAUS officials, well-known hockey reporters, and committee members from the US Olympic Committee.

First, on Christmas Night 1964, the Steers skated to a 3–3 tie against the touring Soviet B squad, prompting the Soviet coach to tell reporters the Steers were undoubtedly the best team the Soviets had faced on the trip. One year later, the Steers buried the Ken

Yackel-coached US national team 10–2 . . . a mere thirty days before that squad went 2–5–0 at the world championships in Tampere, Finland. Even more impressive, perhaps, in December 1965, the Steers dominated the Swedish national team in a 6–2 win, prompting reporters and fans to wonder if the Steers should represent the United States at the 1968 Olympics.

"Before then," Williamson says, "I think most people equated the USHL with a beer league. Hell, back then, the NHL was a beer league. Until Bobby Orr came along, the average NHL player made about as much as a high school teacher. Nobody got rich."

Even if fans and sportswriters wanted the Steers to represent the United States at the Olympics, Williamson had no illusions things would be that simple. "About a year before I became the manager of the US national team, I got a good close look at how things were sometimes decided. Political, I guess you could call it. Or maybe it was just luck."

Earlier that summer, after an AHAUS meeting at the Broadmoor Hotel, Williamson, Walter Bush, Thayer Tutt, and Rochester Mustangs GM Wayne "Bud" Dornack were having a drink at the Golden Bee, an authentic British pub that had been dismantled and reinstalled panel by panel in Colorado Springs. Williamson and the others were swapping stories and talking hockey when Vic Heyliger walked up to their table.

"In strolls Heyliger," Williamson recalls, "chomping that unlit cigar he always had in his mouth, in his normal good spirits, big smile on his face. He sits down, orders a drink, and joins the conversation. Somehow, two hours later, apparently it was decided that Heyliger would coach the US national team at the 1966 World Championships."

Williamson's incredulity is still palpable all these years later.

"Heyliger was a great guy and one hell of a college recruiter," says Williamson. "He knew how to keep his guys happy. But his abilities as a coach . . .? He just opened the gate and turned 'em loose."

In the end, Williamson was right. After getting blown out by a combined 35–9 by the Canadians, Soviets, Swedes, Czechoslovaks, and Finns in their first five games, the US team finally beat East

Germany and lowly Poland, who finished in last place with a record 0–7–0.

The US team had been "hastily assembled," in the words of the *USA Hockey Results Book*, and had only played three games before their world debut in Ljubljana, Yugoslavia.

"It was an organizational disaster," says Williamson, whose St. Paul Steers contributed five players to Heyliger's roster. "At Michigan, he was known as 'Invincible Vic,' but after the Europeans and Canadians took turns soundly trouncing the disorganized US team, I think he learned pretty quickly his reputation as a college coach meant nothing there."

AHAUS leadership was deeply concerned. After a silver medal at the 1956 Olympics and a gold in 1960, the United States hadn't finished higher than fifth place in any world tournament that had included the Soviets and Czechoslovaks. With the 1968 Olympics less than two years away, they needed answers quick.

In May 1966, Tom Lockhart, Thayer Tutt, and Don Clark invited Murray Williamson to make a presentation to the executive committee at the AHAUS annual meeting in San Francisco. They wanted Williamson to share his perspective and ideas about how to select, organize, and manage the 1967 US national team.

"I don't think they really wanted me as their coach, but nobody else had access to the players that I had," Williamson says. "They were in a bind, and they knew it."

At just thirty-one years of age—with a mere three years behind the bench—Williamson was flattered but apprehensive. "I wasn't very polished when it came to dealing with boards and committees," he says. "I couldn't just sit there and tell them what they wanted to hear."

Williamson bought a ticket and flew to California to make his presentation.

In the wood-paneled conference room of the Fairmont Hotel, he began with the basics, listing the best eligible players in the USHL. Next, he singled out a handful of US-born college standouts he thought he could recruit. His idea was to bring thirty to forty players to training camp in Minnesota. As Mariucci had bluntly explained a decade prior, Williamson already knew his core group of ten players. He only needed to find another five or six.

Regardless, everyone on the roster needed to understand this was going to be a full-time five-month commitment, with practices or games almost every day; twice a day at the beginning. "I wasn't going to bend on that," says Williamson. "There's only one way to develop team spirit, morale, and the skills we needed to bring the [United States] back to the level we'd been at in 1960."

> *Regardless, everyone on the roster needed to understand this was going to be a full-time five-month commitment, with practices or games almost every day; twice a day at the beginning.*

After the team was selected, they would embark on a three-month, fifty-game exhibition schedule designed to replicate the rigors of international travel, complete with overnight bus rides, hurried meals in restaurants, and budget hotel rooms. The bulk of the games would be against teams from the USHL. They'd supplement that with games against Division I college teams and any international tournaments AHAUS could arrange. On average, Williamson wanted his team to play one game every two days. Conditioning was key.

"It wasn't revolutionary," he says. "We'd been talking about it for years, but nobody had ever done it."

Mariucci had said the same thing about a week before the 1956 US Olympic team left for Italy, complaining to the press, "Three or four weeks isn't enough time to have a group of individual stars teaming together like a veteran outfit."

Wrapping up his presentation, Williamson dropped the bomb. He needed an Act of Congress to get citizenship for three key players from Canada: George Konik, Bill Masterton, and Lou Nanne.

"All three had attended US universities and were the caliber player we needed, in my opinion, if we hoped to compete with the Canadians and Europeans," says Williamson. "And all three fell short of the five-year residency requirement for US citizenship."

Masterton and Konik were Denver University grads and reinstated amateurs living and working in the Twin Cities on permanent visas, playing for the St. Paul Steers. Nanne had recently graduated from the University of Minnesota and was playing for the Rochester Mustangs. Like Mariucci before him, Williamson thought the Canadian contingent would not only be substantial contributors; they would also help to develop the team's younger players.

"Apparently, at least *one person* on the committee agreed my proposal had merit," Williamson says with a laugh. "Somehow, I'd survived without making a fool of myself."

The committee did express one key concern, however. They said they would be more comfortable with an older, veteran coach whose track record was already known. "They clearly meant Mariucci," Williamson says. "If they'd suggested anyone else, I would've walked out the door."

Williamson left San Francisco cautiously optimistic, ready to launch a new system for training and developing the US national team.

CHAPTER FOURTEEN

THE MAN WHO HIRED AND FIRED JOHN MARIUCCI

Back in Minneapolis, Murray Williamson tracked down John Mariucci, who'd recently been fired by the Gophers. He was also in the middle of a contentious divorce, and his wholesale paper business was on the verge of bankruptcy.

"I knew he'd hit a rough patch," Williamson says. "I was hoping a stint as coach for the US national team would give him a new start."

They met at a bar by Mariucci's office. Williamson sat down across from his old coach and immediately sensed the depth of Mariucci's depression. After two consecutive trips to the NCAA finals in his first two years as head coach, the Gophers had only reached the national tournament once more in the decade that followed. Recently, Mariucci had strung together four straight winning seasons that had all been capped off by appearances in the WCHA playoffs, but they couldn't get over the hump.

In a desperate attempt to keep his own job as athletic director, Marsh Ryman threw Mariucci under the bus. Officially, the Gophers coach had retired "to devote more time to his business," but insiders knew the real story.

"John Mariucci didn't quit as Minnesota hockey coach," Sid Hartman proclaimed in the Minneapolis *Tribune*. "The popular former Chicago Blackhawk, who put the sport on the map at the University of Minnesota, was [pressured] to resign by athletic director Marsh Ryman."

It was likely no consolation that Ryman quickly named Glen Sonmor—who'd been nurtured and developed by Mariucci—as the Gophers' new head coach.

"Hockey was barely a sport when Maroosh took over," says Williamson. "The moment John arrived, all of that changed. Hockey at every level flourished. The number of high school teams exploded. Mariucci made all of that happen."

Feeling a sense of déjà vu, Williamson wrote his offer on a napkin and slid it across the table: $4,000 to coach the US national team at the 1967 World Championships in Vienna.

"Knowing John, even at that point, he probably would've done it for nothing," says Williamson. "But he definitely needed the money."

Mariucci accepted without hesitation, and they got down to business. Williamson pulled a list of players from his pocket, and together, they went through the pros and cons of each one.

Meanwhile, with the public announcement that Mariucci had just left the Gophers, pressure quickly began to mount within the North Stars franchise to find a role for the former coach. A few days later, North Stars President Walter Bush offered Mariucci the assistant GM position under Wren Blair, who'd previously coached and managed the Minneapolis Bruins under Bush.

Things were happening quickly. With two new job offers on the table, Mariucci's fortunes were taking a dramatic turn. The obvious question, of course, was whether Mariucci could handle two high-profile jobs for two different high-profile teams at the same time.

Things started out well enough, but the US national team's exhibition schedule was played almost exclusively on the road. Williamson wanted the team to get a heavy dose of unsympathetic fans and hostile environments.

USHL teams rarely played in newer, A-list arenas. The rinks were dingy and cold, the "glass" was a chain-link fence, and the boards were actual boards—everything from rough vertical 2-by-6 planks to mismatched sheets of plywood nailed to old railroad ties. Once the trip began, the team rarely stopped at home or had a home-cooked meal.

After two months of bouncing around over rugged Midwestern roads, juggling two jobs, not knowing which way was up, Mariucci's morale was flagging. No doubt, it was a letdown for one of Minnesota hockey's true legends and most popular public figures. The loud, colorful Maroosh who commanded people's attention through sheer personal charisma seemed to have vanished. His confidence was shot, dragging down his young players and casting a dark pall over the whole team.

By mid-December, with two international tournaments quickly approaching, the US national team's record against USHL opponents stood at an unimpressive 6–8–3. Not nearly good enough to skate with the Europeans, much less the Canadians or juggernaut Soviets. Things needed to turn around quickly or the experiment would be over before it had even begun.

Intriguingly, the Canadian national team, led by Father David Bauer, was in the midst of its own experiment. Beginning in 1963, Bauer and Coach Jackie McLeod brought many of Canada's top young stars to Winnipeg for rigorous training and a heavy exhibition schedule very similar to the program adopted by Williamson.

Coincidentally, the US national team and the Canadian national team were set to collide in the first game of the 1966 Walter A. Brown Memorial Tournament. Beginning in 1964, the yearly tournament honored Brown's legacy and lasting impact on international hockey. The first two iterations had featured the Soviets, Czechoslovaks, and Canadians, who'd finished both times in that order.

With the Soviet and Czechoslovakian teams prohibited from traveling to the United States by their respective governments, however, the 1966 tournament featured the US and Canadian national teams and a collection of senior league all-stars called the West Canada Selects.

In the first US game, the Canadian Nationals blitzed the United States 8–1, leaving them stunned and discouraged. In their second game, the United States tied the Selects 3–3 before fighting the

Canadian Nationals to a 4–4 draw two nights later. In the final game of the tournament, the US team edged the Selects 4–2, posting their only win.

"It was embarrassing," says Williamson. "We were skated right off the ice by the Nationals and should have handled the Selects easily."

Feeling demoralized, if not completely undone, the US Nationals headed north to Winnipeg for the Centennial Tournament, part of a yearlong celebration commemorating the 100th anniversary of the Canadian Confederation.

Canada beat Czechoslovakia 5–3 to open the tournament on New Year's Eve, before the Soviets swamped the United States 7–1 the following night. The United States then lost 7–1 to the Canadians and 8–2 to the Czechoslovaks. Scoring a meager four goals while giving up twenty-two, the US team failed to be competitive in all three games.

"We were completely outclassed," Williamson says, "not in terms of skill, but conditioning. We literally couldn't keep up. The Soviets and Czechs, in particular, did everything well, and they did it fast. I don't think our guys had ever seen anything like it."

On the last day of the tournament, the Canadians came from behind to beat the Soviets 5–4 and win the tournament. With impressive victories against the Soviets and Czechoslovaks—arguably the best two teams in the world—the Canadians were flying high, riding a three-game winning streak and feeling unbeatable.

The United States, by contrast, had suffered three straight defeats to drop their overall record to 7–12. With a single win against international opponents in their last seven games, US prospects for the world championships in Vienna looked utterly bleak.

Chaos and dissension reigned in the US locker room. Deep down, everyone knew the biggest problem was focus. With better organization, better conditioning—and better coaching—the players felt they could rise to the level of the Canadian and European teams. Perhaps unsurprisingly, some players began to express concerns about Mariucci. They wondered if he had the time, interest, and energy to coach the US team while still maintaining his health, his job with the North Stars, and his sanity.

Meanwhile, Williamson was preoccupied with trying to push through the Act of Congress that would give Lou Nanne instant citizenship. Williamson wanted him to captain the 1968 Olympic team, and time was running short. Nanne would also be instrumental in keeping the national team competitive at the upcoming world championships. He was a vital part of the plan.

With his mind reeling from multiple issues, Williamson was summoned to the Fort Garry Hotel by AHAUS president Tom Lockhart and Thayer Tutt, head of the International Hockey Committee. The moment Williamson walked into the bar, he immediately sensed the severity of the situation.

After the requisite greetings, the two men got right down to business. Obviously, they were disappointed with the US team's recent performance and wanted to know what kinds of changes Williamson might like to see. Almost immediately, Williamson knew they were trying to pin down his thoughts on replacing Mariucci a mere six weeks before the world championships were slated to start.

"They knew John was my friend," Williamson says. "It was obvious neither one of them wanted to upset John or me. So I expressed my own concerns about our lack of success and shouldered some of the blame." In the end, however, it became increasingly clear something needed to change. And that something was John Mariucci.

All three men agreed: In order to minimize disruption and maintain at least some sense of continuity, Williamson would take over as coach and continue to manage the team—effective immediately. Publicly, Mariucci would still have a role, advising the team on personnel and acting as a scout. In practical terms, however, Mariucci's brief tenure was over.

Williamson's first concern was that Mariucci get a check for the balance of his contract. Lockhart and Tutt agreed, signed a check for $3,000, and gave it to the newly appointed manager-coach. Williamson folded the check, put it in his breast pocket, and caught a taxi back to the International Hotel.

"When people ask me, *How the heck did you fire Maroosh?* I tell them it was easy," Williamson likes to say. "I knocked on the door of

Mariucci's room. He said 'Come in.' I opened the door and said, 'John, you're fired,' threw the check at him, slammed the door, and ran like hell."

"I knocked on the door of Mariucci's room. He said 'Come in.' I opened the door and said, 'John, you're fired,' threw the check at him, slammed the door, and ran like hell."

Of course, it wasn't like that at all. The real story is much different, and it's also pure Mariucci.

"Only divorce or death could've been a bigger emotional strain," says Williamson. "John was more than a friend. He was like a father to me. He was the man who brought me to Minnesota. The man who took a chance on me and gave me a spot on his team. The man whose name I'd given my first son, Kevin John. Who knows where Williamson might be if Maroosh hadn't found me?"

Williamson called Mariucci from the lobby of the International Hotel and asked if he was alone. If so, Williamson wondered, would it be possible for the two of them to meet to discuss a problem?

"You're the boss," said Mariucci. "If you want to meet, just say so. You don't need my permission."

"He obviously knew what was coming," Williamson says. "He was trying to make it easy. Not for himself, for *me*."

When Williamson got to Mariucci's room, the coach was reading a book. Williamson started slowly, fumbling his way along, telling Mariucci that he'd just seen Lockhart and Tutt. They were both quite disappointed and thought the team was playing far below its capabilities. They also wondered if Mariucci had enough time to build a winning team.

On top of that, Williamson confessed, there was dissension in the ranks. If something didn't change soon, they might lose some key players and start a chain reaction. Of course, all of that is normal on a losing team, Williamson said. Nothing personal, but maybe John was stretched too thin, spending so much time on the North Stars that he didn't have anything left for the national program. Building a championship team was a full-time job.

"John didn't cut me off," Williamson says, "but he slowly set down his book and suggested I get right to the heart of the problem, helping me find my way through the most difficult task I'd ever faced in my life."

"Beating around the bush won't make it easier," Mariucci told his former player and friend. "If what you need to say makes you uncomfortable, just go ahead and say it and let's be done with it."

"The room seemed so still and quiet," Williamson remembers. "Of course, I respected John's wishes, so I just said, very plainly, 'We're making a coaching change. I'm taking over the team.'"

Williamson took the $3,000 check from his pocket and gave it to Mariucci, explaining it was the balance of his salary for coaching the team. "John hesitated at first," Williamson says, "but I insisted he take it, and eventually he did." Williamson breathed a sigh of relief. "Sometimes John burned hot, but he never held a grudge, and he was loyal as hell. I knew he'd support me and do anything I asked him to do. Two hours later, we went to the Canada–Russia game on the best of terms, like none of it ever happened."

A few weeks later, Mariucci learned Williamson was still having trouble getting US citizenship for Konik, Masterton, and Nanne. He called and told Williamson about an old pal from the Iron Range who'd gone off to Washington and become a big deal. The guy had grown up in Chisholm, about twenty-five miles west of Eveleth. He and Mariucci knew each other from youth hockey and had kept in touch all these years.

That old friend happened to be Lud Andolsek, vice chairman of the US Civil Service Commission and a close associate of Vice President Hubert H. Humphrey. One week later, Williamson flew to DC to meet with Andolsek and spend some time with Congressman John Blatnik—also from Chisholm—to help get the bill back on track.

Once inside the capitol, Williamson went down to the House floor to shake a few hands and help push the bill along. Andolsek had mentioned that once it got through the judiciary subcommittee, it would have to go to the full committee and then to the House. From there, it would go to the Senate and, finally, to President Lyndon Johnson for his signature.

The thirty-one-year-old barber's son from Winnipeg was obviously biting off a big chunk. They got the bill back on track, but time was running out. It was too late for Nanne and Masterton to be eligible to play in the world championships. Konik, in the meantime, had turned pro. It was a blow but not sufficient enough to dampen their enthusiasm. Since the December tournaments they had gotten the team turned around.

"After Murray took over as coach, practices got harder and conditioning was a bigger focus," wrote legendary team physician George "Doc" Nagobads in his memoir *Gold, Silver, Bronze: A Doctor's Devotion to Hockey*. "The team got in better shape. A lot of players from Murray's team familiar with his coaching methods were happier, and everything went a little bit smoother after that."

They now had a well-conditioned squad that was prepared to begin the seven-game European pre-tournament schedule and then go to Vienna. The pre-championship schedule included games in Switzerland, Germany, and Austria, as well as a small tournament in Geneva with the Soviet Army team and Czechoslovakia's championship club team from Bratislava. These were teams from the same leagues that, ten years later, would compete against the NHL.

CHAPTER FIFTEEN

ON TO VIENNA

On March 3, 1967, the US national team left for Europe. The first leg of their tour would take them through Switzerland, where they were set to play two exhibition games against the Swiss national team followed by an international tournament in Geneva.

The first game was in Basel on an outdoor open-air rink with artificial ice. When the game started, the sun was still shining and the US players had trouble seeing through the glare. Even worse, as the game went on, the rink was soon covered in slush and pools of water.

"That was my first introduction to European hockey," says Williamson. "I was simultaneously impressed and amazed. I was impressed by the skill of the young Swiss players and amazed what they'd learned with such basic facilities. It was like playing on a Winnipeg park rink in late February, where the sun melts all day and refreezes overnight."

The US team fell behind 2–1 in the early going, but once the sun went behind an apartment building, they took control. With the score tied at two, North Dakota defenseman Don Ross scored the go-ahead goal when Denver All-American Marty Howe stopped quickly in front of the Swiss net and sprayed a shower of water onto the goalie. With the goalie unable to see, Ross's shot sailed by and hit the back of the net. The United States won 4–2, excited to win their first game overseas.

From there, the team went to Geneva for an international

tournament against the champions from the top Czechoslovakian and Soviet leagues, as well as the Swiss National team, to battle for the Perrot Duval Cup. The tournament favorite was Spartak Moscow, the 1967 Soviet League Champions. Right behind them was Slovan Bratislava, winners of the Czechoslovak Extraliga, the top professional league in Czechoslovakia. The USs and Swiss teams were the clear underdogs, expected to battle it out for third and fourth place.

The first game of the tournament pitted the US national team against Spartak Moscow, the team coached Vsevolod Bobrov—leading scorer and star of the 1956 Soviet gold medal team. By then, Williamson had faced numerous Soviet teams and knew their game plan focused on controlling the puck and making quick, accurate passes. Williamson's counterstrategy was simple in theory but harder to execute on the ice. Nonetheless, with a young, courageous team, he thought he might have the answer.

"If we could catch them and hit them," he says, "I knew it would disrupt their passing attack. We also decided to play a very conservative forecheck, sending just one man deep and lining up the other four on our blue line to prevent the Russians from breaking in."

With strong discipline and great goaltending by Carl Wetzel, the strategy worked, keeping the Russians scoreless for two full periods. Meanwhile, goals by former Boston College All-American John Cunniff and John Rendell put the United States 2–0 heading into the final frame.

"That gave our young guys lot of confidence," says Williamson. "The more they saw our strategy working, the more tenacious they got." The teams traded goals the rest of the way, and the United States hung on for a 4–2 win. "By the third period, we were literally matching the Soviets stride for stride and goal for goal," Williamson says. "It was incredible. I don't think I'd ever been more proud of my team."

The Czechoslovaks handled the Swiss with ease and advanced to the championship round two nights later.

On the heels of their unlikely win over the Soviets, Williamson planned to use the same basic strategy against the Czechoslovaks. Unsurprisingly, the Czechoslovaks had studied the US team's first round game very closely. After a single practice, they'd reorganized their breakout and completely revised their offensive strategy.

"Instead of their usual short-passing attack, they opted for long breakout passes, quickly pushing the puck through the neutral zone," recalls Doc Nagobads.

"The Czechs got on the board first and dominated play through the first two periods," Williamson says, "but we never fell behind by more than one goal." With the United States down 4–3 midway into the third period, they tied the score at four. At that point, "the fighting American spirit" took over, according to Williamson. "The Czechs were more skillful," he says, "but they were unemotional. Our guys just wanted it more."

With three minutes left in the game, John Cunniff broke through the defense and scored, putting the Americans up 5–4. At that point, at least one Czechoslovak defenseman could no longer suppress his emotions. Just after Cunniff shot, the frustrated defender pushed Cunniff from behind, sending him crashing into the boards and knocking him out of the game with a separated shoulder.

"That tournament win served notice," Williamson says. "This US national team wasn't some kind of patsy outfit on a European vacation. We weren't there to frolic. We were there to play hockey."

> "This US national team wasn't some kind of patsy outfit on a European vacation. We weren't there to frolic. We were there to play hockey."

Unfortunately, the team would be without Cunniff for at least a week. "It was a great victory for us but also a huge loss," says Williamson. "John was a former All-American at Boston College. Losing that kind of player just three days before the world championships was a very tough blow."

Williamson left Geneva with mixed emotions. On one hand, the United States had won their first international tournament convincingly, with impressive back-to-back wins over the Soviets and Czechoslovaks. On the other hand, with John Cunniff out of the lineup, Williamson was down to just sixteen players as his team headed into a brutal stretch of seven games in ten days against the best teams in the world. He knew his squad was overmatched in terms of skill, but they'd somehow been getting by on hustle and determination. He only hoped it would last.

On the morning of the US team's first game, Williamson went to the rink to watch the Soviets practice. On the way back to the hotel, he shared a cab with two players from the Swedish team, the US opponent later that night. As the three of them chatted in the back of the cab, it occurred to Williamson the two Swedes didn't know who he was.

"I decided to wage a little psychological warfare," he says. "I introduced myself as an American sports journalist and proceeded to give them a detailed report on the most animalistic, violent group of players to ever represent the United States."

A few of the players, Williamson said, were known to beat their opponents nearly unconscious if they tried to interfere with the US goalie. Of course, the "journalist" confessed, he didn't like it one bit. Such behavior was not only unfair; it was embarrassing. He wasn't proud to call himself an American when his team was on the ice.

"That night, at the opening face-off," Williamson laughs, "there wasn't a single Swede without a helmet. And most of them wore mouthpieces too"—both of which were uncommon in 1967.

After the game began, it was incredible how well Williamson's psychological tactics seemed to work. The Swedes were shooting from far away and barely went after their rebounds, hesitating before they went into the corners or avoiding them altogether.

"We bounced those speedy Swedes every chance we got," says Williamson. "We hustled, scrambled, and scratched our way through the first two periods, keeping the score as close as we could."

Midway through the third period, Tom Hurley from Clarkson College tied the score at three. Then, Marty Howe took charge. In the midst of a penalty kill, the former Denver Pioneers star scored a spectacular shorthanded goal. With a 4–3 lead, the United States hung on for the last ten minutes to win.

First World Junior Team, before boarding the plane to the Championships in
Leningrad, Russia.

1974 World Junior Championships in Leningrad.

1974 Inaugural World Junior Team. Front row (seated): Mike Dibble, Mark Lambert, Steve Roberts, Murray Williamson, Andre Beaulieu, Gary Sargent, Mike Zimmerman. Middle row: Mike Radakovich (Assistant Manager), John Shewchuk, Tom Funke, Dave Hanson, Craig Hammer, Paul Holmgren, Dave Heitz, Pete Roberts, Jeff Hymanson, Steve Short, Mike Wong, Steve Ulseth, Al Mathieu (Trainer). Back row: Dan Bonk, Greg Woods, Dave Geving, Jim Warner, Buzzy LaFond, Jim Kronschnabel. Others: Don Madson, Earl Sargent, Tom Ulseth.

Junior ice loop seeks writ against NCAA

By DAN STONEKING
Minneapolis Star Staff Writer

Murray Williamson, executive director of the Midwest Junior Hockey League, said today the league will seek an injunction against the National Collegiate Athletic Association's ruling that that the MJHL is a professional league.

Williamson

"We want due process," said Williamson when the NCAA officially declared the MJHL a professional league today.

"From the beginning of the Midwest League we have operated above board with the NCAA. As a new and growing organization we realized there could be pitfalls and we wanted to avoid all of them. We laid things wide open.

"One of our principal goals was protecting the college eligibility of our players."

Williamson said that in August of 1973 he met with the NCAA's Warren Brown, assistant executive director, to outline the purpose and operations of the MJHL. "He pointed out some discrepancies at that time, and we changed them to conform with NCAA rules," said Williamson.

Williamson said his last meeting with Brown was on April 8, after the league had finished its first season.

"He told us at that time that if there were any problems the NCAA would get back to us within a week," Williamson said. "We never heard from them again and naturally assumed there weren't any problems. I have felt that our communications with the NCAA were excellent. But apparently Henry Kissinger would have trouble communicating with them."

The crux of the NCAA's case against the MJHL is that the league received direct payments from the National Hockey League, instead of through the American Amateur Hockey Association.

Williamson claimed the NCAA was informed of that in the April meeting. "We gave Mr. Brown a statement which showed financial allocation of the

NHL to the Midwest Junior League, the American Amateur Hockey Association, the National Association of Intercollegiate Atheletics (NAIA), the Canadian Amateur Hockey Association and the United States Olympic hockey program," said Williamson.

"Apararently then there was no objection," said Williamson.

Williamson said apparently there were no objections, because he didn't hear from Brown within the week. However, that statement proved to be the evidence on which the NCAA made its decision that the MJHL is professional, Brown told The Star today.

Last week Williamson got wind that the NCAA was going to declare the MJHL professional.

"We immediately asked to have our attorney present at a meeting they held last Friday to see our case was presented properly. Obviously Mr. Brown has not done that. But they refused and held a closed-door, kangaroo court session."

Williamson says he has considerable documentation to support the MJHL's position as keeping within NCAA rules.

"For example we sent them a copy of a form our player's sign that spells out just how much they can be compensated. It is right out of the NCAA rule book. All they receive is for actual and necessary expenses. The amount cannot exeed $50 a month."

Williamson to Fight NCAA Ruling on Loop

By Greg Wong
Staff Writer

Gopher hockey coach Herb Brooks is breathing easier today than he was 48 hours earlier, his fight nearly ended, but Murray Williamson is ready to don his boxing gloves.

Brooks was relieved by the National Collegiate Athletic Association's ruling Wednesday that his four Midwest Junior Hockey League recruits would be eligible to play despite the MJHL's being declared a professional league by the NCAA.

Joe Baker, Mark Lambert, Ken Yackel Jr. and Paul Holmgren must sign an affadavit testifying that they received nothing more in expenses than what is called for under NCAA guidelines.

"That's no problem," Brooks sighed. "The kids have told me they received nothing more."

The NCAA's ruling said that each case would be determined individually, that no group or class action ruling would be made.

Meanwhile, Williamson, executive director of the MJHL, said the league will seek an injunction against the NCAA's allegation that the league received money directly from the National Hockey League.

"That's false," Williamson said. "The monies went through the proper channels — to the American Amateur Hockey Association and then to the Midwest Junior League. The NCAA does not have its facts right.

"They've made such a bad mistake in not allowing Hal Trumble (director of the AAHA) to represent the other side of the story. I feel they'll eventually withdraw their allegation, that there won't be a need for legal action.

"If there is, we have the country's most knowledgeable attorney in terms of NCAA legalities — Gordon Martin of Boston.

"We feel we're entitled to due process before the NCAA can make such a ruling I just don't understand how they can make that decision without hearing our side. It's incredible."

The fight to save the Midwest Junior Hockey League,
August 29, 1974.

NCAA may drop hockey

By DAN STONEKING
The Star's Sports Editor

The National Collegiate Athletic Association is considering dropping hockey as an intercollegiate sport, The Minneapolis Star has learned.

The NCAA's action is based upon its concern of payments made by the National Hockey League through the Amateur Hockey Association of the United States to help develop U.S hockey programs.

The NCAA feels that these payments are turning U.S. amateur hockey professional.

The Star has obtained a copy of a NCAA letter stating the possibility that intercollegiate hockey could be dropped.

The letter was signed by Warren Brown, assistant executive director, under the name of Walter Byers, NCAA executive director. The letter reads:

"This is to advise you that the NCAA officers have placed on the agenda of the NCAA Council on its October, 1974, meeting and the Executive Committee Meeting at its Jan-

nary, 1975 meeting, the question of whether the National Collegitate Ice Hockey Championship be discontinued and the NCAA Ice Hockey Committee be disbanded. This of course would require action by the Annual Convention.

"This decision reflects the growing concern about the threat of all the association's amateur rules and practices in ice hockey. Specially, the Amateur Hockey Association of the United States in conjunction with the National Hockey League are turn-

ing amateur hockey in this country into a professional operation insofar as the generally accepted interscholastic and intercollegiate rules of the United States are concerned.

"There is a strong feeling that unless these people dedicated to intercollegiate ice hockey are prepared to take a stand against the NHL-AHAUS subsidy pattern and also abide by the NCAA rules in Canadian recruitment, that ice hockey will be rejected as an intercollegiate sport by the NCAA membership."

The NCAA has been involved in several disputes recently concerning the application of its rules to amateur hockey programs subsidized by the NHL through the AHAUS.

The NCAA lost a court fight with Boston University players Pete Marzo and Jak Buston, two Canadian players declared ineligible last season because of their junior A hockey background.

The **Midwest Junior Hockey League** was declared by the NCAA to be a professional because of

NHL subsidization in August. But two weeks later, the NCAA reversed that verdict.

More recently the NCAA lost a suit by Reed Larson whom the NCAA had declared ineligible to play hockey at Minnesota because of a violation on its rule covering agents.

The NCAA has a meeting scheduled Monday at its Shawnee Mission, Kan. headquarters to discuss intercollegiate hockey.

Only about 70 of the more than 700 NCAA-member schools play hockey.

If it were dropped by the NCAA as an intercollegiate sport, those schools would probably band their hockey programs under a new governing organization and create their own national championship.

If the NCAA would eliminate hockey it is unclear what effect it would have upon hockey players receiving scholarships.

NCAA officials were unavailable to comment about the letter.

NCAA may drop hockey due to concerns of league funding from National Hockey League, October 10, 1974.

1980 United States Olympic Hockey Team.

John Mariucci, Murray Williamson, and Maurice "Rocket" Richard at
Hobey Baker Awards, 1983.

The All-American team (from inception through 1965) wall collage located
in Mariucci Arena.

Kevin Williamson, Gordie Howe, Murray Williamson, in 1992 at Warroad, Minnesota, celebrity golf tournament.

Twenty-fifth reunion of the 1972 Olympic Team at the Decathlon Athletic Club in Bloomington, Minnesota. Missing only Buddy Kessel, equipment manager.

By Harry Thompson
Photos By Pacific Stars & Stripes

CLOCKWISE:
HENRY BOUCHA
TIM REGAN
PETER SEARS
MARK HOWE

REMEMBERING '72

*The Successes Of Others And Years Of Anonymity
Can't Tarnish The Bonds Of The Silver-Medal
Winning 1972 Olympic Hockey Team.*

THE TEAM THAT TIME FORGOT

USA Hockey Magazine article by Harry Thompson, November 2004.

Murray with Hall of Famer Ted Lindsay at one of the
Hobey Baker banquets.

The Caraccioli brothers, writers of *Striking Silver*, introducing the book to
Massachusetts Governor Mitt Romney in 2006 with members of the
1972 US Olympic Team.

Jack Kelley, former Boston University hockey coach and Hartford Whalers
general manager and coach.

USA Hockey recognizing former Olympic coaches left to right:
Murray Williamson, Lou Vairo, Tim Taylor, Katey Stone, Peter Laviolette,
Ron Wilson, Ben Smith, and Mark Johnson.

Murray Williamson with family, 2015.

Visiting with Walter Bush at the 2017 Hobey Baker banquet.

With legendary doctor Doc Nagabods prior to his induction into the M Club
Hall of Fame, June 2017.

Olympic Hockey Chairman Bob Fleming at Jax Cafe celebrating a night with Doc Nagabods, 2017.

After the game, some of the players were so exhausted they could barely hold themselves upright. It was the biggest international win by the US hockey team since the 1960 Olympics. Ten thousand people stood as the organist played "The Star Spangled Banner" and the American flag was hoisted. With a dramatic win over Sweden in their first World Tournament game, Williamson and his young team suddenly thought they might have a shot at doing something big.

After a recovery day, it was time to face the high-powered Soviets. Williamson's team was both excited and nervous. Beating Spartak Moscow was one thing; somehow stealing a win from the Soviet national team would be a much more difficult task. As the young Americans stepped onto the ice, the atmosphere was electric. Even during warm-ups, the sellout crowd made it clear: they were rooting for the Americans.

When the smoke finally cleared, the Soviets had won 7–2. With classic machine-like precision, the Russians were up 2–0 a mere 6:23 into the game. They stumbled and gave up two goals in a ninety-second span to make the score 5–2 but slammed the door shut after that.

The game was hardly as close as the final score might suggest; but in a postgame press conference, Soviet assistant coach and general manager Anatoly Tarasov praised the US team's "spirit, hustle, and courage."

"The Americans have a tough team," added Coach Arkady Chernyshev. "It takes much hard work to get the better of them ... They must have been more tired than we were because they played earlier Saturday."

Aside from losing the game, the United States lost two more players. Defenseman Marsh Tschida hurt his back, and forward Jerry Melnychuk suffered strained knee ligaments. The roster was reduced to just fourteen healthy players.

> *"The Americans have a tough team," added Coach Arkady Chernyshev. "It takes much hard work to get the better of them ..."*

"It felt like Doc Nagobads was becoming the most valuable person we'd brought on the trip," says Williamson.

For the game against the Czechoslovaks, Williamson asked his "least injured" players to suit up—"even Johnny Cunniff, with his separated shoulder, in case we needed him to sit out a penalty," Williamson says. "We went into the game badly outmanned, but that only proved to be a huge inspiration for our incredible goalie, Carl Wetzel."

The United States lost by a score of 8–3, but Wetzel turned away an unbelievable seventy-five shots, in the words of the Associated Press, "to prevent the game from becoming a complete rout." Many of Wetzel's saves "were of a spectacular nature," they added.

"None of our guys ever gave up," says Williamson. "They fought to the very end despite the lopsided score and manpower disadvantage."

The Associated Press agreed: "Although the Czechs were impressive in victory, it was the Americans who stole the limelight. Our aggressive skating and fighting spirt drew loud cheers from the gallery of [ten thousand] spectators who jammed into Vienna's modern Stadthalle Ice Palace."

Things didn't get any easier for the Americans when they drew the undefeated Canadians for their fourth opponent. Fresh off a 13–1 shellacking of West Germany two nights prior, the Canadians were clearly favored.

"Our record at that point wasn't great," says Williamson, "but our guys never acted like they were the underdogs. They still had a lot of fire."

In fact, the United States scored first to take a 1–0 lead.

"The Yanks drew first blood in the second period when Craig Falkman took a perfect pass from Marsh Tschida and rifled the puck past the Canadian goalie," wrote the AP. In the final frame, however, twenty-year-old right winger Morris Mott became the unlikely hero by scoring a pair of unanswered goals to give his Canadian squad the 2–1 win.

"If nothing else, it was a moral victory," Williamson said at the time.

"That was the toughest game the Americans played against us in five years," said Canadian netminder Seth Martin.

"The Americans are real fighters," added Canadian coach Jack MacLeod. "They are having a great tournament."

The United States' next three games were against East Germany, Finland, and West Germany. With a record of 1–3–0, the US team needed to win *at least* one more game to qualify for the 1968 Olympics.

"The Americans are real fighters," added Canadian coach Jack MacLeod. "They are having a great tournament."

They tied East Germany 0–0 in the first game, but the team's bad luck streak continued. Terry Casey and Art Miller were both knocked out of the game with knee injuries. The local press began referring to the United States as "the skating wounded." Depleted but undeterred, Williamson decided to dress Cunniff against the Finns despite his separated shoulder, rigging up a brace to make sure the shoulder wouldn't be hyperextended.

Thanks to another brilliant performance by Wetzel, the United States blanked Finland 2–0 to earn a qualifying berth to the 1968 Olympics.

"US goalie Carl Wetzel became the first netminder to get two shutouts in the tournament," wrote *The Canadian Press*. "The two have come in consecutive games, giving him a record of 127 minutes and 43 seconds of shutout hockey since Morris Mott scored on him in the third period Thursday."

Two nights later, the United States beat West Germany 8–3 in its tournament finale. For once, the game wasn't all on Wetzel. "The US team wrapped up Tuesday's contest in the first period with a flurry of four goals within six minutes, twenty-eight seconds," wrote the AP. "The score rose to 7–0 midway through the second stanza with three more goals in a three minute, four second span."

In the meantime, Russia beat Canada 2–1 to finish undefeated and win its fifth straight world championship. After the game, Canadian players and coaches complained the first goal was a fluke and the second was clearly off-side.

"I saw it. We all saw it," said Canadian coach Jack MacLeod, "but nobody called it."

Asked for comment by the press, Anatoli Firsov—whose goal from the blue line seemed "more like a tennis lob or a baseball pop fly than a hockey shot"—simply smiled and said, "I was damn lucky to get that in," proving himself to be a class act both on and off the ice.

"The [United States] managed to share in the glory, however," wrote UPI from Vienna, "as goalie Carl Wetzel of Detroit was named to the tournament All-Star team." The twenty-seven-year-old net-minder, they said, "was largely responsible for the American team's opening day upset of Sweden, and he became a favorite of the crowds in the Vienna Stadthalle with his acrobatic saves."

Finishing strong with two wins, one tie, and no losses, the United States placed fifth overall—its best result in seven years—securing an automatic bid to the 1968 Olympic Winter Games in Geneva. They still hadn't cracked the Big Four, but it was a dramatic reversal from their anemic tournament performances in Colorado and Winnipeg. AHAUS officials were pleased. The new national development program looked like a success.

CHAPTER SIXTEEN

THE ROAD TO GRENOBLE

By the mid-1960s, the year-round state sponsorship of Soviet, Czecho-slovakian, and Swedish hockey programs had become an open secret.

"All of those national teams were heavily subsidized and even paid their players a salary," Williamson says, "but of course they all denied it when it came time to sign the Olympic Code. 'We're soldiers,' they would say, or 'teachers' or 'civil servants.' The government would give them a paycheck, but all they did was play hockey."

"Russians play hockey nine months of the year . . . take a couple of months' vacation on the Black Sea and go back to hockey again," wrote sports columnist Harry Missildine in Spokane's *Spokesman-Review.* "Come to think of it, Russia's hockey players are more pro-fessional than National Hockey League players, especially in their attitude toward conditioning."

The *Ottawa Journal*'s Bill Westwick thought the Canadians should simply copy the European system. "It will cost money," he wrote, "and it will mean being about as professional as the next party. But if that's the custom . . . that's what is needed. After all, since when was Cana-dian hockey squeamish about paying amateurs?"

Sports columnist Jack Dulmage, by contrast, complained that until Canada was allowed to use its NHL players, a world title would remain out of reach. "The domination of world-class amateur hockey has been seized by the Communist nations of Europe," he wrote in the *Windsor Star*. "Father David Bauer's noble experiment has had a good run . . . and he deserves commendation . . . but his team has not produced a winner, and I will be amazed if it does . . . Either we somehow bring our best athletes (the pros) to bear, or Russia will stampede everybody in the world . . ."

"You've got to realize those are the number one through number eighteen hockey players in Russia," said Walter Bush, newly appointed president of the Minnesota North Stars. "Even Canada can't match it. Their 600 best players are in [professional] Canadian and American hockey leagues, so they start with number 601."

Back in Minnesota, Coach Murray Williamson wasn't interested in debating any of that. He'd had a taste of success and wanted to build on it. He knew skill and conditioning were the foundation; but without continuity, camaraderie, and extensive game experience, it would be nearly impossible to build a championship program.

Williamson hit the ground running. "I knew we needed to play a heavier domestic schedule," he says, "so my first order of business was to put together a budget. I needed money for stipends, room and board, travel. No more jobs for the players. I needed their full attention. We'd learn how to push the envelope but not violate the Olympic code."

Williamson's budget called for thirty-seven exhibition games between October 21, 1967, and January 21, 1968—about one game every three days. On tour, they'd collect at least $30,000 in guaranteed gate receipts, to be placed into a separate account for player salaries and expenses. By the time the team left for Europe, a projected surplus of $11,000 would be credited back to AHAUS to cover its donation to the US Olympic fund.

> Williamson couldn't help but marvel at the fact his team would train and essentially play an entire season for less than the price of two NHL player salaries.

After a thorough review, the Olympic Committee granted Williamson a total of $44,500 to cover five months of expenses. Williamson couldn't help but marvel at the fact his team would train and essentially play an entire season for less than the price of two NHL player salaries. *Pros in the Olympics?* he thought. *Not without a budget at least ten times bigger.*

With a full-time commitment to the US national team, Williamson realized he'd need to make a decision about what to do with his St. Paul Steers franchise. "By then, most of my players were actually on the US national team," he says.

Rather than abandon the franchise, Williamson and the league decided to turn it into an informal national B team. "Not just a roster of spares to fill in for injured players," Williamson says, "a true development squad who could push the guys on the main team." He chuckles. "Yeah. Those were some grandiose plans. Putting together *one team* would be a major chore. Implementing a farm team more than doubled my workload."

Williamson set about the task of signing and recruiting players for the national program with the idea of having them play and train with the A team or be ready for immediate recall from the ranks of the B team. He'd kept his job as employment manager at Honeywell Aerospace, which actually worked in his favor.

"I traveled around the country on the company dime," he says, "recruiting players as I went." John Rendell, the former Michigan star from Williamson's childhood neighborhood, was the coach of the B team.

Williamson had been unsuccessful in his earlier attempt to push through the Act of Congress granting Lou Nanne and Bill Masterton citizenship. Nonetheless, the bill wasn't dead. With tighter eligibility rules for the Olympic team, however, Masterton was a no-go since he'd played professionally three years prior.

Nanne, on the other hand, still hadn't signed a pro contract. As the first and only Gophers defenseman to ever win the WCHA scoring title, Nanne was a potential pillar of Williamson's roster; so it was well worth the time and energy to get the job done. Ten months out from the 1968 Winter Olympic Games, Williamson rededicated himself to his legislative effort.

After first identifying their fellow committee members'

objections, Representatives John Blatnik and Clark MacGregor were able to enlist the help of Minnesota Senators Walter Mondale and Eugene McCarthy. Mondale and McCarthy, in turn, were able to recruit Senator Philip Hart of Michigan, Everett Dirksen of Illinois, and Edward Kennedy of Massachusetts. A coalition was building, and the bill was picking up steam. Williamson's dogged persistence was finally paying off.

By the third week in June, the bill had passed through the House and Senate and was signed into law by President Lyndon B. Johnson on June 26, 1967.

"When the dust finally settled, the whole thing seemed a little surreal," Williamson says. "Can you imagine an Act of Congress to give a Canadian hockey player US citizenship? Just so he could play for the US Olympic team? It seems like the kind of thing that could actually start a riot."

In fact, it nearly did.

After a great deal of expense—in terms of both time and money—Williamson had finally succeeded in getting Nanne citizenship. Nanne had signed his contract to play for the US Olympic team, and Williamson thought things were set. He breathed a sigh of relief and moved on to other issues.

In the meantime, Nanne had become fixated on the idea of playing for the hometown North Stars once the Olympics were over. By September, he'd convinced Wren Blair, the North Stars' colorful coach and GM, to give him a tryout. Blair's big claim to fame was finding and signing a fourteen-year-old phenom by the name of Bobby Orr, and he couldn't pass up the chance to get a little publicity while establishing himself as Minnesota's hockey guru.

Nanne had a great reputation as an All-American college defenseman and was very well-known around town. Needless to say, Williamson was concerned that Nanne was attempting to divide his time between the two huge commitments while toying with his amateur status. He also wasn't about to give special consideration to any one player.

"I called Louie and told him it would cost him fifty bucks every time he suited up for the North Stars and reminded him he'd lose his eligibility if he played even *one* exhibition game with an NHL team," Williamson says.

Of course, this message was relayed to Blair and the stage was set for the fireworks. Both the national team and the North Stars often practiced at Wakota Arena in South St. Paul. One afternoon, the national team was wrapping up and the North Stars were getting ready to go on next. Williamson had just left the arena and was in the parking lot when Mariucci called out the door and asked him to return to the rink. Blair wanted to talk about the Nanne situation.

The moment Williamson stepped inside the arena, he was confronted by Blair, who was already running hot. Blair demanded to know what the hell Williamson was doing tampering with Nanne. He told Williamson that Nanne was on the North Stars' negotiation list, and they had no intention of letting him play anywhere else.

Williamson repeated the edict he'd issued to Nanne earlier and loudly reminded everyone that things were in Lou's lap. Williamson said he didn't care one way or the other what Nanne decided, but the issue had to be settled.

At that point, Blair blew up.

"Anybody who ever knew Blair understood how his moods could shift instantly without warning," says Williamson. "You'd be having a conversation and he'd suddenly be wild-eyed and ranting."

Blair threatened to make it public that Williamson was paying his players *beyond* mere living expenses. The raucous verbal exchange was on the brink of getting physical when Mariucci stepped in.

"By then, all the North Stars players had gathered at the boards to watch the two bantamweight fighters skirmishing over a player," Williamson says. "They were doubled over in laughter, enjoying all the fuss."

At that point, Williamson turned and started to leave, but he'd couldn't pass up the temptation of a last parting shot. Shouting loud enough for everyone to hear, he yelled, "If the North Stars want to settle the problem, maybe they should pay Nanne $30,000 per year." At the time, the typical NHL salary was about $10,000 per year.

Superstar Bobby Orr, in his second year with the Bruins, was only making $35,000 per year. The hugely inflated figure was an obvious taunt. Williamson walked out the door and didn't look back.

The next day, Blair and Williamson met by chance in downtown Minneapolis, where the North Stars had their temporary offices. They both said hello to each other, exchanged pleasantries, and went about their business as if nothing had happened.

"That was typical of Wren," Williamson says. "He'd blow up at someone one minute and forget it the next. It drove some people crazy but, I have to say, I always admired and respected that about him."

Somewhere along the line, Blair had agreed to leave Nanne alone until after the Olympics and the national team began its four-month, thirty-five-game exhibition schedule. Williamson was in the midst of crisscrossing the country when he ran into Wren Blair at the Boston airport. Blair looked startled at first, then bowed his head and told Williamson the tragic news.

In Bill Masterton's second shift of the North Stars game the night before, he'd carried the puck across the blue line, angled to right as he entered the zone, and sent a backhand pass to right wing Wayne Connelly. Seconds later, he was flat on his back, sprawled motionless on the ice.

"I've never seen anyone go down like that," said Blair. "We heard the crash from the bench, and we knew it wasn't good."

"It sounded like a baseball bat hitting a ball," teammate André Boudrias told reporters.

In the following days, players, fans, and the press disagreed about exactly what happened. Some say Masterton lost his balance after getting his feet tangled in a stick and spun backward onto the ice, unable to break his fall. Others say he collided with Seals defensemen Larry Cahan and Ron Harris, both of whom were converging on the puck as Masterton let go of his pass. Others say Harris delivered a hard, clean check while Masterton had his head turned and Masterton fell over Cahan, his legs cut out from under him, striking the back of his head on the ice.

However it actually happened, Masterton left the rink on a stretcher, bleeding from his nose, ears, and mouth. Team doctors treated him briefly in a Met Center dressing room, and he was taken by ambulance to Fairview Southdale Hospital, seven miles away. By the time he arrived, the swelling in Masterton's brain was so severe that surgery was no longer an option.

Doctors flooded his system with steroids and diuretics in a desperate attempt to reduce the swelling. They put him on a ventilator. His wife, Carol, who'd been in the stands, held her injured husband's hand and prayed.

After landing at the airport, Williamson rushed to Fairview Southdale. Walter Bush, the North Stars' team president, was pacing the waiting room. Other family members sat with their heads down, desperately trying to console each other.

Williamson quietly stepped into his friend's hospital room and immediately felt his heart sink. Masterton's head was heavily bandaged. He lay motionless on the bed, his chest moving only slightly as he inhaled and exhaled.

Two years earlier, Williamson had brought Masterton to the St. Paul Steers. Masterton had been playing for the Cleveland Barons in the Montréal Canadiens system. Williamson's pitch was easy: he'd get Masterton a job at Honeywell and give him a roster spot on one of the best teams in the USHL. Masterton said yes, and the two had been close friends ever since.

Williamson spoke quietly to Carol. Earlier, the doctor had told her that Bill would never regain consciousness. The man she knew and loved was already gone. After hearing about the tragic accident, Masterton's parents had flown down from Winnipeg as soon as they could. Together, they made the decision to remove Masterton from life support. He died at 1:55 a.m.

"Masterton died early Monday morning of a massive brain hemorrhage received in a game against Oakland Saturday night," wrote the UPI. "The 29-year-old center did not regain consciousness during the thirty hours between the accident and his death."

Masterton's tragic death sent shockwaves through the entire

Minnesota hockey community. Many of his former teammates had seen him not long before he died. It was an incomprehensible loss.

The following Monday, Williamson put on a brave face and announced his final eighteen-man roster to the press. Herb Brooks, Craig Falkman, Len Lilyholm, Don Ross, and Pat Rupp all carried over from the 1967 national team. Thirteen others were new, including recently naturalized US citizen Lou Nanne.

"Fully half the squad comes from Minnesota," wrote the AP. Further down in the article, they quoted Williamson describing the 1968 team as "bigger, faster, and stronger than last year."

> Further down in the article, they quoted Williamson describing the 1968 team as "bigger, faster, and stronger than last year."

In summary, the coach said, "I feel their size, shooting, and skating are strong points, but we still lack experience."

Friday, January 26, the team left for Munich to play four final tune-up games before the Olympics began, with two in West Germany, one in Lyon, France, and the fourth in Geneva.

The first game was in Bad Tölz against the West German national team in front of an exuberant sellout crowd. In a largely defensive struggle, the United States won 3–1 on goals by Tom Hurley, Larry Stordahl, and Herb Brooks. Even so, the coach wasn't pleased.

"I thought the Germans were bush league," Williamson says, "and the crowd was just egging them on. Elbows and sticks were flying and it got worse as the game went on."

Doc Nagobads agreed, writing in his memoir, "We won the game, but we didn't enjoy it at all because the West Germans were quite chippy, hooking and slashing our players—a sign of things to come."

Two nights later, in Garmisch-Partenkirchen, Doc's prediction came true. The way Williamson tells it, Herb Brooks and a German player were in a scrum in the corner when the German suddenly spit in Brooks's face.

"Herb was about the last man to ever get into a scrap," says Williamson, "but he dropped his gloves and just went after the guy."

Moments later, the German goalie raced from his net, leapt on Brooks's back, and both benches cleared.

"Suddenly, out of nowhere," Nagobads writes, "the West German goalie joined the fray and hit Herb over the head with his stick."

"Bob Paradise leveled the German goalie," Williamson adds, "and Johnny Cunniff chased their biggest guy right off the ice. German players were scrambling back onto the bench in full retreat."

Naturally, the international press told a different story.

"West Germany had taken a 2–0 lead in the third period when Herb Brooks was penalized," wrote the United Press International. "Brooks, who had been in and out of the penalty box throughout the exhibition contest, refused to go. Two German players told him to leave the ice after he ignored the Czech referee. It touched off a slugfest as both teams emptied onto the ice. After the melee was halted, the players started brawling again and spectators threw beer bottles and debris onto the ice."

"That development scared us," Williamson says. "We had trouble getting back to the dressing room without getting hurt." The US coach quickly locked the door and refused to continue the game without reassurance the German fans wouldn't attack his team.

Several German officials, the two Czech referees, Williamson, and the German coach all met in an empty locker room to determine how to proceed. After a lengthy conference, everyone agreed both teams would receive two penalties each. Brooks and the German goalie would be ejected. Both teams would line up on the blue line, raise their sticks to salute each other, shake hands, and resume the game.

The coaches went back to their benches, the two teams lined up as discussed, and the hostile crowd fell silent. Both teams halfheartedly saluted each other, and the fans began to applaud as the players all shook hands. When they announced the penalties, though, things went awry.

"Our two penalties were both ten-minute majors," Williamson says—his frustration still apparent more than half a century later—"while one German player got a five-minute penalty and the other a lousy two minutes."

Williamson looked at the German bench, searching in vain for some kind of explanation. "All of them were smiling," he says. "I'd been completely duped."

For the rest of the game, the United States had to play short-handed. "In a way, it was a blessing," Williamson says. "The game was an exhibition. It didn't mean anything." He went down the bench and told every player, "Be smart. Stay in control. Don't do anything stupid. And for God's sake, *don't get hurt.*"

Ten days later, incidentally, the United States got revenge, trouncing the West Germans 8–1 to secure its first Olympic win.

Prior to their next game against West Germany, the United States had to face each of the Big Four, beginning with the Czechoslovaks. Fresh from the mayhem in Garmisch-Partenkirchen and worried about his team's reputation for rough play, Williamson urged his players to keep it clean.

Instead, "The Czechs toyed with the Americans through much of the game," according to the Minneapolis *Star*. "At one time, in the third period, they seemed to be having batting practice against goalie Pat Rupp as they set up and fired the puck at him repeatedly."

"We never know how much body checking the officials will let us do, so we played cautiously and lost," said Williamson after the 5–1 defeat. "If we had roughed up the Czechs, maybe we would have won."

> "We're a mad team now," he said. "We'll win our game against Sweden."

Undeterred, he told reporters the loss would actually inspire his team. "We're a mad team now," he said. "We'll win our game against Sweden."

Midway through the game two nights later, Williamson's optimism seemed well justified. With Sweden up by a slim 1–0 margin in the second period, Craig Falkman scored on a perfect feed from Len Lilyholm to tie the game. Fourteen seconds later, Falkman returned the favor, dishing the puck to Lilyholm, who banged it home.

Sweden quickly responded, retaking the lead 3–2, but as the US team was resurgent, disaster struck. Skating hard to avoid an icing, Falkman slipped and crashed feetfirst into the end boards.

"As I ran onto the ice, I saw Craig's foot was almost 90 degrees out of its normal position," wrote Doc Nagobads. "I stabilized the ankle with one hand, grabbed the skate with my other hand, pulled down hard, and turned the foot back to its normal position."

Falkman was in less pain, but he was carried off the ice on a stretcher and rushed to Grenoble Military Hospital. The United States lost the game 4–3 *and* the services of their star forward for the remainder of the tournament.

"It hurt us," Williamson told reporters after the game. "He was playing great, and we were forced to use a defenseman on the attack after that."

Effectively out of contention for an Olympic medal, Williamson pinned his hopes on defeating the Soviets. "We thought we should have beaten Sweden, but the squad knows if they can beat the Russians, it will be a successful Olympics," he said.

Needless to say, the Soviets envisioned a different outcome... even if it meant they had to resort to psychological warfare.

"Both we and the Russians had games Wednesday night," Herb Brooks told reporters. "When we were trying to get out of bed this morning, they were running and doing exercises right outside our window. It's quite demoralizing."

Williamson wasn't surprised. "There isn't a professional team that trains as hard as they do," he said. "They could give any NHL squad a good game."

The following night, the Soviets scored four goals in the first six minutes, running the score to 6–0 before the first period ended. The United States, on the other hand, had notched six penalties by the time the first frame concluded.

"The Americans started out with heavy body checks," said the AP, "hoping to throw the Russians off balance." That tactic backfired, though, and the United States lost 10–2.

Williamson was irate, but not from his team's performance. "This was absolutely the worst refereeing I have ever seen in hockey," he told reporters. "The Russians won the game 4–2, but the first period went to the referees. We deserved penalties at times, but nothing like that."

The United States went on to lose a tightly contested game to the Canadians two nights later before finally posting their first win—a satisfying 8–2 rout of West Germany. "We lost that game in Garmisch-Partenkirchen," Williamson says, "but we beat them when it counted."

Mathematically, the United States could still finish as high as fifth place; but by then, the damage was done. It would be impossible to crack the top four. In their final two games, the United States beat East Germany 6–4 and tied Finland 1–1 but still placed sixth over-all—their lowest finish ever in Olympic play.

Despite Czechoslovakia's stunning 5–4 win over the Soviets—a loss that snapped the Russians' streak of thirty-nine straight wins in world championship play—the fight for the gold medal came down to the final game of the tournament: Canada versus Russia.

On the eve of the final showdown, Tarasov invited Williamson to watch his team's pregame routine in the Soviet locker room. Over the past two years, the two coaches had become close friends.

The Russians were notorious for suiting up before they left the hotel. Williamson was in the Soviet dressing room when the team arrived—in everything but their skates and helmets—less than half an hour before the opening face-off.

"The next twenty minutes amazed me," Williamson says. "I'd never seen anything like it." Without any instruction that Williamson noticed, every player cycled through a series of calisthenics at a rapid pace, never stopping to rest or even regather themselves.

"Tarasov was walking around with a stopwatch in his hand, barking orders and raising hell with any player he thought wasn't fast enough. The entire dressing room was like a beehive. The only way I can describe it is 'organized confusion.' Everyone did their own thing, oblivious to the others."

Williamson was shocked. As someone who'd been trained to believe a dressing room should be quiet before the game, it didn't make any sense. "The contrast was enormous," he says. "The players didn't talk, but they moved constantly, and Tarasov *never* let up. He was after them the whole time."

The Canadians kept it close for the first two-thirds of the game. They gave up a single goal in each of the first two periods, but the Soviets were too much too handle in the final stanza. Pumping in three straight goals to take a 5-0 lead, the Russians coasted the rest of the way for a shutout victory.

"At least three of the Russian forwards—Anatoli Firsov, Viktor Polupanov, and Vyacheslav Starshinov—could step right into permanent jobs with any team in the NHL," wrote Jim Coleman in the *Calgary Herald*. "Comrade Anatoly Tarasov rather smugly announced his team is ready to challenge the Montréal Canadiens or Chicago Blackhawks, and many of us in Grenoble are prepared to agree with him."

At the post-Olympic hockey banquet at the Chateau de la Chartreuse—north of Grenoble, where the famous liqueur is made—the Russians once again dominated the proceedings.

"They challenged all of us to an endless series of toasts using a mixture of Scotch and that greenish-yellow chartreuse," Williamson says. "Those who were foolish enough to accept the challenge didn't stand a chance." Even in the cellars of Chartreuse, the Soviets were determined to vanquish their rivals just as they had on the ice.

CHAPTER SEVENTEEN

RESTORING US HOCKEY TO A POSITION OF RESPECTABILITY

As a player, John Mayasich was in a class by himself.

In his four-year high school career, he never lost a game. He led Eveleth to four state championships while posting a ridiculous record of 79–0. In college, Mayasich won the Western League scoring title twice and was named an All-American three years in a row. To this day, he remains the Gophers' top scorer with a Wayne Gretzky-like average of 2.68 points per game.

Prior to the 1960 Olympics, Mayasich led the Green Bay Bobcats to a 20–4–0 record, ending the Rochester Mustangs' five-year reign as national senior champions. Five days after that season ended, he notched a hat trick and two assists in a surprising 7–5 win over Czechoslovakia, jumpstarting the United States' improbable gold medal run in Squaw Valley.

When asked to describe Mayasich after coaching him on the Gophers and 1956 US Olympic team, John Mariucci said, "The words to describe the boy haven't yet been invented. When I say he's the best, that's totally inadequate."

Despite Mayasich's unrivaled feats as a player, his bewildering 0–10–0 record behind the bench at the 1969 World Championships is a stark reminder how far and how fast the US national team had fallen behind. After the Soviets won the 1954 IIHF World Championship, the Soviets, Czechoslovaks, and Swedes took home a combined eleven of sixteen gold medals, ushering in a new era, where continuity and training were the keys to long-term success. Individual skill was no longer enough.

To their credit, Walter Brown and Bob Ridder noticed this sea change early and adapted accordingly, with tryouts and training camps, a sizable exhibition schedule, better financing, and pre-Olympic tours of Europe against some of the top regional teams. The United States had fallen behind but seemed to be gaining ground.

Brown's unexpected passing in 1964 coupled with Ridder's near full-time involvement with the Minnesota North Stars created a leadership vacuum. In stepped Tom Lockhart, the original founder of AHAUS, who'd spent the early years running the organization from his apartment "when the paperwork fit in a shoebox." As the founding president, his opinions held considerable sway . . . though they weren't necessarily aligned with those of Brown and Ridder.

Lockhart had come up through the ranks of distance running and competitive cycling, highly individualized sports where athletic prowess was key. His first exposure to hockey had come as a young promoter at Madison Square Garden, booking challenge matches between East Coast amateur teams who were amateur in name only. Players were "reimbursed" for expenses and "lost wages" from playing hockey. Lockhart had come of age promoting marquee players—many of whom were Canadian—rather than teams. Somewhere along the way, he seemed to end up believing his own sales pitch.

By finishing with a mark of 2–4–1 in Grenoble in 1968, the US national team confirmed Lockhart's biases. He'd never thought an amateur team stocked with unknown players could hope to compete against world-class players, no matter how long the team had trained and played together. He thought time and money spent developing young players was a decidedly poor investment. The only way to win, in his mind, was to support the country's top teams and develop superstars.

Ignoring any progress the national development program had made—not to mention the lessons learned—Lockhart abruptly changed course. Outlining a vastly different organizational philosophy, he sent a rambling letter to Williamson in June 1969.

From what Williamson could tell, Lockhart's argument hinged on the thesis that a unified development program discouraged the overall growth of senior amateur leagues. With one geographically centered, full-time national team, Lockhart reasoned there was no incentive for senior teams from New York, Boston, Maine, Michigan or anywhere else to keep improving. Much like Vic Heyliger in the late 1940s, Lockhart seemed to believe a national tournament—with an Olympic bid as the grand prize—was the only guaranteed way to motivate the country's best players.

After a mere two years, Murray Williamson's vision for a sustainable and continuous US development program had apparently run its course.

Lockhart's grandiose idea of a national senior amateur tournament notwithstanding, as the New Year approached, AHAUS leadership publicly named John Mayasich head coach of the 1969 US National team, with Wayne "Bud" Dornack as manager. Ostensibly, Don Clark and Jack Riley would lead a five-man commission in charge of selecting the players, but the real plan appeared to be combining players from Mayasich's Green Bay Bobcats and Dornack's Rochester Mustangs.

"I'm not sure why they did it that way," Williamson says, "but you can't argue with the fact there were some damn good players on the final roster."

In fact, seven of the team's eighteen players were later enshrined in the US Hockey Hall of Fame, including Keith Raymond "Huffer" Christiansen, Paul Coppo, Lefty Curran, Gary Gambucci, Bob Paradise, Larry Pleau, and Tim Sheehy—not to mention Mayasich himself.

"Team chemistry is tricky," Williamson says. "I think that's one of the biggest lessons that Tarasov and the Soviets taught us. You can have all the top players; but if they don't work together, what difference does it make?"

In its classic understated style, the *USA Hockey Results Book* doesn't speculate as to *why* players were chosen from only two USHL teams.

Instead, it simply notes, "Due to the problem of obtaining players for an extended period of time, the team did not practice together as a unit before departing for Europe."

Prior to that departure, Mayasich tamped down expectations. "Under the circumstances," he told reporters, "if we can beat the Finns and surprise one other team, I think we'll be doing well. For us to do better than that would be expecting an awful lot."

Williamson won't disagree. "I don't think it's fair to say Mayasich was not a good coach," he says. "I think AHAUS leadership created an impossible situation. It was a fiasco right from the start."

Thanks to a circuitous route, Mayasich and his team landed in Prague after twenty-six hours of travel. There, they were scheduled to play a pair of exhibition games against Czechoslovakia's top two teams. It was the first—and only—chance for the US team to play together before the world tournament started.

With barely enough time to unpack, much less sleep or relax, the team went straight to the rink . . . where they were promptly shellacked 11–0 by the Czechoslovakian A team in front of eighteen thousand screaming fans.

Nearly falling asleep in the locker room after the game, according to the *Canadian Press*, Lefty Curran told reporters, "They don't shoot all that hard, but they work in so close and they just keep coming at you. They showed us a lot. The score proves that."

"That's the measure of how badly this team needs to practice together," said Bud Dornack. "That was the first time they ever played together as a team. How can you expect them to do well?"

Williamson is still incredulous all these decades later. "There was no preparation," he says. "They all just hopped on a plane and went to Europe like it was winter vacation. I thought we'd made some real progress during the two previous years. They threw it all out the window."

Twenty-four hours later, the result was little better. Playing the same style as their elders, the Czechoslovakian junior team controlled virtually every aspect of the game, cruising to a decisive 6–1 win.

Two days later, "the battered United States amateur ice hockey team" arrived in Stockholm and immediately drove to the rink for their first game of the tournament. The United States faced the defending champion Soviets. Ten minutes into the contest, the score was tied 0–0, even though the US skaters were struggling to keep up. "In that early spell, goalkeeper Mike Curran . . . performed heroically as the Russians swarmed around the cage," wrote the AP.

Eventually, Vyacheslav Starshinov tallied twice to give the Soviets a 2–0 lead before the first period ended. Still, the United States had kept the game close and the team remained optimistic.

Things changed abruptly, however, when the second period started. The Soviets scored two goals in the first thirty-six seconds to take a 4–0 lead. After that, the Soviets peppered Mike Curran as the defense around him imploded. By the second period buzzer, the Soviets had pumped in a whopping ten more goals to give them a comical 14–0 lead.

The Russians had never scored more than thirteen goals in a single world tournament game. They'd just broken that record, and there was still a full period left. The final tally was 17–2, the Soviets' biggest margin of victory in world tournament history.

Mathematically, of course, the US team was still alive. Psychologically, they were already done. "If we'd had the possibility to work out and play together before the tournament," Mayasich said, "I'm sure we would have had a much better start."

As the tournament continued, Mayasich's complaints grew louder and more insistent. After taking a 2–1 lead against Sweden in the first period, the United States surrendered seven unanswered goals in the final two frames for an 8–2 loss.

"We played a good first period tonight, but then our game just fell to pieces," Mayasich said. "It seems we're not in condition. We can't skate."

Facing Canada two nights later, the pattern was repeated. Behind 1–0 after two periods, the United States conceded four straight goals in the final twenty minutes to take a 5–0 loss. After the game, Mayasich grumbled, "If the United States is going to support its team on a B level, then that's where we belong."

His comments were blunt but prophetic. After dropping a must-win game to Finland—the only other winless team—relegation seemed inevitable.

"The bottom team will not be included in the 1970 World Championships in Canada," the AP explained. "That was why it was vital to Mayasich and his squad to beat the fast-skating Finns."

One week later, the United States had lost four more games and were set to face the Finns for the second time. Incredibly, even with a record of 0–9–0, they still had one shot left: beat the Finns by two or more goals. In the standings, the United States and Finland would be tied with one win each, but the Americans would hold the tie-breaker—a better goal differential in head-to-head matchups.

On paper, it seemed doable. On the ice, it was more of the same. Tied 1–1 as the first period ended, the Finns scored five unanswered goals in the second period and coasted to an easy 7–3 win.

"With ten losses in ten games," the AP noted, "that drops the Americans into Group B for next year's international competition while East Germany, winner of Group B this year, moves up into Group A."

Frustrated and embittered with his squad's winless performance, Mayasich lashed out in the press. "I feel sorry for the boys," he said, boarding the team bus after the game. "Tom Lockhart, the president of AHAUS, was in Stockholm and didn't have the courtesy to come around and pat the boys on the head . . . He hasn't visited the team and hasn't done anything for us during the whole tournament."

As it turns out, Lockhart was only in Stockholm for a total of three days. For the rest of the two-week event, he was home in New York, supervising the playoffs of the Eastern Hockey League, a money-making venture that he also controlled.

Asked if relegation to Group B might change AHAUS's perspective, Mayasich replied, "I doubt it. They'll probably sleep until next March when it comes time to pick another fifteen or so boys to send over." With visible frustration, he added, "The whole system will have to change if we're going to have a chance to get back into the A group and fight for the title."

Even with low expectations, the United States had performed worse than anyone could have imagined. They not only lost every game; in the process, they surrendered a whopping seventy-four goals in ten games, scoring just twenty-four. With a total goal differential of -50, the United States had lost by an average of five goals per game. They weren't simply beaten; they'd never stood a chance.

Referee Hal Trumble—recently back from Stockholm, where he'd officiated eight of the world tournament contests—found the US approach doomed to fail from the start. "The [United States] sent over a part-time pickup team who had to play opposition wholly subsidized by their governments," he told the Minneapolis *Tribune*. "This is no way to compete.... The biggest blunder was breaking up the program established two years ago by Murray Williamson. Murray wanted a permanent team based in Minnesota. This required an outlay of money ... Instead, Lockhart broke up the team and was satisfied to send over a team recruited from playing weekend hockey."

Referee Hal Trumble—recently back from Stockholm, where he'd officiated eight of the world tournament contests—found the US approach doomed to fail from the start.

Relegation to Group B meant an Olympic bid was no longer guaranteed.

"*That* sure got people's attention," Williamson says. "Red lights started flashing. Horns were going off. A lot of people were panicked."

AHAUS Director Bob Fleming sure sat up and took notice.

Like Murray Williamson, Fleming had grown up in Winnipeg. He'd also played varsity hockey for the Minnesota Gophers while earning a BA in business. After graduation, he moved to Rochester and played for the Mustangs. As his hockey career wound down, he got a job at the Mayo Clinic. Over the next three decades, he steadily rose through the ranks and ultimately became chief administrative officer.

Nearly a decade prior, Fleming had helped organize the 1960 gold medal team. He subsequently managed the 1961 and 1962 teams coached by Connie Pleban. He was elected to the AHAUS board of directors in 1964 and continued to hold that position for the next thirty-three years.

Fleming called Williamson and suggested the two of them meet at the Black Stallion Supper Club in Cannon Falls, about halfway between Rochester and the Twin Cities. Williamson agreed, and a few days later, the two of them talked for hours over dinner and drinks.

Fleming had not been involved directly with player selection or team management for several years, but he couldn't sit idly by as the national program hit rock bottom. His twofold goal was simple: get the former coach's thoughts about how to prepare for the 1972 Olympics and figure out a way to make it happen.

First off, Williamson volunteered, AHAUS's vision for the national team was too shortsighted, too inflexible, and too arbitrary.

"I never thought it was favoritism," Williamson says in retrospect, "but it got political in a hurry. Seniority was a big factor. If you'd coached for twenty-five years and were coming off a big season, the attitude was, 'Okay, you're next in line. Let's see what you can do.' There's nothing wrong with that, I suppose, but it doesn't prioritize winning."

The more Williamson and Fleming dug into the problem, the more it became clear AHAUS didn't have the desire, much less the capacity, to organize, manage, and finance a true national development program. Bob Ridder had made it work back in the 1950s, but he was far too busy with the Minnesota North Stars and his other business ventures. As president of the North Stars and head of the burgeoning USHL, Walter Bush couldn't do it either.

There had to be someone else, but Fleming needed a way to find him; so he drew on his corporate background and decided to form a commission. He would gather the best hockey minds and charge the group with devising a plan for the upcoming Winter Games in Sapporo, Japan.

Soon, Fleming had recruited heavy hitters Bush and Ridder as well as James Fullerton, head coach at Brown and winner of the 1965 NCAA Coach of the Year award; Marsh Ryman, the Gophers athletic director; and Vic Weber from Bemidji State, president of the NAIA Hockey Coaches Association.

Fleming also reached out to Art Lentz, executive director of the US Olympic Committee since 1965. Lentz was intensely aware of the deepening crisis in US hockey, which he viewed as a symptom of larger systemic failure. He shared Fleming's concerns and vowed to secure financing for a long-term development program. In fact, he'd already tripled the 1968 Olympic budget, raising over ten million dollars for 1972.

As Lentz told the press not long after he and Fleming had spoken, "The old methods are no longer valid . . . Other countries have national teams in many sports. It's a darned good idea. But we have always had trouble forming national teams because of the battle over who would run them. The AAU is jealous. The NCAA is jealous. The NAIA is jealous and the Armed Forces are jealous . . . Somebody has to take the lead in this . . . We can no longer expect to maintain a major influence in the Olympic sport world by continuing the simple but antiquated one-season affair in preparing for each Olympic games."

Lentz didn't call out AHAUS specifically, but the implications were clear. The USOC was done with interorganizational bickering and managerial bumbling. They were going to take over and throw their power and money behind a new, centralized system for developing athletes and building teams.

Energized and inspired, Fleming organized a meeting of the Olympic Hockey Committee and AHAUS in Chicago at the end of the summer. He invited Williamson to attend to present his ideas to the joint committee. Williamson accepted with one crucial caveat: if other coaches and managers would be making their presentations too, Williamson was out. The joint committee could interview all the candidates they wanted, but Williamson would not be among them.

"I guess my attitude was they either wanted me or they didn't," he says. "They knew what they'd be getting, so why try to play that game . . . ?"

Sometimes, Williamson likes to describe himself as "the Billy Martin of hockey," referring to the infamous Yankees manager who was fired and rehired five times by George Steinbrenner. While some people might agree Williamson knew how to "make a bad situation worse," Fleming, Bush, and Ridder were not yet in that camp.

Williamson stood at the front of a large conference room in a tall office building in downtown Chicago, feeling out of place and a bit intimidated by lots of men in gray suits. He presented his long-term vision for building a national team as earnestly as he could, but something kept bugging him.

Grandiose plans aside, the first and biggest concern was winning the Group B World Championship in Bucharest, Romania. And with the tournament just six months away, he feared they were behind already. Putting together a world-class team—even to compete in Group B—would be a monumental task, especially when so many of the country's top prospects had already signed to minor league pro teams and D1 college programs.

To further complicate matters, Williamson no longer owned and managed the St. Paul Steers. That talent pool had long since scattered. He wondered why all of them were sitting in a conference room, chatting, when they could be holding tryouts and playing scrimmages, building a team. It wasn't complicated. They just needed to get out there and do it.

"I was never one for chalkboards and strategy and talking about what you're going to do," Williamson says. "Most of the time, it comes down to one thing: surround yourself with people who aren't afraid to work hard and *cannot stand* to lose. I think that's really it. The guys I wanted on my team were the ones who hated to lose."

Williamson's tireless work ethic and fierce competitive spirit must have come through in his presentation, because the joint commission was sold. They appointed him head coach through the end of the 1972 Winter Olympic tournament.

A few days later, Robert Fleming announced a long-range plan "to restore the United States to a position of respectability in international amateur hockey competition." He also established the immediate goal of winning the 1970 World B Championship and returning to Group A for the 1971 Championship.

On the surface, the initial stage of Williamson's ambitious three-year plan looked a lot like the slapdash system used to select Mayasich and Dornack's team. With little time to spare and limited prospects to choose from, Williamson worked the phones, calling everyone he knew to get their thoughts on the best American players who were still available *and* eligible.

Tryouts were held over Christmas break at the Met Center in Bloomington. That way, things were opened up to current college players whose coaches might see fit to release them. Williamson was optimistic. If it all worked out, they might even be able to squeeze in a few February exhibition games before they left for Europe.

Generally, things went according to plan, and by the time the new year arrived, Williamson had cobbled together "a patched-up conglomeration of players" from the previous national team, US-born skaters from Europe, three kids from Bemidji State, four players on leave from the army, two reinstated pros, and a handful of veterans from various Midwestern senior league teams.

"It was a makeshift operation," Williamson says, "but I thought with some hard work and maybe a little luck, a Group B championship wasn't out the question."

The team reassembled in February for a week of practice and two exhibition games before departing for Switzerland. After two uneventful contests against WCHA opponents, the club had yet to jell, let alone work as a team.

"They were still introducing themselves as we boarded the flight to Geneva," Williamson says. "That's when I felt the pressure. America's hockey prestige was hanging in the balance."

In Geneva, the United States opened with a 5–2 win over the Swiss national team. "The score doesn't reflect it," Williamson confesses, "but our guys really struggled." On the eve of their final tune-up, he was still searching for some kind of spark, something to bring them together and ignite their competitive spirit. In their second match against the Swiss team, the coach finally got his wish.

The arena in La Chaux-de-Fonds was boiling over with enthusiasm. Horns were sounding, and fans were chanting a full thirty minutes before the game was scheduled to start. Williamson could feel the tension as the two teams took to the ice. Then, he looked over and noticed two German referees were scheduled to work the game. Of all the European officials, it seemed like Germans disliked the North American style more than anyone else. The game would be called very tightly. Williamson grew concerned.

The Swiss came out flying and took a 1–0 lead five minutes in the game. The overflow crowd went wild. The US players looked rattled, but Williamson reminded them to stick to the style they knew, playing tough in the corners and forechecking hard.

Suddenly, the US team's George Konik and Swiss superstar Michel Turler met in a head-on collision at center ice. A roar went up from the crowd, prompting the referee to call Konik for charging. Turler lost his cool and retaliated with a slash, also drawing a penalty. A shower of plastic bottles rained down on the ice as the crowd booed and jeered, complaining about the call. With the referees on edge, the fans soon took over and controlled the tempo for the rest of the game. Every time they roared, the referees blew the whistle.

By the end of the second period, the score was tied 3–3. The game was rough and intense, but Williamson was pleased. United by the adversity and viciousness of the crowd, the team was coming together, bonding as a unit.

The third period began with the Swiss scoring a power play goal to take a 4–3 lead. Midway through the period, Gary Gambucci scored the equalizer and the United States took control. With thirty seconds left in the game, it was fire-wagon hockey when Gambucci sprang loose on a breakaway. The last Swiss defender caught up and hauled him down from behind. The referee's arm shot up, and he blew the whistle. Two minutes for tripping.

Williamson yelled and argued, demanding a penalty shot. Bottles showered the ice, and the referees sent the teams to their dressing rooms, desperate to regain control. After a long delay, the two teams returned. There were five seconds left. The referee dropped the puck, Henry Boucha won the face-off cleanly and sent a pass to his winger. Konik gathered the puck and blasted it into the net for a shocking

5–4 win.

The US players went wild. Suddenly, they had arrived.

On to Bucharest, Romania, for the World B Championship.

The United States drew Japan as their first opponent. In some ways, it felt like a one-game tournament. Going into the World B Championship, Japan was heavily favored. They'd recently completed a successful tour of Canada, followed by a month of training in Czechoslovakia with some of the country's best coaches.

West Germany was thought to be a strong contender along with Switzerland, who'd also been alternating between Group A and Group B in recent years.

The night before their opening game, no one on the US national team slept very well. In warm-ups, the players seemed tense. They all knew if they didn't start strong, it might be nearly impossible to claw their way back into Group A. There was little margin for error. One loss might be too many. Everything was on the line.

Thankfully, two minutes into the game, Gambucci scored from a scramble. Everybody breathed a tremendous sigh of relief and eased into the game. Even when Japan scored on its very first shot, everybody stayed calm, focused, and confident. They were keyed up but no longer worried. Their confidence was growing. Williamson could feel them coming to life.

By the end of the first period the United States led 4–1. In fact, after Japan's first goal, they never scored again, and the US team cruised to a dominant 11–1 win. From there, the United States never looked back, reeling off six more wins to take the World B Championship easily, with a perfect mark of 7–0–0.

The United States scored 70 goals while yielding only 11, for an average margin of victory of 8.4 goals per game. On top of that, they won the Fair Play Cup for being the least-penalized team in the tournament, something no one ever expected from a North American squad. Perhaps it really was the dawning of a new era.

CHAPTER EIGHTEEN

FIGHTING TO GET INTO THE 1972 OLYMPICS

Fresh from a 7–0–0 sweep at the World B Championship, Williamson was eager to launch the second phase of his plan: beefing up his roster to make a legitimate run in the 1971 Group A World Tournament. Beyond restoring prestige to the US hockey program, a higher tournament finish meant a weaker opponent in the Olympic qualifying match, dramatically increasing the chance of earning a bid to the Winter Olympics.

Twelve players carried over from the 1970 squad, including scoring leaders Henry Boucha and Gary Gambucci. After holding tryout camps in Boston, Detroit, and Minneapolis, nine new players were added, including future US Hockey Hall of Fame inductee Tim Sheehy.

The team assembled in late October at the Met Center in Bloomington for a week of training camp before embarking on a grueling fifty-one-game exhibition schedule. With almost four additional months to practice and play together, Williamson had high hopes. Unlike years past, however, when the majority of games were against teams in the USHL and WCHA, this year's exhibition schedule included some less familiar opponents in more hostile environments.

"I think about two months in, we started asking ourselves what representing our country was all about," Williamson says. "If we won, the local fans were offended—we just took down their hometown squad. If we lost, we were unfit to call ourselves the national team. Sometimes, it just felt like every possible outcome was bad."

Decades later, there are still a handful of memorable games that rise to the top. "The first one that comes to mind was against Fred Shero's Omaha Knights," Williamson says. "Back in those days, the Knights were the New York Rangers' top feeder team. They were also a typical Fred Shero squad: hell-bent on intimidating everyone they played, especially a bunch of US Olympians."

To make matters worse, bruisers André "Moose" Dupont, Jack Egers, and Rick Newell were trying to establish themselves as fearless young enforcers, hoping their ability to bloody an opponent's nose would be their ticket to the big time.

"We were leading 2–1 when Dupont sucker punched Henry Boucha out of the blue," Williamson remembers. "At that point, I said to myself, 'Well, we've got a few scrappers too.' So I sent out Tim Sheehy."

At six feet tall, 190 pounds, the two-time All-American—who also happened to be legendary tough guy Bronislau "Bronko" Nagurski's nephew—wasn't easily intimidated. "He went straight after Newell and did a real job on him," Williamson says.

With the game tied 3–3 and the play getting rougher and rougher, Williamson chirped the referees for being too intimidated. Using a barrage of his favorite expletives, the coach strongly suggested the refs might want to start calling penalties on the ferocious Omaha squad.

Moments later, Williamson was ejected.

"I don't have any regrets," Williamson says. "It was ridiculous. That team was all gooney birds."

Williamson was deep in the tunnel somewhere when Kevin Ahearn scored the game winner late in the third period. "I didn't know which team had scored until the guys started filing into the locker room. I'm not sure I even cared. I just wanted to get the hell out of there."

With a game against Cornell on the Friday after Thanksgiving, Williamson knew the guys wouldn't want to be on the road, but he also knew they'd understand. It was a high-profile game against a big-time opponent. It was a chance for the national team to make a statement, and the arena was sure to sell out, providing a much-needed cash infusion.

No one on the team demanded red carpet treatment. They did, however, expect a modicum of respect. Instead, when they got to campus on Thanksgiving afternoon, the place was deserted.

Eventually, they tracked down a security guard, who called a residential assistant, who led them to a dorm. Inside, it was empty and cold. Worse, the players were expected to sleep on double bunk beds, four to a room.

Williamson promptly asked his manager, Hal Trumble, to bring him the contract for the game. Skimming through it, he quickly realized Cornell had agreed to pay the national team a mere $500—from a projected sellout crowd—plus a percentage. Williamson was incensed. The normal guarantee for college exhibition matches was $2,500-plus. It felt like Cornell was stealing from the national team.

Williamson ordered his team back onto the bus and demanded rooms at a nearby hotel. After several phone calls to various Cornell officials, Williamson was begrudgingly accommodated, and the Nationals finally left to get a good night's sleep.

Cornell was coming off an undefeated season the year before. They'd won twenty-one regular season games, the ECAC Holiday Hockey Festival, the Syracuse Invitational, and the NCAA National Championship for a stellar mark of 29–0–0. All of that was under Cornell's previous coach, Ned Harkness, who'd subsequently left to coach the Detroit Red Wings. Regardless, first-year coach Dick Bertram was in no mood to end Harkness's winning streak, least of all this early in the season.

The following morning, when the national team's trainer and equipment manager went to the rink to set up for practice, the arena manager told them he'd never received their request. He told them the ice was booked and there was no other time to practice before the game that evening. Two hours later, the trainer came back to report he'd never seen anyone on the ice.

When the main event finally began, diminutive skill player Huffer Christiansen threw a textbook body check at his offensive blue line four minutes in, and the crowd went wild. The referee called Christiansen for an illegal hit.

"*What*?" Williamson objected. His agreement with college teams specified *international rules*. It was the only way he could prepare his team for the world championship tournament. Besides, Cornell's roster was packed with Canadian players. They, more than anyone else, were accustomed to rules that permitted body checking in all three zones. US college players could only check in their defensive half of the ice, but that wasn't the game's agreement.

The referees told Williamson that Bob Kane himself had advised them before the game to play under college rules. The capacity crowd was in an uproar. Williamson was furious and called a halt to the match until the matter could be resolved.

The PA announcer paged Kane and asked him to report to the scorekeeper, but he didn't show. Meanwhile, the crowd kept booing and jeering, and they were only getting louder. Rather than fuel the controversy, Williamson conceded, and the game resumed under college rules.

The national team was fired up, but the first period ended with the score tied 1–1. After the buzzer sounded, Trumble and Williamson were escorted to a back office for a conversation with Kane. The Cornell athletic director read them the riot act and reminded Williamson his team was Cornell's guest. Williamson was done taking further abuse and demanded to know whose side Kane was on. The barbs flew back and forth until, finally, "the Billy Martin of hockey" told the esteemed athletic director to take a hike.

After that suggestion, the debate promptly ended and everyone dispersed.

Cornell kept the game close through the end of the second period, down by a score of 3–2. In the third period, though, the better-conditioned national team ran roughshod, pumping in four unanswered goals for a 7–2 victory. Cornell's winning streak was over.

Williamson later found out Cornell's athletic department had retroactively designated the game a scrimmage purely to keep their streak intact. Even worse, Kane wrote several letters condemning

Williamson's behavior. Bob Fleming stood firm, however, and refused to sanction Williamson, much less think about his dismissal.

Eventually, Kane coughed up another $1,500 to avoid further allegations of using the Olympic squad to fatten Cornell's coffers.

"And he still got off cheap at that price!" says Williamson.

After their decisive win over Cornell, the Nationals headed three hours east to take on the RPI Engineers, another perennial ECAC powerhouse. RPI hung around for much of the first period, but in the end, it was no contest.

"Goalie Terry Jordan held off the US Nationals hockey team for the first seventeen minutes Saturday," wrote the Minneapolis *Tribune*, "but the [United States] finally broke through on Pete Fichuk's goal and cruised to a 9–0 triumph, their ninth without a loss this season."

By mid-December, the Nationals had run their winning streak to twenty-one games before they finally took a 4–2 loss against the Flint Generals, a minor pro team in the International Hockey League.

"This columnist marvels at what Williamson has done with the team," wrote Paul Foss of the *Tribune*. "All the sharp ex-Gopher All-American has done is organize and coach a team in a three-month period to a point where it is able to defeat almost all of the college sixes and most of the semipro teams around the country."

"We think this team is better than the one which won the 1960 Olympic gold medal," Williamson boasted. "We're going to play good, hard hockey. I think this time, we might turn in a surprise."

> "All the sharp ex-Gopher All-American has done is organize and coach a team in a three-month period to a point where it is able to defeat almost all of the college sixes and most of the semipro teams around the country."

Once the team got to Europe, however, it felt like more of the same.

After a series of flight delays and itinerary changes, the team finally landed in Prague, physically drained and mentally sapped. Williamson had scheduled a morning skate, but they'd already missed it. In fact, they'd lost an entire day. They would be lucky to have enough time to check into the hotel, get something to eat, and rest briefly before they had to leave for the rink.

Meanwhile, the Czechoslovaks had been sequestered for a week at their mountain training retreat. The game was completely sold out and set to be televised throughout the country. The US team was fresh meat for the hungry Czechoslovaks, bent on dethroning the Russians on the world stage a week later.

As soon as the game began, the Czechoslovaks erupted, pouring in four quick goals within the first eight minutes. Less than halfway through the first period, Williamson and his team were on the brink of disaster. Determined to retain some semblance of morale and confidence, the coach decided his team's only hope was to slow down their highly skilled opponents with heavy body checks and physical intimidation. He turned his players loose, encouraging them to be as rough as possible, just shy of fighting.

Within minutes, the referees had lost control. Three Czechoslovaks were limping, and the rest wouldn't come within twenty feet of the US net. The Nationals failed to score, but the team only surrendered two more goals the rest of the way, taking a 6–0 loss.

After the game, Czechoslovak Coach Vladimír Kostka was visibly upset. Williamson shrugged off the criticism, knowing full well that if he'd encouraged his team to play "friendly," they would have been blitzed, giving the Czechoslovaks a huge psychological edge.

"He didn't like the fact we refused to roll over," Williamson says. "The two of us were friends, but at the postgame banquet, his superiors made it clear: *this was not a friendly match.*"

Williamson was playing the long game, getting ready for the matches that counted, quietly laying the groundwork for the following week's world tournament.

Coincidentally or not, the Americans and Czechoslovaks met in the first game of the 1971 IIHF Group A World Championship. In pregame press interviews, Williamson publicly stressed his plan to stifle the Czechs at both ends of the ice with rough physical play and tight checking.

Meanwhile, he quietly told his players to use a different strategy. He instructed his defensemen to stand up at the blue line while the wings covered wide and the center hovered high, near the opposite blue line, waiting for a loose puck.

Once the game began, Williamson's system worked well. Like the Soviets, the Czechoslovakian strategy centered on creating odd-man rushes. With no clear advantage as they moved the puck through the neutral zone, the Czechoslovaks retreated to regroup and try again.

Unlike North American teams, the Czechs were reluctant to shoot the puck into corner and fight to regain control. To them, it seemed like a gamble. Their passing was simply too good to willingly give up the puck.

Late in the first period, the Czechs' patience was wearing thin. They were losing 1–0 to what they considered a lesser team. Finally, the Czechs tied the score and thought they might have some momentum. The United States quickly countered, however, scoring two more goals to take a 3–1 lead.

Down 4–1 in the third period, the Czechoslovaks abandoned their game plan and started dumping the puck into the zone. But with vivid memories of crunching hits from the week before, the Czechoslovakian players were hesitant to go hard in the corners. Williamson's tactics were working. He'd intimidated the Czechs and knocked them back on their heels.

The United States won the game 5–1. It was not only a shocking upset but a loud, unambiguous message: this was not the US team that had been swept at the 1969 Group A World Championship. Team USA was back.

It was not only a shocking upset but a loud, unambiguous message: this was not the US team that had been swept at the 1969 Group A World Championship.

Later that night, after his own team's resounding 11–2 win over West Germany, Soviet Coach Anatoly Tarasov summoned Williamson to his hotel room to celebrate their victories with vodka and raw fish. Tarasov was exuberant. His friend, the American coach, had knocked off the

Soviets' biggest rival in the tournament's opening game. A full two points ahead of the Czechs after one night of play, Tarasov knew the Soviets were well on their way to winning their ninth consecutive world title.

Next up for the United States was Sweden. In one of the tournament's more memorable games, the score was tied 1–1 after the first period and 2–2 after the second. Suddenly, in the midst of a furious third period, forward Henry Boucha sprung loose for a breakaway. He drove in hard with the puck, made a subtle fake with his shoulders, and flipped the puck past the goalie for the apparent go-ahead goal.

Seconds later, however, as Boucha and his teammates were celebrating, the goal was waved off. From his vantage point deep at the far end of the ice, the Polish referee claimed the US team had been off-side, even though no whistle was blown.

"I still don't know what he saw," Williamson says. "One of our players was standing there waiting to make a change with one leg dangling over the boards, but his foot never touched the ice. He wasn't even part of the play."

Williamson objected, but the call stood, dealing a crushing blow to the deflated US squad who'd been giving it all they had. Minutes later, Sweden scored to take a 3–2 lead. Then, with less than two minutes left, US goalie Mike Curran bobbled a clearing attempt. Swedish center Håkan Wickberg quickly scooped up the puck and scored his second goal, securing the 4–2 win.

"They had strength for three periods. We did not," Williamson told reporters after the game. "We had a decisive advantage in the first period. After that, we ran out of gas."

Looking ahead to the next game, the coach appeared to shake off the loss. "We will come back," he said. "The word 'lose' is not allowed in our dressing room. We're not afraid of the Russians or anyone else."

With strong showings in their first two games, the United States was attracting attention. Despite their tremendous skill and nearly incomprehensible winning percentage, the Soviets were despised by most European fans and reporters. Most hockey insiders hoped the plucky US squad might be the Cinderella team who could take down

The Big Red Machine.

Williamson's game plan was to slow things down as much as possible, freezing the puck along the boards and creating other delays. With the help of the raucous proAmerican crowd, Williamson was hoping his team might pull the upset.

For a while, it seemed to be working.

"For twenty minutes the game was wide open," wrote the UPI. "The Russians had problems with the Americans, who used tough forechecking and plenty of body contact to keep the Russian skaters off balance."

Then the roof caved in.

The Russians scored seven goals in the second period to take an invincible 8–1 lead. When the smoke finally cleared, the Soviets had won 10–2 and Williamson felt humiliated.

"I doubt any other team will be able to upset the Russians if they play like they played against us in the second period," he said.

Two nights later, the Finns thumped the US team by a score of 7–4, setting the Americans on a collision course with the winless West Germans. Sitting alone in last place, the West Germans had surrendered thirty-one total goals in their first four games while scoring only eight, nearly half of which came against Finland. The United States was heavily favored . . . which, in the end, only made the sting worse.

"West Germany clobbered the United States 7–2 at the world hockey championships in a battle of the tailenders," wrote the *Canadian Press*.

"It was the first victory for the West Germans and the fourth straight setback for the Americans after an opening game triumph over Czechoslovakia," the AP added.

"The Americans shocked the experts with a 5–1 opening game victory over the Czechs but have grown steadily more inept since then," jabbed UPI.

After routing Sweden 8–0 to take sole possession of first place in a game played that same night, Tarasov knocked on Williamson's door, bottle of vodka in hand and interpreter in tow. He handed Williamson a can of caviar and suggested the two should talk.

"After what may have been the single most bitter defeat of my coaching career, he'd come over to console me," Williamson says. "It wasn't even surprising. That's the man I knew."

Williamson found some glasses, Tarasov opened the bottle, and vodka started flowing. "We drank it straight, 'in the Russian style,'" Williamson laughs, "chased by caviar that you ate off the back of your hand."

During the tournaments in Vienna and Grenoble, the Soviet and American coaches had become especially close. Their relationship had evolved into something almost familial, though Tarasov made it clear who was the master and who was the student.

"He was as competitive as anyone I've ever met. But deep down, he was a teacher," Williamson says. "He was like Herbic that way. Neither one of them *ever* stopped thinking about hockey."

As though underscoring Williamson's point, Tarasov once told reporters, "A coach never gets bored. You might get bored with your wife, but not with coaching."

As the night wore on and the bottle of vodka emptied, Tarasov became more generous with sharing information. "He was like a king holding court," Williamson says. "I would ask a simple question, and the amount of detail he would give me was just staggering."

For Tarasov, it always started with training. "Your players are in good condition *by Canadian standards*," he said, "but we know we will outlast you."

"He kept going back to training," Williamson says. "That was his refrain. He was very passionate about it, leaning in close one moment, leaping to his feet the next, waving his arms and speaking quickly."

Tarasov tried to explain his dryland conditioning program and the numerous off-ice drills he'd invented, but he was having trouble making himself understood. The interpreter couldn't keep up. Finally, Tarasov said, "For you to understand, you must come to Moscow. You will understand when you see Russian camp."

No one from North America—and very few Europeans—had

been given the opportunity to watch the Soviets train. There were rumors and speculation, but most of it remained shrouded in mystery.

Williamson said yes, and Tarasov told him to come for the first two weeks of August when training camp began.

The invitation was there. Now, it was just a matter of making it happen.

CHAPTER NINETEEN

TUTELAGE UNDER TARASOV

Shortly after WWII, the Soviet Central Committee issued a brash proclamation: "Soviet sportsmen in upcoming years will surpass world records in all major sports."

For generations, Russians had played the winter sport they called *khokkei*, known to English speakers as "bandy" or simply "hockey on ice." With a mixture of rules derived from field hockey and soccer, a bandy rink is the size of a typical soccer pitch, with low boards along the sidelines.

The game is played with a hard round ball. There are eleven skaters per side, and rules regarding off-side are like those found in soccer. The players' sticks are short and heavy, shaped like a capital *J*, and swung like a golf club. The goalie plays without a stick, defending a large goal at the end line, which doesn't have any boards. Notably, physical contact is limited, and checking is not allowed.

Historically, bandy had also been popular throughout Finland, Sweden, the Netherlands, and parts of the United Kingdom. Still, it could hardly be considered a "major sport." More importantly to Soviet leadership, bandy wasn't sanctioned by the International Olympic Committee, a designation that seemed unlikely to change. Thus, in 1946, the Soviet Sports Committee turned its attention to the game called "Canadian hockey," promptly appointing a panel of young player-coaches to convert the country's elite bandy players to "puck hockey" instead. Among the young appointees was a proficient bandy and soccer player who'd recently graduated from the Moscow Institute of Physical Culture and Sports: Anatoly Tarasov.

Armed with little more than a rule book, a miscellaneous collection of game film, and boundless enthusiasm, Tarasov and his colleagues formed an experimental ice hockey league; and in winter 1947, they played their first public match.

The following morning, the daily paper *Sovietsky Sport* wrote a glowing review. "The first game showed that Canadian hockey can swiftly gain the sympathy of fans and players with its tempo, quickly changing momentum, and intensity of play."

Less than a decade later, internationally unknown visionary Anatoly Tarasov and his hard-nosed, detail-oriented fellow coach Arkady Chernyshev led the Soviet national team to an undefeated mark of 6–0–1 to win the 1954 IIHF World Championship title.

Seemingly out of nowhere, the Soviets had burst onto the scene with a perplexing, creative style that was so unfamiliar one Canadian reporter could only say the Russians "pass too much, check too little, and skate too fast."

On the receiving end of a startling 7–2 upset in the de facto gold medal game, Canadian forward Eric Unger echoed this blunt assessment. "Their slowest player skated more quickly than our fastest player," he told reporters after the game. "I don't know if I should say this or not, but they dominated us by more than the five-goal margin."

Despite the lopsided margin, Canadian pundits remained unfazed. They blamed the loss on everything *except* Soviet skill and prowess. Instead, Canadian sportswriters mocked the Soviet squad by calling out "their jerseys that were too long, their homemade sticks, and their bicycle helmets." Canadian coaches, for their part, denigrated the Soviets' "pass-happy" style and alleged fear of physical contact—perceptions that endured for decades.

Incredibly, the Soviets didn't open an indoor ice arena until 1956. Most of the year, Tarasov was forced to improvise, creating dryland programs that included everything from long distance running and swimming to weightlifting and ballet, not to mention a heavy dose of other team- and individual-sports.

"A hockey player can't be only good at hockey," Tarasov said. "He must also be a great soccer player. He must be good at basketball. He must play a lot of tennis."

North American sportswriters, coaches, and players could mock and belittle Tarasov's unconventional methods and strategies as much as they wanted. Williamson was convinced the blueprint for championship hockey lay behind the Iron Curtain. So when Tarasov extended a personal invitation in 1971, the American coach didn't need to ask twice. It was time to go to Moscow.

Less than an hour after landing in the Soviet Union, Williamson was exhausted, wandering aimlessly through Sheremetyevo International Airport and contemplating his next move. He'd gotten off the airplane hoping to see Tarasov's beaming smile. Instead, there'd been nobody there.

> Williamson was convinced the blueprint for championship hockey lay behind the Iron Curtain. So when Tarasov extended a personal invitation in 1971, the American coach didn't need to ask twice. It was time to go to Moscow.

Williamson had made all the travel arrangements himself. AHAUS Vice President Thayer Tutt had sent multiple telegrams to the Soviet Ice Hockey Federation confirming Williamson's travel plans, but no one ever responded. Even so, not wanting to jeopardize his incredible, once-in-a-lifetime opportunity, Williamson prepaid all his travel costs in Moscow—including food and lodging—which Tarasov had promised to handle.

"The Olympic Committee couldn't tell me whether or not they'd pay my expenses, but I couldn't get caught up in the details," Williamson says. "So I borrowed $2,000 from the Bemidji Hockey Camp and made preparations to arrive in Moscow on the last day of July."

Before crossing the Atlantic, however, Williamson stopped in Boston to meet with—and recruit—Tommy Mellor, a Boston College All-American. Mellor's coach, Snooks Kelley, had been trying to convince Mellor to forgo the Olympics and stay at BC for his senior year. Williamson was optimistic that if he made a verbal commitment Mellor wouldn't be cut in the midst of tryouts—missing both the Olympics *and* his senior season—the kid would choose Team USA.

After hours of heart-to-heart conversation, Williamson got his wish and Mellor committed to the US Olympic team. In the meantime, however, the coach had missed his flight. Without any way to call Tarasov or anyone else, Williamson was booked on a flight from Boston to Shannon, Ireland, with the faint hope of reconnecting with his original plane.

When that plan failed to work, Williamson ended up on a flight to Japan that had a layover in Moscow. That flight, however, landed six hours later than his original arrival time. Plus, nobody knew he was on that flight, anyway. Williamson was worried the Russians had come to meet his original flight but assumed the whole thing was off since the plans were never confirmed and he wasn't on the plane.

Suddenly, all of it seemed like a really bad idea.

"I couldn't find anyone who could speak English, and I couldn't read or understand any of the signs around me," says Williamson. "It was just about the most helpless feeling in the world." He was beginning to get a little frantic when two Soviet policemen approached. "They took me by the arm and whisked me down the hall to this dark, tiny office. It felt like something out of a movie. I halfway expected them to put me in handcuffs."

Instead, Williamson was greeted by a man named Vasilie Pepkin. He spoke very good English, though his demeanor was terse and stern. Pepkin told Williamson that Mr. Tarasov and Mr. Mayoroff—the former captain of the Soviet hockey team—had come to the airport hours ago to meet the flight from Boston. After the plane was empty and Williamson wasn't there, they'd given up and left.

Eventually, they gathered Williamson's luggage and Pepkin drove them to the Hotel Metropol, where they ordered drinks and dinner. Waiting for their food, Pepkin began to pepper Williamson with questions. How did he feel about Nixon's upcoming visit to China? What were his thoughts on the US intervention in Vietnam?

"It felt more like an interrogation than a conversation," Williamson says. "It was also obvious this Pepkin character didn't know or care about hockey."

Pepkin launched into a lengthy monologue about the structure of Russian sports. The Soviet Union was divided into fifteen separate republics, he said. Each of those republics appointed its own sports committee, which was responsible for organizing and managing all sports within that republic. Each of those committees was led by a committee chairman, who in turn reported to the State Committee for Sports and Physical Education of the USSR. The chairman of *that* committee was a prominent member of the *Politburo*, the highest policy-making body in the Soviet Union.

Finally, almost as an afterthought, Pepkin mentioned that Tarasov was out of town on official business. He would be back on Monday. Williamson could meet him then. The Soviet hockey team would begin its training on Tuesday. Until then, Pepkin would show Williamson the beautiful sights of Moscow.

Sunday, Pepkin arrived at the Metropol at 11:00 a.m. and took Williamson on a tour of the Kremlin and Lenin's tomb, a short walk from the hotel. Pepkin was still full of questions and continued to be perplexed how Williamson had gotten there without any assistance from the US government or Soviet officials.

"I faked my way through the process," Williamson says. *"I didn't know anything about visa applications or immigration forms. I just tried to make it all sound official, and somehow I pulled it off."*

"I faked my way through the process," Williamson says. "I didn't know anything about visa applications or immigration forms. I just tried to make it all sound official, and somehow I pulled it off."

Later that afternoon, Pepkin arranged a meeting with the chairman of the sports committee from the Soviet Republic of Georgia. Pepkin and the chairman outlined the Soviet hockey program in greater detail. They said that the chairman of the Soviet Sports Committee had complete control over player selection for the Olympic team and seemed to take great pride in the notion that the coaches did not have the final say about who was selected.

"I found that pretty hard to believe," says Williamson, "but I didn't want to argue."

After hearing the men describe how the sports committee actually worked—with a guaranteed subsidy, youth leagues and feeder programs and top-down control of all the country's best players while they were teenagers—Williamson realized how wildly different the US and Soviet systems were.

Every year, AHAUS scrambled to raise money to fund the team, and still there was no guarantee they could get all the players they wanted. Some might have turned pro. Others had full-time jobs; some were going to college; and still others had families. Things were constantly shifting, and there was little a coach could do to keep his roster intact.

The top Soviet players, by contrast, traded their autonomy for a guaranteed annual salary, housing, and other perks. Once they were part of the national Soviet system, they didn't leave by choice. They stayed with the team until they were either cut or retired.

The following morning, Williamson was eating breakfast by himself at the Metropol when he looked across the room and saw someone headed his way. It was Anatoly, carrying a brown paper bag full of bright yellow flowers, a big smile on his face. He hugged and kissed Williamson in the effusive Russian style and then handed him the bag. It was a bottle of vodka buried in a bouquet of Russian dandelions. Williamson guessed the flowers were there to hide the bottle, so he thanked Tarasov for the flowers and the two men sat down.

Tarasov was thrilled to see his American colleague and told him there was a practice beginning in one hour. Williamson was surprised. He'd been told things wouldn't start until the following day. He hurriedly finished his breakfast, grabbed his notebook and pen, and they drove across town to the multipurpose Soviet military sports complex.

Pulling into the parking lot, Williamson was struck by how plain everything looked, especially by American standards. The colors were dull and uninspired, and there was hardly any indication they'd arrived at an ice arena. Inside, the dressing rooms were stark and simple, although a little untidy and disorganized. There was little in the way of equipment, and the lighting was dim.

Nonetheless, Tarasov swelled with pride as he showed Williamson around and introduced him to every player and all of the coaches and trainers. He had assembled his top twenty-eight players from the Soviet Army system, he explained. Fourteen would begin practice at 11:00 a.m., and the other fourteen were scheduled to take the ice at noon. All twenty-eight would convene at 1:00 p.m. for a two-hour scrimmage.

He'd broken them into two groups, so he could closely observe each player. Also, they would all work harder and be more conscientious knowing that he and the other coaches were watching intently.

In total, the first day's practice would consist of three hours' ice time for each player, interrupted only by one fifteen-minute break. Tarasov also noted this was a lighter day than normal because it was everyone's first day back after a one-month layoff. He assured the American coach the next day would be more rigorous and representative of a typical practice. Williamson should be prepared to watch very carefully if he hoped to understand the key to Russian hockey.

After practice, they left the rink and returned to the hotel for a late afternoon lunch. They were met by a new interpreter, who seemed much more familiar with the Soviet hockey program and sports in general.

"I got the impression Pepkin had only been there to screen me," Williamson says. "He never let go of the fact that I'd gotten to Moscow on my own. I don't think he believed me. He was convinced I worked for the CIA. He was determined to interrogate me before I met Tarasov and the rest of the hockey people."

Williamson found the new interpreter to be far less serious and much more informative. Meanwhile, Tarasov had ordered two bottles of vodka, which were prominently placed in the center of the table.

Tarasov then poured everyone a drink. They toasted Williamson's arrival and began to talk hockey philosophy.

"He viewed hockey as a performance," Williamson says. "He thought of it like a ballet. The coach was the choreographer; and practice was learning the steps, repeating them endlessly until they were perfect—but also leaving room for some improvisation."

According to legend, Tarasov was out walking in Moscow when he heard classical music and what sounded like people jumping. Drawn by the strange combination of sounds, he looked through the window and saw a ballet rehearsal. He was immediately captivated by the dancers' strength and grace. All of their movements were fluid and seemed effortless. They coiled their legs tight, then exploded, soaring high into the air as though unburdened by gravity.

The instructor noticed Tarasov watching and gestured for him to come in. Standing silently in the corner, Tarasov wrote pages of notes describing the dancers' movements and the position of their bodies. The mechanics inspired some of Tarasov's first drills, which he continually perfected over the years.

As in their past encounters, the more the vodka flowed, the more passionate Tarasov became. Before long, he asked Williamson to help arrange exhibition matches between the Soviet national team and the NHL's top clubs. It was his lifetime ambition, he said. After twenty-five years of Soviet hockey, it was time for the biggest test. He wanted to silence the critics and prove the Soviets were capable of beating anyone. Williamson agreed it was sure to be a great series and promised to pass the request to his NHL contacts as soon as he returned.

Tarasov also wanted to visit an NFL training camp. He wanted to study the sport of football to see if the training techniques could be applied to hockey and the Soviet team. Williamson suggested Minnesota Vikings Coach Bud Grant was sure to be interested, since he was also a hockey fan. William would call Grant directly and work something out. They concluded their epic meal with one final toast, and Williamson wandered up to his room to shake off the effects of warm vodka and too many toasts.

The next morning, Tarasov drove them to a Soviet Army base

different from the day before. In addition to the national team, Tarasov also coached CSKA Moscow, known colloquially as "the Central Red Army team," considered to be one of the top hockey teams in Europe. Once again, he'd assembled a total of twenty-eight players. This time, however, Tarasov split the players into three separate groups. Today's focus was dryland training.

As Williamson had seen six months prior in the Soviet locker room, the players began their warm-up without any explicit instructions. One minute, it was quiet; the next, players were rolling and jumping. Some were jogging in place. Others were hopping up and down while tossing five-pound weights back and forth.

After fifteen minutes, one group assembled at the far end of a crude wooden basketball court and began to hop the length of the floor while passing medicine balls underneath their legs. A second group did a series of skips while playing catch with heavy free weight discs.

The final group had assembled on the outdoor basketball court. They were stickhandling with weighted hockey sticks. There were taut elastic ropes looped around each player's waist. The other end was attached to a stationary pole at the edge of the court.

Each player extended himself as far as he could from the pole, stickhandling rhythmically. There were several marks on the floor. The players extended toward one of the marks while stickhandling quickly, then retreated and moved onto the next. One player lost his balance and was snapped back viciously by the elastic.

The exercises and drills went on for an hour and a half. After each group completed the entire cycle, everyone reassembled on the basketball court. There, they performed a series of stickhandling drills while carrying another player on their back. Williamson was dumbstruck. It was a phenomenal display of discipline and strength.

Tarasov watched intently but intervened only once. During the slightest lull, he ran down from the stands, jumped onto the basketball court, and began to wave his arms at a faster tempo. Everyone stopped and stared as he chewed out the players who'd slowed things down. He gestured wildly like some kind of manic conductor, shouting for everyone to pick up the pace. Finally satisfied, he climbed back into the bleachers and sat down next to Williamson.

"Have you yet detected the key to our training system?" he asked. "Do you understand the vital secret to Soviet hockey?"

Williamson was still trying to process everything he'd seen in the past two days. It was all so unique and different. How could he pick one thing? Instead, he shook his head no.

"There is only one law in life," Tarasov said, his voice booming over the noise of his players' rapid stickhandling, "and this one law says *movement*." He paused for dramatic effect before continuing on. "You must do everything with tempo. Speed. Intensity. Always maintain the same rhythm. If you *practice* at a slow pace, you will *play* at a slow pace."

Tarasov never used the phrase *overspeed training*, but that's what American sports physiologists later came to call it. Half a century later, Dr. Jack Blatherwick, strength and conditioning coach for the 1980 US Olympic team, summarized the concept beautifully: "Developing athleticism requires training that looks and feels athletic—fast, explosive, coordinated, rhythmical movement—poetry in motion. And endurance means keeping up that fast, poetic movement for as long as it takes."

Tarasov was a scientist, so he understood the importance of things like mechanics and muscle memory. His appreciation for ballet turned Russian hockey into an art form. He believed every part of the game must be rapid and rhythmical. His players were like performers working in sync, driven by the same metronome.

"Even during practice, Tarasov believed that maintaining flow and tempo were more important than stopping a drill to make corrections," Williamson says. "If a player made a mistake, he did a quick recovery drill and got back into the flow without interrupting the others. Tarasov only stopped when the whole tempo was less than perfect."

After Tarasov's brief intervention, the lightbulb went off in Williamson's head. Suddenly, he saw it: the key to the Russian system. Every drill they did, every movement they made—on or off the ice— was performed at maximum tempo. The focus was never on quick stops and starts or sudden bursts of speed. Every player pushed himself to perform *beyond* his comfort zone, maintaining maximum intensity throughout the entire practice. Eventually, that level of pace and intensity was so deeply ingrained that the Soviet players felt awkward when they played slower. It literally didn't feel right.

Suddenly, he saw it: the key to the Russian system. Every drill they did, every movement they made— on or off the ice—was performed at maximum tempo.

As Blatherwick later wrote in *Let's Play Hockey*, "Forget Hollywood's overemphasis on the endless stops-and-starts that Coach Brooks would pull out of his hat when he got mad . . . Those lapses were outside his true plan for conditioning. The goal was to play hockey in the high-speed comfort zone that the Soviets developed . . . As a veteran of two Olympic teams, Brooks had experienced the discomfort of playing the Soviets on their terms. It was much too fast for teams that hadn't practiced for months at an 'overspeed' pace."

Tarasov pushed his players to skate with the same intensity late in the third period as they did on their first shift. They came out fast and maintained it throughout the entire game. There was never a dip or a lull, and rarely were Soviet players sidelined with pulls or strains.

"If you want fast, skillful execution, your entire practice has to be high-quality skills executed at the fastest possible tempo," wrote Blatherwick. "When it is no longer physically possible to keep up the quality, practice is over. Do something else. Lift weights in an air-conditioned room. Watch films. Go swimming . . . But never practice poor skill at a slow speed."

After completing their morning dryland training, Tarasov let his players engage in a rollicking basketball game. Here, too, the fast tempo was clearly ingrained in their system. The players took it seriously but were also having fun. When the basketball game was over, the players quickly changed into their hockey gear and immediately hit the ice.

"I've heard plenty of people try to analyze and dissect the Soviet system over the years," Williamson says. "Most of the time, their descriptions focused on generic concepts like strict discipline, intense conditioning, endless repetition, an obsessive focus on basic skills. None of that is wrong—you saw it when you played them—but it also wasn't really what made the Soviets unique.

"The word I keep coming back to is *flow*. That's how they achieved such high levels of skill and precision. Their players were often criticized for behaving like machines, but their sense of flow was incredible. The geometry of North American hockey was predictable and simplistic. Tarasov imagined the rink as a blank canvas with diagonal lines and circles. We'd never seen anything like it."

Later that afternoon, the players reassembled for a two-hour scrimmage. Tarasov sat in the stands with a microphone in his hands, closely watching each player. His voice was amplified through a portable loudspeaker that sounded like a megaphone. He almost never blew the whistle but frequently barked corrections over the loudspeaker, calling the player by name and pointing out his mistake.

"It was incredible," Williamson says. "The Russian players worked very hard to avoid being corrected over the loudspeaker. Tarasov, from his vantage point, could see everything that happened anywhere on the ice, and the players knew it. They played carefully but incredibly fast. None of them ever wanted to be called out for a mistake. You could see how much it meant to them to not let their teammates down."

After practice, Tarasov was holding court outside the arena, philosophizing about his unique training methods. Suddenly, he noticed a woman cutting tall weeds with a sickle. Seizing the moment, he rushed over and asked to borrow the sickle. She agreed and he took over, crouching instead of stooping, cutting more rapidly, swinging with his whole body. Several players laughed at his act of showmanship and he handed back the sickle, satisfied he'd made his point. As Tarasov walked back to the group, the woman went back to work, her whole body engaged, working at a much faster clip.

That evening, Tarasov invited Williamson to join him at a Russian bath. Clearly, he was having a great deal of fun showing the

American coach the Soviet way of life. Pepkin and Boris Mayoroff, the former captain of the Soviet national team, were also there. Tarasov gave everyone an old felt hat and instructed them it was the only clothing they would wear in the sauna.

Completely undressed and unashamed, Tarasov carried four bottles of beer and a pail of water to the Russian steam bath, or *banya*. He proceeded to instruct everyone on the finer points of how to experience the perfect banya. He poured a mixture of beer and water over the hot coals, and everyone was engulfed in a thick cloud of steam.

After about ten minutes, Tarasov opened the door and gestured for everyone to step outside and join him. Earlier, he'd unloaded several armloads of small, leafy branches. He'd gathered them into bunches, which were known as "bath brooms" (*venik* in Russian). Tarasov explained how the leaves were dipped in cold water and smacked all over the body. Each man grabbed a bunch of branches and took turns beating another.

Back inside the steam room, Williamson was amazed how the tall, 240-pound coach moved about like a cat, preparing the steam bath again, tending to every detail. After another ten minutes, they all left the sauna, scampered through the gym, and jumped in a pool. It was very cold but refreshing.

They repeated this ritual five or six more times until everyone except Tarasov was driven out by the heat. As always, he delighted in being the lone survivor.

"I couldn't shake the idea that he looked like an overgrown version of one of Snow White's seven dwarves," says Williamson. "But there he was, Russia's hockey pioneer, sitting alone on a wooden bench, wearing nothing but a felt hat."

After the Russian bath, the four men went to Tarasov's apartment for a large traditional Russian meal. On the way there, Pepkin took center stage, explaining Moscow's finer points and bragging about the Soviet lifestyle. Russians were quite well behaved, Pepkin explained, unlike many people in the United States and Europe. Crimes like stealing, vandalism, violence, or public drunkenness were nonexistent. The Soviet people looked out for each other.

When Tarasov pulled into the parking lot of his apartment, however, he carefully removed his car's windshield wipers and side-view mirrors and locked them in the trunk. Pepkin was embarrassed but looked down at his shoes, not saying a single word.

As Tarasov prepared the food, he assigned Williamson the task of dropping fresh lemon peels into one of the three types of vodka they would drink with dinner. Mayoroff set out the hors d'oeuvres, which consisted of caviar, pork, bread, cucumbers, mushrooms, and many other Russian delicacies.

Tarasov invited everyone to start eating and poured champagne. He called for a toast and thanked his American friend for joining him in Moscow.

Next came roasted potatoes, smoked fish, pork chops, steak tartare with raw egg, and several other side dishes, all prepared exclusively by Tarasov. Soon, Williamson fell behind the pace in terms of both food and drink.

"The amount of vodka we consumed was *astronomical*," he says, "but Tarasov never seemed to be affected in the least. He just kept calling for toasts."

Eventually, they took a break and Tarasov pulled out his scrapbook. It dated back to the earliest days of Soviet ice "puck hockey." Williamson found it fascinating, but the others soon grew tired of pictures they'd seen before. Tarasov put away the book and called for yet another toast: to the NHL and NFL and professional American sports.

By this time, Pepkin was getting drunk and insisted on talking about Nixon's upcoming visit to China, Vietnam, the evils of capitalism, and other political topics Williamson would rather avoid. Meanwhile, Tarasov and Mayoroff promptly excused themselves and disappeared into the kitchen.

After fifteen minutes of deflecting Pepkin's criticism and endless badgering questions, Williamson lost his patience. He turned the tables and demanded to know why the Soviets had invaded their supposed ally Czechoslovakia. Pepkin quieted down after that, and they managed to avoid talking politics the rest of the night.

Later that same evening, Pepkin told Williamson an intriguing fact about Tarasov's fondness for the American hockey coach—Tarasov thought Williamson bore a striking resemblance to famous Russian cosmonaut Yuri Gagarin.

Until Gagarin's tragic death in 1968, he and Tarasov had been close friends. In fact, the two had seen each other a few short days before Gagarin's fighter jet crashed. Whenever he saw Williamson, Tarasov was reminded of his dear friend, whose sudden loss he still mourned.

On the final day of Williamson's stay in Russia, Tarasov arranged a special scrimmage in his honor. As a result, over two thousand fans turned out to watch the Russian national team's intrasquad scrimmage.

As the game progressed, Williamson expressed his admiration for a defensemen by the name of Vladimir Lutchenko. He was tremendously agile and strong and had amazing control of the puck. He was also a great body checker, a very rare skill at the time for prominent Russian players.

Soon, Williamson was kidding Tarasov that he was planning to take Lutchenko back home to Minnesota to play in the NHL. Tarasov look at him quizzically, then reprimanded him sternly: "Why will you take only one when there are many Russians who would be superstars in your league? Firsov and Kharlamov and plenty others could play for *any* NHL team."

Also on the ice at the time were goalie Vladislav Tretiak, the first player born and trained outside North America to be inducted into the Hockey Hall of Fame; defenseman Alexander Ragulin, star of the 1972 Summit Series; and forward Alexander Maltsev, who still holds the world record for most career goals in international competition with an astounding 215.

"I really love my guys," Tarasov told the American press when he was asked about his relentless off-ice training and grueling practices. "That is why I demand from them what no one else could ever do."

On the day of his departure, Williamson was overcome with emotions. He knew the things he'd learned would be invaluable as he prepared his young team for the upcoming Olympics. Beyond that, he'd solidified his friendship with one of the greatest strategists and mentors to ever coach the game of hockey.

"I think I learned more on that trip than any other time in my life," Williamson says. "It was incredible. I'll treasure that trip forever. I wish I'd had more time, but I was also very excited to get back to Minnesota and start putting into practice everything that I'd learned. I think *one* Tarasov practice covered more ground than a pro team did in a week."

> "I wish I'd had more time, but I was also very excited to get back to Minnesota and start putting into practice everything that I'd learned. I think one Tarasov practice covered more ground than a pro team did in a week."

Unfortunately, whether by accident or nefarious intervention, Williamson's three rolls of pictures were completely blacked out. The visual record was lost, never to be recovered.

Though he was mocked at first, it's now widely understood that Tarasov was years ahead of his time, blending kinesthetic science with wildly imaginative drills often born from necessity.

"The coach always needs the ability to invent new exercises," Tarasov said, "to hold one training session after another in a high emotional mood. Nobody will forgive a coach, even if he is experienced and famous, if he conducts his classes sluggishly, without novelty, in an uninteresting way."

Tarasov's vision and methods were revolutionary—in practice and in games—and his results clearly speak for themselves. By the time he was demoted from coach of the Soviet national team by his political bosses, Tarasov had won three Olympic gold medals, nine IIHF World Championship titles, and eighteen Soviet League championships. In 1974, he became the first European inducted into the Hockey Hall of Fame. In 2008, he posthumously received the Wayne Gretzky International Award from the US Hockey Hall of Fame for his "major contributions to the growth and advancement of ice hockey in the United States."

CHAPTER TWENTY

SILVER IN SAPPORO

Williamson returned from Moscow a much wiser hockey coach, his head spinning with ideas for new skill and conditioning drills—both on and off the ice. He was excited to get back to work and begin the final year of his three-year plan. Nonetheless, with only eight players returning from the 1971 team, the first step was building the roster.

Unlike the Soviet Union—where Tarasov had the luxury of working with the same core group of players eleven months of the year—after each world championship or Olympic tournament ended, American players were thrown to the wind. Some went back to work; others returned to their original teams. Some retired, others signed pro contracts. There was no reliable structure or pattern. Every year, the recruiting began all over again.

During the past offseason, two of the team's top players had signed professional contracts. Gary Gambucci had gone to the North Stars, and Craig Patrick had signed with the California Seals. Herb Brooks, George Konik, Len Lilyholm, Don Ross, and Carl Wetzel had also opted out. Any further losses would be a significant blow to the team's continuity and undermine Williamson's plan. Meanwhile, the coach hope to add another eight to ten quality players from open try-outs in Boston, Minneapolis, and Detroit.

Behind the scenes, however, Williamson was dealing with a bigger, more urgent problem. For months, US Olympic Hockey Committee Chairman Bob Fleming had been unable to get the USOC to sign off on the hockey team's budget.

As with Bob Ridder's original plan nearly two decades before, the team's exhibition schedule was designed to cover the team's operating expenses. Still, they needed money for player stipends and living expenses. Without guaranteed money from the USOC, the team would suffer a devastating $50,000 shortfall. Williamson knew he couldn't ask his players to sign their contracts without funds from the USOC.

With the issue still unresolved by September 2, Fleming had lost his patience. "In all the time I knew him, I never saw him so worked up," Williamson says. "He called to let me know he was ready to issue an ultimatum: if the USOC didn't approve his budget within [twenty-four] hours, he would tender his resignation."

Needless to say, Williamson did not want to see Fleming resign his position . . . but he also understood the committee chairman's gambit. If he didn't force the USOC's hand, they may not approve the budget until it was too late.

"His gamble must have worked," Williamson says, "because about ten minutes later, he called me back and said they'd approved it on the spot."

With the financial piece in place, Williamson was able to take twenty-two players north to Bemidji State University for a Russian-style training camp. Away from the press and prying eyes, the coach worked his players hard, incorporating much of what he'd learned from Tarasov. In addition to twice daily practices, there was also plenty of dry-land training, with everything from stretching and weightlifting to swimming, soccer, tennis, and basketball.

> *Like his friend Tarasov, Williamson hoped to create a group of athletes first, a team of hockey players second.*

Like his friend Tarasov, Williamson hoped to create a group of athletes first, a team of hockey players second. They had just ten days to prepare for their first series of games against three of the country's top NHL farm teams, but the last thing he wanted to do was sacrifice long-term gains for short-term success.

"Everybody talks about how much the 1980 team trained and played an extended exhibition schedule," says Jim McElmury, who played defense on three of Williamson's national teams. "We did that in '72."

After two solid weeks of training, playing, eating, and living together, the team hit the road for an ambitious forty-seven-game exhibition schedule beginning with the Omaha Knights, Cleveland Barons, and Denver Spurs.

First up was a two-game stint against the Minnesota North Stars' farm club, the Cleveland Barons. In Bemidji for the first game, the national team beat the Barons 5–3. The following night, in Duluth, the Nationals kept rolling, outskating the Barons for a dominant 6–2 win. Before the final buzzer sounded, some of the more frustrated minor leaguers dropped their gloves and went after their younger opponents. Williamson was impressed by how his young team responded, refusing to back down or be intimidated in the least. It was a sign of things to come.

Six days later, during his team's afternoon skate around, Williamson stood on the end boards, watching his players prepare for their game against the Omaha Knights. Near the end of the session, several Omaha players sauntered in. They'd come directly from the New York Rangers' tryout camp. They started laughing and ridiculing the younger, smaller national team players.

"It's gonna be fun to knock those little punks around," said one.

"Yeah," said another, "I bet they won't even want to finish the game."

Williamson glanced over the Omaha roster. It included some outstanding former Junior A stars. The name that really jumped out, however, was *Steve Durbano*, the feisty defenseman nicknamed "Mental Case" who'd carved his name in the Junior A record book for most career penalty minutes with the Toronto Marlboros.

"At that point," Williamson says, "I decided to start the game with 'a thousand pounds of beef and a goaltender.'" The coach sent out his five biggest bruisers: Charlie Brown, Tommy Mellor, Frank Sanders,

Tim Sheehy, and Dale Smedsmo. "Sure enough," Williamson continues, "the game wasn't two minutes old when Omaha started in with the rough stuff."

With little provocation, Omaha's Steve Vickers squared off with Frank Sanders. "Frank cut his face so badly, Vickers was forced to leave," Williamson says. Within minutes, Smedsmo and Durbano met near the center line for the main event.

"That fight lasted five minutes," says the coach. "Smedsmo was getting the best of it, too, until Durbano suddenly headbutted the kid and knocked him down."

As the first period came to a close, Sheehy was provoked and ended up fighting one of the Knights to a draw.

"None of our guys backed down," Williamson says proudly. "Fighting was not our style, but that night we made it clear: we'd earned the right to be there, and we weren't going to let anyone intimidate us."

The next night in Duluth, the two teams played a much cleaner, hard-fought game. Down 4–3 with a minute to go, the Nationals fought back for a 4–4 tie when Boucha drove home the equalizer.

"That two-game series was huge," Williamson says. "Right out of the gate, it gave us the confidence to know we could skate with anybody. Whether mucking it up in the trenches or playing end-to-end hockey, we knew we could make it work."

By Christmas break, their record stood at 26–5–3. Along the way, the national team had beaten some of the country's best minor pro teams, several top senior league teams, and many of the perennial powerhouse college teams. Preparing to face the Russians five times in less than two weeks at five separate venues across the country, Williamson was feeling a mixture of optimism and dread.

"My main goal was to not get embarrassed," says the coach. "I knew how good that team was, even if nobody else did. Kharlamov, Mikhailov, Maltsev, Firsov, Tretiak—that might've been one of the best rosters ever assembled. Those guys went toe to toe with a team of Canadian all-stars at the Summit Series nine months later, and they came within one minute of ending the series in a tie. I never expected to win; I just hoped we'd stay within a few goals."

Instead, two days after Christmas at the Broadmoor, the Soviets blitzed the Nationals 13–3.

"Yawn," wrote the Colorado Springs *Gazette-Telegraph*, describing the game as nothing more than "a long practice session" for the visiting Russians. A mere 1:27 into the game, Valeri Kharlamov made US goalie Tim Regan "look like a child playing blind man's bluff."

Gathering up a rebound, Kharlamov darted behind the net, faked a move to one side, quickly swooped the other way, and slipped the puck in the open net. After that, "the world champions kept the statisticians working overtime by scoring five goals in a little over four minutes" to open up a 7–1 lead.

"But for some ironic reason," the paper continued, "US coach Murray Williamson wasn't upset by his club's play."

Rather, the coach insisted, "That's only the first time we faced the Russians. By the time we get to the fifth game, we'll know what to do with them."

Williamson remained unconcerned because he knew firsthand the Soviets were in a class by themselves. Even as sportswriters, NHL players, and coaches continued to mock and deride the Russians, Williamson kept watching and learning. Their players were talented, no question about it, but there was also something deeper going on. Williamson had gotten a glimpse at their training camp in Moscow. Now, he was determined to figure out what it was.

Back at the Broadmoor after the game, Williamson got a bottle of vodka and went straight to Tarasov's room. The lopsided score was one thing. The part that drove Williamson nuts was how the Soviets kept springing their forwards on solo breakaways with pinpoint stretch passes.

"It was like the bomb in football," Williamson says. "We'd be forechecking deep in their zone. One of their defensemen would get the puck and—*boom*—breakaway." He didn't know if it was Tarasov's new strategy or if he'd seen a major weakness in the American forecheck.

The two men greeted each other like long-lost brothers, and the vodka started flowing. Naturally, Tarasov brought out some caviar. After a bit of small talk and several toasts, Williamson finally asked,

"Anatoly, what was that? What did you see out there? What's the flaw in our forecheck?"

Tarasov was evasive at first, praising the American players for their dogged determination and spirit.

"I appreciate your compliments," Williamson told his friend, "but I want to know how to correct it." Eventually, Tarasov promised to reveal his secret. First, he needed to teach his American friend a few more lessons.

In St. Louis three nights later, the United States managed to tighten the score but ended up losing 7–3. "Either the Soviets were flat, or my pleas for mercy were answered," Williamson says.

Both teams arrived in Minneapolis on New Year's Eve. Williamson invited Tarasov to his home for dinner. Tarasov graciously accepted but insisted they have a Russian bath first. Williamson laughed and explained there was a sauna in the North Stars dressing room, but it was nothing like the Russian baths in Moscow. They could pour beer on the rocks, but there was no cold pool, much less any tree branches.

"That's exactly what Anatoly had been waiting to hear," Williamson says. "With a devilish smile on his face, he dug deep into his equipment bag and brought out a bundle of tree branches he'd brought from Moscow."

The branches were a little dried out, but they did the trick. Coincidentally, not long after the two coaches had swatted each other's backs for the second time, Walter Bush arrived. He was in the process of giving a tour to Günther Sabetski, president of the German Hockey Federation, when he opened door of the sauna. There were several towels on the floor, dry leaves all over the place, and empty beer cans on the rocks. The place looked like a disaster. All Williamson could do was laugh and introduce the famous Russian coach, whom Sabetski was pleased to meet despite the awkward circumstances.

After dinner at Williamson's house, Tarasov agreed to tell the American coach how his team had managed to get so many breakaways the first night. He detailed the pass pattern the Russians had used in their own zone to suck in and distract the US defenders.

Meanwhile, Kharlamov had been skating full speed up the far side, unnoticed.

"And then," Williamson says, "with the pinpoint precision only the Russians possessed, they'd hit Kharlamov in stride and it was off to the races. No one could ever catch him."

Tarasov leaned forward, a mischievous glint in his eye, and assured Williamson that all of this no longer mattered. The Czechs would be scouting the next game, so the Soviets would use entirely different tactics. The Czechs would never see that same play again.

As the New Year began, Tarasov's strategy may have been different, but the result was exactly the same.

"The USSR put the game out of reach early in the first period," wrote the UPI, "as veterans Anatoli Firsov, Boris Mikhailov, and Vladimir Zikulov scored on a beleaguered US goalie Tim Regan ... within the first six and a half minutes of play." It was the third straight Soviet win on American soil and their sixty-first victory over the United States in sixty-three games.

For the fourth game, the two teams traveled to Philadelphia, where they played in front of 13,864 fans at the Spectrum. New venue, same old story. The Soviets won 11–3, but the pummeling continued for days. "The newspapers the next day were brutal," Williamson says. "They may not have liked the Russians, but they didn't exactly lavish our team with praise."

"The Russians can handle the puck, but they're not being checked," said executive director of the Pittsburgh Penguins, Jack Riley. "If you're not being knocked on your tail, it's easy to give a little dipsy-doodle."

"Sure, the Russians are showing a lot of pretty stuff," echoed Flyers GM Keith Allen, "but anybody can look pretty if you stand around and let them."

"There's no way that club could ever beat us," said a supremely confident Gary Dornhoefer (who only ever played two career NHL games). "I'd bet a whole year's salary on that."

"Maybe two or three of their players could play in the National

Hockey League, but I couldn't be sure," Allen concluded.

Two decades later, Sergei Fedorov and the "Russian Five" dominated the NHL, leading the Detroit Red Wings to three Stanley Cups in six years. Honestly, there's no telling what the Soviet superstars from the 1972 Olympic team may have accomplished if they'd been given the chance.

"We learn just by playing them," Williamson said after his team's 11–4 loss in the series finale. "But it's a hard way to learn. Every time you make a mistake, they seem to cash in."

By the time the five-game series concluded, the Soviets had outscored the United States by a margin of 51–14, but Williamson was undaunted. He'd simply wanted his younger players to get a good look at the competition.

"The Russians did some things our guys never saw before," he said. "Sure, we got beat; but we learned a lot." It also didn't hurt that the five-game series earned $200,000—money that flowed directly to AHAUS to cover training expenses.

"Sometimes when you get your butt danced around the ice a little bit . . . you raise your game to another level, concentrate a little bit more, work a little harder in practice," said Bruce McIntosh in *Striking Silver*, underscoring the ingenuity of Williamson's plan.

Deep down, the coach knew his players would rise to the challenge. They were young and resilient and always fought to final buzzer, no matter what.

"I was very nervous when we first played against [the Russians]," said Stu Irving. "Now I feel we can keep up with them and maybe even beat them."

"I'm not so sure about that," Williamson says. "My plan was to fly under the radar. Don't attract attention. Just keep getting better. Peak at the right time. The only games that counted were the ones in Sapporo. Everything else was just filler."

With less than a month to go before his team left for Sapporo, Williamson was still searching for a left wing. At the time, his top two candidates were Denver's Tom Peluso and Harvard junior Dave Hynes. Discussions, however, seemed to be going nowhere.

Williamson thought back to their game against the Junior Red Wings five days before Christmas. He'd been impressed by Mark Howe, the sixteen-year-old son of hockey immortal Gordie Howe. He'd undergone knee surgery in the offseason and spent the fall rehabilitating. That night was his season debut.

One year prior, the tenth-grade phenom had led the Southern Ontario Junior Hockey League with an astonishing 37 goals and 107 assists in 44 games. Even on a night when the Nationals skated all over the Junior Wings in a 6–1 rout, Howe had caught Williamson's eye.

In his 6 games since then, Howe had notched 6 goals and 4 assists for a blistering average of 3.27 points per game. Williamson was convinced Howe's firepower would be a great addition to the national team. He invited the high-school superstar to Bloomington to work out with the team.

"I'm all in favor of Mark playing in the Olympics," Gordie told the *Detroit Free Press*. "It'd be a terrific experience for him."

Both Gordie and his wife, Colleen, were thrilled about their son's offer; but they wanted some assurance Mark wouldn't join the team only to be cut three weeks later, before the Olympics even began. Nor did they want him to spend a month traveling with the US team only to be given little or no ice time once the Olympic tournament started.

"Of course, I had to tell them I couldn't make any promises," Williamson says. "That kind of deal wouldn't be in the team's best interest or the best interest of their son. Mark's parents both understood that, and things kept moving forward."

Meanwhile, Williamson was also getting hit from the other side. "A lot of sportswriters seemed to think I had a hidden agenda," says the coach. "Some of them said it was all a publicity stunt. Others said I was playing favorites, angling for a job with the Red Wings. There were all kinds of crazy theories. I can only say I firmly believed Mark Howe was the best available athlete. He was raw. He was nervous. He was

"I can only say I firmly believed Mark Howe was the best available athlete. He was raw. He was nervous. He was inexperienced. But his talent was off the charts."

inexperienced. But his talent was off the charts."

Howe played well in his first game with the national team, posting one assist in a 7–4 win over the Minnesota Gophers. "I've been impressed with Mark since he joined us," Williamson told the *Detroit Free Press*. "Not only with his tremendous hockey ability but also as a young man." Nonetheless, the teen superstar was far from a lock.

"After his first workout with us, Mark told one of the players that it was the hardest practice he's ever had in his life," Williamson noted. "And, really, it was one of our lighter sessions. If I can get him far enough along in his conditioning, he'll go to the Olympics . . . He has about a fifty-fifty chance."

Howe scored two goals in his next game, a 9–2 rout of the Saginaw All-Stars. Gordie and Colleen were there. After the game, they met with the US coach to see if he'd made a decision. They were anxious. Should Mark return with them to Detroit and join his Junior A team or fly back to Minneapolis with the national team?

Williamson calmly explained that he still needed a few more days. Mark had impressed him thus far, but he was also in discussions with a few other players. As the coach, he needed to focus on what was best for the whole team. Mark's parents understood, but they were clearly disappointed. They'd assumed their son's two-goal performance was enough to seal the deal.

The three adults turned toward Mark, awaiting some kind of response. The sixteen-year-old stared at his shoes, thinking carefully. In calm, measured words, he said he would ride back to Detroit with his parents, pack enough clothes for three weeks in Japan, and fly to Minneapolis. There, he would work his tail off to make the squad and travel to Sapporo for the Winter Olympic games. If he somehow fell short, it was his problem, nobody else's. He would accept the consequences.

"I was stunned by his maturity," Williamson says. "So were Gordie and Colleen. I could see how relieved they were. I think in that moment, all three of us knew Mark would make the team. For me, his response tipped the balance. This kid was ready to work."

By January 10, all the pieces were in place but one: goalie Lefty

Curran. Curran and Williamson had parted on bitter terms after the 1971 World Championships. Curran had been hurt, opted out of the remaining games, and even asked to be sent home. That move didn't sit well with the coach at all as he tried to guide "the walking wounded" across the finish line. Plenty of guys played hurt. Williamson questioned Curran's commitment.

In the off-season, Curran had knee surgery and returned to the Green Bay Bobcats. "I kept an eye on him," Williamson says. "Every coach has that guy you keep in the back of your mind. You know he's part of the plan; you're just not sure when to bring him in."

As expected, Curran impressed Williamson when the Nationals played Green Bay. "He and I were like oil and water, but we worked out," Williamson says. "Curran was a team guy. I knew that. The team always came first. So we brought him in and told the team he was coming to Sapporo."

On January 25, the team flew to Anchorage and then on to Tokyo, where Williamson had scheduled two final exhibition games. "The first one was against Poland," Williamson says, "considered by most people to be very chippy. They were also more experienced and resented our younger squad. Our guys were a little bit nervous."

Early in the second period, the Nationals were down 5–2. Williamson wasn't concerned at all about the score, but he was apprehensive about the rutted ice surface. Additionally, the Poles were using their sticks in almost every confrontation. Suddenly, Craig Sarner—one of the least penalized players on the national team—collided with a Polish player and knocked him to the ice.

The Pole lashed out with his skate and tried to kick Sarner in the face. Sarner was so shocked, he jumped up and chased the Pole to the players' bench. For some reason, Curran joined in, and a brawl erupted.

"I never saw one of my teams react so quickly and with so much determination to defend a teammate," Williamson says.

The national team came back soon after that, scoring four straight goals to take a 6–5 lead, going on to win 7–5. "Even if they didn't fully respect our ability," Williamson says, "I knew they definitely had respect for our toughness and determination."

The next night, they faced the Czechs, who won 4–1. Williamson was pleased by his team's performance even though they'd been outskated by a smooth, well-disciplined hockey machine.

"Mark Howe was crushed by Václav Nedomanský in the middle of the second period," Williamson says, "but he never missed a shift." Later, Howe mentioned to Doc Nagobods that he had a headache and his vision was a little blurry. Doc pulled him off the ice and told Williamson the boy was concussed. By then, Howe had played well over a period without complaining once.

"At the time," Williamson says, "I thought it was a real display of courage. Now we understand he never should've gone back out there."

When they arrived at the Olympic Village in Sapporo, the Japanese were warm and extremely polite. They escorted the team to the housing complex, where the players would sleep three to a room. On the other side of the building were the North Korean athletes. They watched the Americans arrive with a great curiosity. It seemed to the US players that some of the North Koreans might want to be friends, but the North Koreans were prohibited from making contact or communicating at all.

The next morning, the team went to the rink for their first training session. The ice was smooth, and the boards were glass—a new experience for everyone at the time. They trained hard for two hours and got ready for their qualifying match against Switzerland.

Notably, every Olympic hockey team—except for the world champions from the previous year—was required to play a qualifying game against one of the B teams. If the United States lost, they would be knocked out of the Olympic A tournament, and Williamson's three-year plan would be entirely for naught.

Once the qualifier finally started, the United States came out strong and took a 2–0 lead before the game was ten minutes old. After that, however, Swiss goalie Gérald Rigolet became a brick wall. By the end of the second period, the United States had taken forty-three shots but were only winning 3–2.

Williamson was scared.

"It always drives a coach crazy when you have the better team but their goalie is red hot," Williamson says. "A hot goalie can make all the difference. He can start to get in the guys' heads. No matter what they do, they can't seem to put the puck in the net."

> "A hot goalie can make all the difference. He can start to get in the guys' heads. No matter what they do, they can't seem to put the puck in the net."

The United States repeatedly swarmed the offensive zone, pouring shots on the net, and yet they desperately clung to a slim one-goal lead. To start the third period, even that lead evaporated. The Swiss scored on a deflection to tie the game 3–3. Suddenly, the Swiss were dominating every phase of the game as the US team clanged multiple shots off the goal post and another off the knob of Rigolet's stick.

Even then, nobody panicked. "Don't worry, Coach, we'll do it," said Robbie Ftorek—and Frank Sanders scored on the very next shift. It was firewagon hockey until the final minute, when Stu Irving scored the insurance goal for the 5–3 win. The next day, the local press referred to the US squad as "the gutty Yanks."

After just sixteen hours of rest, the United States faced the Swedes, who opened with two goals in the first six minutes of play before cruising to a 5–1 win. Much better thaN 17–2 . . . but still a loss.

It was time for the high-flying Czechs. Both teams started slowly, and the first period ended in a 1–1 tie. In the second period, though, the United States caught fire and netted three unanswered goals. The US players shut out the Czechs the rest of the way for a 5–1 win to shock the hockey world. The US team's youth and conditioning were starting to pay off in a big way.

In the next game, the United States hung tough, but the Soviets were just too much. Since the 1960 Olympics, the Soviets had won sixty-one straight games against the US national team in venues around the world, and they definitely weren't ready to change things up. The Americans scored twice, but the Soviets had scored five goals by the time US team got on the board.

Despite a final score of 7–2, Williamson was pleased. Four weeks prior, Tarasov had benched his top five stars. Here, he had no such luxury.

"Whatever the scoreboard showed," says Williamson, "I honestly think that was the best game an American team played against the Soviets since the 1960 Olympics. We had officially matured from a bunch of inexperienced 'gutty Yanks' into a courageous, experienced team of young men. After three years of hard work, our team had earned what I consider to be the highest compliment: respect from Tarasov and the Soviets."

Perhaps if the 1972 and 1980 Olympics had happened back to back, the silver medal in Sapporo might be viewed as the natural springboard for the 1980 gold medal. Maybe that gold medal win in Lake Placid wouldn't seem like some kind of one-in-a-million aberration, but a natural evolution. Bob Fleming, Walter Bush, Bob Ridder, Don Clark, Murray Williamson—all had painstakingly rebuilt the US National hockey program, bringing it up to the level where it belonged in the conversation with the Soviets, Czechs, and Swedes.

In their last two games of the tournament, those scrappy kids showed how good they were, blowing away the Finns and Poles by a combined margin of 10–2. All they needed to win an Olympic silver medal was for the Soviets to beat the Czechs.

In the twenty-five years since Tarasov passed away, his grandson Alex seems to have confirmed a rumor that had been circulating for years—a rumor that Williamson heard from Tarasov himself.

"I know that in the 1972 Olympics in Sapporo, in order to improve relations with our Czechoslovakian 'friends,' they told my grandfather not to win and to arrange a tie," Alex says in the documentary *Of Miracles and Men*. "He could never do that."

At the rink before the game, Tarasov said to Williamson, "Soon, I will be a general without an army."

For the Soviets, the game was literally meaningless. Whether they won, lost, or tied, they would still win the gold medal. For the

Czechs, however, winning or losing was the difference between finishing second or third. If the Czechs won or tied, they would win the silver medal and knock the United States down to bronze; but if the Soviets won, the scenario would be reversed. The Americans and Czechs would both finish with a 3–2–0 record, but the Americans held the tiebreaker since they'd already beaten the Czechs in head-to-head competition.

Tarasov's orders were clear, but he refused to throw the game. The Soviets beat the Czechs 5–2, the United States finished ahead of the Czechs, and Tarasov was summarily fired.

"He was sent into retirement at age fifty-four because he would not be controlled," said his daughter Tatiana. "He was scarred in his heart and his soul."

"I think Tarasov got too famous," Williamson says. "The Soviets needed a cog, and Tarasov could never be that. He was bigger than the system, and the party bosses wouldn't allow it. He was generous, vivacious, charismatic, and full of life. He was one of a kind. There will never be anyone like him."

As the US team left the Olympic Village, there was a tremendous rainstorm. When they finally got to the airport, their flight was delayed six hours.

Eventually, they made it back to Anchorage, where they learned they'd received a telegram from President Richard M. Nixon. Tim Sheehy read it aloud:

"Heartiest congratulations on winning the silver medal. Your superb performance on the ice has won the admiration of all sports fans in America."

Everyone on the plane clapped and cheered. They gave the team a standing ovation.

Asked to comment on Tarasov's firing, Williamson told reporters, "Without Tarasov, Russia will be like Green Bay without Lombardi. Tarasov put Russia on the hockey map. It may be the end of the

greatest coaching dynasty I've ever been exposed to. He revolution-
ized hockey to the point nobody could beat Russia."

All these years later, Williamson says, "If Tarasov had coached
the 1980 Soviet team, I'm not sure there'd even be a Miracle. Herb
was a brilliant coach, but so much of what he did was inspired by the
things Tarasov had developed. As Tarasov liked to say, you can't pass
your competition when you follow them down the same road. Tarasov would have kept innovating and creating. That's what he loved to
do most."

CHAPTER TWENTY-ONE

I'M NOT HERE FOR MY HEALTH:
THE WHA CHANGES THE GAME

In the three decades after WWII, the NHL maintained near complete control over its labor market. Carefully crafted sponsorship deals gave its franchises the unequivocal rights to promising young prospects before they even understood their options. Ironclad contracts that favored team owners essentially locked players in for life and stripped them of their bargaining power. Over time, the NHL had effectively starved its competition of talent and become a cartel.

On June 27, 1972, ten-time NHL All-Star Bobby Hull obliterated this system with the stroke of a pen.

"In a deal of such magnitude that it had to be consummated in two countries," wrote Gerald Eskenazi on the front page of the *New York Times*, "Bobby Hull jumped from the National Hockey League to the World Hockey Association for a package worth at least $2.5 million."

The carefully choreographed "flying press conference" began when Hull and his wife Joanne, along with their three oldest sons, took a chartered flight from Winnipeg to Minneapolis with thirty-six newspaper, TV, and radio reporters in tow. After landing in Minnesota, Hull and his family were whisked into a 1934 Rolls-Royce Phantom—one of only three in the world—and escorted by local police to downtown St. Paul.

Thronged by reporters and fans, the thirty-three-year-old star with Hollywood good looks and schoolboy charm smiled broadly and waved as he emerged from the shiny black limousine. Flashbulbs popped and reporters shouted questions as Hull made his way up the red carpet into the Minnesota Club.

Inside, World Hockey Asssociation (WHA) President Gary Davidson presented the Golden Jet with an oversize cardboard check in the amount of one million dollars—an up-front cash guarantee Hull was allowed to keep even if the WHA folded.

Hull then sat down and signed the no-trade, no-cut contract that made him the exclusive property of the Winnipeg Jets for the next ten years.

Known as much for his bleach blond hair and photogenic smile as he was for his blistering slap shot and pulse-pounding end-to-end rushes, Hull was far and away the biggest star yet to leave the NHL for the upstart WHA.

"Until yesterday, the highest paid player in hockey was Bobby Orr with an annual salary estimated at $180,000," wrote the Montréal *Gazette*. Simply by switching leagues, Hull was set to make over $250,000 per year in salary and incentives. Hull's total compensation package not only eclipsed that of the great Bobby Orr, it changed the economics of pro hockey forever.

"So many people didn't think I could do it," said Jets owner Benny Hatskin. "I know that months ago, when I first mentioned the Winnipeg Jets would try to sign Bobby Hull, everybody thought it was just a publicity stunt. But I've never been more serious about anything in my life."

As a savvy entrepreneur who'd also played professional football for the Winnipeg Blue Bombers, Benny Hatskin had known exactly what he was doing from the start. It was more or less his idea to launch the WHA in the first place.

With a diverse array of business interests in everything from corrugated cardboard boxes and lumber to coin-operated jukeboxes,

Hatskin had previously tried to win an NHL franchise for Winnipeg when the league first expanded in 1967. When that bid was rejected, the feisty businessman turned his attention to the Junior A Winnipeg Jets and the newly reorganized Western Canada Hockey League.

At the same time, out in Vancouver, an ownership group spearheaded by telecommunications executive Cyrus McLean, former Vancouver Mayor Fred Hume, and Foster Hewitt—the legendary radio voice of "Hockey Night in Canada"—had also failed to land an NHL expansion franchise. Rebuffed but undefeated, the group completed construction on the distinctive 15,000-seat Pacific Coliseum, which promptly became the home of the minor league Vancouver Canucks of the Western Hockey League.

Meanwhile, the NHL's Oakland Seals—one of the more improbable expansion franchises in the NHL's first wave—had been struggling financially ever since they first hit the ice. With a poor record and lousy attendance, the Seals' majority owner, millionaire socialite Barry Van Gerbig, publicly threatened to move the team from California to Vancouver a mere fourteen games into their debut season. Embarrassed and unwilling to set such a precedent, the NHL's powerful board of governors quickly squelched the idea, sparking a rancorous legal showdown that wasn't fully resolved until 1976.

In the interim, in an overt attempt to de-escalate the situation and avoid further lawsuits, the NHL committed to awarding one of its next two franchises to Vancouver. In the three short years since its first expansion, however, the cost of an NHL franchise had tripled. With a price tag that now stood at a cool six million USD, McLean and his co-owners balked. Instead, they countered with a bold new plan: NHL expansion into four new cities—Baltimore, Buffalo, Cleveland, and Vancouver—at the cost of only three million per franchise. The NHL wasn't impressed. They rejected the compromise and started looking for someone who was willing to pay the full franchise fee.

Enter Walter Bush, then president and co-owner of the Minnesota North Stars, one of the NHL's 1967 expansion teams. Bush called his friend Tom Scallen, a freewheeling entrepreneur with twin passions for show business and closing deals. Scallen's far-flung assets—held under the incongruous name Medicor—included the Ice Follies, a New York ad agency that specialized in entertainment, multiple minority stakes in Broadway musicals, and a three-year contract with figure skating sensation and Olympic gold medalist Peggy Fleming.

Bush wondered if Scallen might want to add an NHL franchise to his eclectic portfolio. By the time Bush had line-listed Pacific Coliseum's seating capacity, proposed ticket prices, and projected player salaries, Scallen was sold.

"I'll do it," he said. "They won't have any trouble making money up there."

At the next board of governors meeting—with the backing of John David Molson from the Montréal Canadiens and Bill Jennings of the New York Rangers—Walter Bush suggested Tom Scallen and Minneapolis-based Medical Investment Corporation as the best viable option to replace Cyrus McLean and his skittish ownership group. With a self-imposed December 1 deadline looming, the board of governors swiftly agreed, publicly announcing their intent to launch expansion franchises in Buffalo and Vancouver at a press conference in early September. The only remaining hurdle was the formal transfer of assets between the two ownership groups.

"Medicor is not only acceptable to the NHL as the Vancouver hockey operator," reported the *Vancouver Sun* in October 1969, "it was the league that put Medicor into the picture and insisted the Vancouver ownership group make a deal and make it quickly."

Though not exactly apologetic for rejecting the Vancouver proposal in the first round of expansion, "the governors remain convinced this city is by far the best unoccupied territory on the continent and decided any further expansion excluding Vancouver would be a mistake." One way or another, the NHL was fiercely determined to seize control of Pacific Coliseum. "Even if they have to become marriage brokers in a shotgun wedding," according to the *Vancouver Sun*.

Feeling personally snubbed by the NHL establishment yet again, Benny Hatskin was both incensed and newly reenergized. With a population of over five hundred thousand and a passionate hockey fan base, Hatskin knew Winnipeg was ripe for a top-level professional team—even if Clarence Campbell and the rest of the NHL brain trust failed to see it. Having previously shared his frustrations and indignation with friend and colleague William Dickenson "Wild Bill" Hunter, Hatskin began to hatch the idea of forming a world-class professional league to rival the NHL.

Hunter not only owned the junior league Edmonton Oil Kings, he also coached and managed the team. On top of that, he was the founding chairman of the Western Canada Hockey League, the breakaway "outlaw league" he and others had launched after a fierce dispute with the Saskatchewan Junior Hockey League. Clearly, Hunter was no absentee owner looking to make a quick buck. He was absolutely as feisty as his nickname implied; but above it all, he loved and understood the game of hockey.

Hatskin and Hunter flew to Southern California determined to shake up the world of pro hockey. They scheduled a meeting with Dennis Murphy, Gary Davidson, and Don Regan, the three young hotshot lawyers who'd started the American Basketball Association four years prior. By 1971, the three lawyers had been squeezed out, but a looming NBA merger promised big paydays for team owners and players alike. It was a strategy akin to trading "pump and dump" stocks. For some franchise owners, the only reason to have a team was to stir the pot and then cash out.

Hatskin and Hunter were different. For the two of them, a big windfall wasn't the point. As Toronto-based author Gare Joyce writes in his book *The Devil and Bobby Hull*, "Starting a new league wasn't the goal but a means to an end, a way to force a merger and bring NHL teams to Winnipeg and Edmonton." The trick was to establish the one thing the ABA lacked: credibility.

> "Starting a new league wasn't the goal but a means to an end, a way to force a merger and bring NHL teams to Winnipeg and Edmonton." The trick was to establish the one thing the ABA lacked: credibility.

With its innovative three-point arc, freewheeling style, and distinctive red-white-and-blue ball, plenty of basketball fans were immediately drawn to the new league. For traditionalists, however, the ABA was little more than a hokey, gimmick-filled version of "real basketball." Whether despite or because of this fact, the ABA had failed to land a major TV contract, shutting off a significant source of potential revenue.

In the end, according to Regan, everyone agreed to follow the same basic blueprint as the one devised for launching the ABA... with one notable exception: "Early on, they determined that for the league to succeed at the gate and get a television contract, they needed a superstar."

It was a message that resonated with Benny Hatskin most of all. Almost immediately, he set his sights on Bobby Hull, arguably the best active hockey player in the world. With 604 career goals at the time as well as a stellar .538 lifetime goals-per-game average, Hatskin viewed the fabled left winger as the cornerstone of not just his own Winnipeg franchise but the entire league.

"The other owners won't be sorry," Hatskin said, the Golden Jet's contract in hand. "Bobby Hull will sell hockey in every one of our franchise cities."

Whether or not the WHA ultimately managed to sell tickets and survive in the long run, the short-term impact was clear. Prior to Hull's landmark contract, the average annual NHL salary sat somewhere below $30,000 per year, the lowest of the four major sports. For those who followed Hull's lead and joined the WHA, the sudden increase was substantial, coming in at an average $53,000 per year.

For certain marquee players, the bump was even bigger. Goalie Gerry Cheevers, for example, saw his salary jump from $47,500 per year (tending goal for the 1972 Stanley Cup champion Boston Bruins) to $200,000 per year with the Cleveland Crusaders. Meanwhile, Cheever's teammate Derek Sanderson saw his salary skyrocket from $50,000 per season to a whopping $300,000 per year to suit up for the Philadelphia Blazers.

Though many sportswriters, hockey purists, and casual fans had yet to take the WHA seriously—especially in the cities populated by one of the iconic "Original Six" NHL clubs—everything began to unravel the moment Hull signed his contract. As much as it pained the owners, even the players who stuck with their NHL teams saw their salaries jump to $40,000 per year.

Of the 246 players on WHA rosters in its first year, 76 had played in the NHL the prior season. Some called it an exodus.

For team owners and managers, it felt more like a feeding frenzy.

For certain lucky players, it was payday.

In a strange coincidence that sounds like it was written by a Hollywood screenwriter, on the very same day the US team beat Poland and put themselves in a position to win the silver medal, the World Hockey Association held its first ever amateur player draft. Even as Team USA was trouncing the Poles and celebrating late into the night, the Minnesota Fighting Saints claimed the rights to goalie Lefty Curran—who'd previously been placed on their secretive "preferred player list"—as well as defensemen Jim McElmury, Bruce McIntosh, and Frank Sanders; and forwards Henry Boucha, Huffer Christiansen, and Craig Sarner.

In the following weeks, once they'd returned from Japan, forwards Kevin Ahearn and Tim Sheehy both accepted offers to play for the New England Whalers; defenseman Dick McGlynn became a Chicago Cougar; and defender Wally Olds signed with the New York Raiders.

Meanwhile, forward Tom Mellor, who'd been drafted by the Red Wings in 1970, and Henry Boucha, who'd also been claimed by the Detroit as the sixteenth overall draft pick in 1971, both opted to go with the NHL.

All told, a dozen different US team players signed deals with either the WHA or NHL. "Perhaps one or two were ready for major pro hockey at that time," Williamson says, discreetly declining to clarify *who* was ready and who wasn't.

One after another, Williamson's players were signing contracts and cashing big checks. Williamson couldn't help but focus on the math. Curran, for example, left the Green Bay Bobcats and his $12,000-per-year salary as a teacher to sign with the Fighting Saints. Without thinking twice about it, the Saints nearly tripled Curran's pay, signing him at a cost of $35,000 per year.

Williamson remembers meeting with Winnipeg Jets owner Benny Hatskin one year prior. At the time, the Jets were still a Junior A team and they had Henry Boucha under contract. Williamson was asking for Boucha's release so the young winger could play in the upcoming IIHF World Championships.

In the midst of that conversation, Hatskin had expressed his disappointment and frustration with the NHL. The NHL was paying almost one million dollars per year to help subsidize major Junior A hockey in Western Canada. Hatskin thought it was chump change. He said it wasn't nearly enough to offset the value Junior A players created for the NHL. They deserved a bigger piece of the pie, and the NHL knew it. Maybe having to compete with another major pro league would get NHL owners to open their wallets.

"One million dollars?" Williamson asks rhetorically. "Are you kidding me? At $100,000 per year, we could've created an American Junior A league and financed the national team for a decade."

Not long after the WHA player draft, Williamson got a call. It was the WHA's publicity director, Lee Meade. He wanted to know if Williamson had any interest in coaching a WHA team. Williamson said he was willing to listen.

Meade started buzzing about a brand-new franchise that was going to Philadelphia. The Miami Screaming Eagles—a WHA charter member—proved unable to build an arena. The league voided Miami's contract and decided to focus on Philadelphia instead.

Two prominent Philadelphia businessmen, Bernard Brown and Jim Cooper, had bought the Screaming Eagles and turned them into the Philadelphia Blazers. Somewhere along the line, the franchise had acquired veteran goalie Bernie Parent, the first NHL star to sign with the "rebel league." Curious but cautious, Williamson flew to Philly.

"I arrived at the Blazers office and somebody led me straight to club president Jim Cooper," Williamson says. "He was on the phone, talking very fast and literally operating with a checkbook on his knee. I hadn't been there twenty minutes when he offered me a yearly package worth $50,000 in salary and incentives. He also promised me 'unlimited funds' to sign top-notch players."

Cooper had only been running the franchise for a month, and he was learning on the job. He had no experience owning a pro hockey team and didn't know the sport well. His focus seemed to be purely on keeping pace with the rest of the league. He was in the midst of ten other things and needed Williamson's answer within the next two hours.

"It felt like my head was literally spinning," Williamson says. "I took a deep breath and tried to call Walter Bush." Unfortunately, Walter was on his way to Montréal for meetings with his NHL colleagues. He hadn't yet called his office and likely couldn't be reached until later than evening.

Williamson remained noncommittal but began to review the team's roster.

In the meantime, the team's other financial backer, Bernie Brown, had arrived. Brown was the proud owner of a large New Jersey trucking firm and was clearly excited about the idea of owning a hockey team. His partner Jim Cooper, however, had only shared vague details about what it took to finance a pro franchise.

Unlike Cooper—who clearly flew by the seat of his pants— Brown was calm and even-keeled. Williamson was impressed with his manners and quiet style and wondered how the two partners had come to work together.

Brown told Williamson that over the past several weeks, he'd been listening to vague pitches full of grandiose promises. Brown knew Williamson was a "hockey man" through and through. All Brown really wanted was to understand the basics. He wanted to hear Williamson's perspective as an experienced GM and coach.

Williamson decided to lay it all on the table. Even though he'd only gone through it briefly, the numbers didn't look good. Basic expenses alone would quickly eat up their margin. The players' high salaries would throw everything out of whack. As far as Williamson could tell, even if they sold *every seat at every home game* at a price of $10 per ticket, the franchise would still lose two million dollars in its first year.

Brown looked completely shocked. It was obvious that Cooper was chasing pie in the sky. In their frenzy to sign young, promising prospects and older, experienced pros, the WHA had inflated player salaries to the point where it would be nearly impossible to turn a profit. Even mid-tier pros with little to no name recognition were overpriced.

> "I got the strong impression that the big winners were the agents and the players," says Williamson, "and the losers were going to be the owners and the sport of hockey itself."

"I got the strong impression that the big winners were the agents and the players," says Williamson, "and the losers were going to be the owners and the sport of hockey itself."

As if on cue, Cooper came rushing in to say that negotiations were underway with Derek Sanderson, the flamboyant Boston Bruins center. Within hockey circles, many sportswriters and NHL fans equated Sanderson with NFL star "Broadway Joe" Namath, the brash young quarterback who played for the New York Jets.

In the chaos, Cooper also mentioned that he'd set up training camp at a rink in New Jersey, contrary to Williamson's wish to hold the camp in Minnesota. On top of everything else, Cooper stated that he'd scheduled a press conference for the following morning, when he would present Williamson to the public as the Blazers new head coach—"even though," Williamson notes, "I still had not put my signature on a contract."

Everything happened so quickly and with such little thought that Williamson was feeling more and more unsure. He knew these types of decisions should take weeks and months of planning with clear communication. In this case, however, every decision was followed by three more decisions, a constant string of knee-jerk reactions. By the time Walter Bush called, Williamson's head was spinning.

Up in Montréal, Bush had spoken with Ed Snider, the Philadelphia Flyers team president and the man who'd built the 17,000-seat Spectrum, the new state-of-the-art arena that had lured the NHL in the first place. Snider confided to Bush that the Flyers were struggling. If they couldn't turn a profit, how on earth could Philadelphia possibly sustain *two* pro hockey teams?

Through Bush, Snider strongly advised Williamson to decline Cooper's offer. For his part, Bush assured the coach there would be a place for him somewhere in the NHL, possibly even Minnesota.

One wild afternoon on the Blazers roller coaster was more than enough to convince Williamson that Philadelphia wasn't the right fit, even at $50,000 per year—the cost it took to run his entire US national team.

Williamson hung up the phone and called Cooper to decline the offer, assuring the Blazers owner it wasn't about the money. He wanted to return home to Minnesota and a more stable environment. Cooper flew into a panic, begging Williamson to take the job for two weeks. Cooper simply needed enough time to get through the pending press conference, he said, in order to avoid a complete PR disaster.

Williamson paused and said, "That isn't how it works. To do that wouldn't be proper." Then he packed his bags and caught a plane for Minneapolis that very night. He knew there was no way the Blazers would turn a profit. He also knew there would be a few coaches and plenty of players who would make a nice chunk of cash before the team eventually folded.

With a belly full of champagne, on the flight back to Winnipeg to sign the second part of his record-breaking contract, Hull earnestly stated, "My concern now isn't bonuses or money. My job is to help get this league off the ground. As much as money is and was an important factor, the challenge is to help prove this league."

Seeing the plan he'd pursued doggedly from the start finally come to fruition, Benny Hatskin struck a more pragmatic tone. "I've loved my association with the game so far, but I'm not here for my health. There's also a chance to make money." Lest anyone in the press forget why they were all there, he added with a sly smile, "We got him. Season tickets go on sale tomorrow at nine."

CHAPTER TWENTY-TWO

THE MIDWEST JUNIOR HOCKEY LEAGUE
AND THE NCAA

After Murray Williamson's brief but surreal stint as "Manager for a Day," he returned to Minnesota under no illusions about what hockey had become. In the five years he'd been away coaching the US national team, hockey had exploded on both the professional and college levels. In North America and beyond, the sport was becoming Big Business.

The NHL's first wave of expansion, in 1967, had doubled the size of the league. Seemingly overnight, the Original Six became twelve. In 1969, in a largely defensive move, the NHL awarded new franchises to Buffalo and Vancouver to prevent the World Hockey Association from staking claims in those cities. In 1972, the WHA finally got off the ground and major league professional hockey doubled in size yet again. With fourteen franchises in the NHL and sixteen in the WHA, pro hockey had grown to an astonishing thirty teams.

With desperate GMs and coaches frantically trying to fill nearly three hundred new roster spots, competition for quality players was as hard-fought as the games themselves. Under increasing pressure to find and sign hot young players, NHL scouts headed south of the 49th parallel in search of talented US-born players.

In September 1972, Walter Bush made good on his promise and gave Williamson a job with the Minnesota North Stars. Murray's official title was director of special projects. "Great," thought Williamson. "What the heck is a *special project*?"

One month later, he found it. "Williamson will work under president Walter Bush in areas involving junior and international hockey," wrote the Minneapolis *Tribune*.

He and Bush were reviewing a request for financial assistance from the four-team Can-Am Junior League. Ever since the North Stars began, they had given generously to regional junior teams. Every year, it seemed, the requests got a little bigger and the pleas got a little more urgent. They needed a long-term solution. The more they discussed the problem, the more it began to center on a bigger philosophical question: Was there even a role for junior hockey within the American system?

For decades, the NHL had subsidized Canadian Junior A teams. Until the late 1960s, those teams had been the primary source of new players for NHL teams. As the need for players expanded, however, the Junior A leagues did not, creating a significant gap.

In Minnesota, however, this dynamic was reversed. High schools across the state were graduating almost one thousand new hockey players each year. The top college teams, by contrast, could only provide about one hundred roster spots per season. In the past, former American high school players couldn't quite compete with the older, more experienced players who came from the Canadian junior leagues. American players needed somewhere to further develop. The obvious missing link was a well-organized, professionally run *US-based* junior league.

Historically, efforts to form a top-tier junior hockey league on par with Canada's had been sporadic at best. Harry Brown, Win Stephens, Bob Somers, Robert "Red" Kairies, Ken Austin, and others had made unselfish attempts to create and sustain such a program. The problem was always the same: expenses outweighed enthusiasm. Without substantial support—and legitimacy—from the NHL, the league would never get off the

US junior hockey was at a crossroads. It was time to go big or go home.

ground. US junior hockey was at a crossroads. It was time to go big or go home.

By September 1972, Bush had enlisted support from the NHL board of governors, who contributed start-up funds of $59,000 to get the league up and running. Meanwhile, Williamson reached out to rink operators and city officials in ten Midwestern hockey cities to gauge their interest in joining the Midwest Junior Hockey League (MJHL). Eight cities expressed interest in hosting a franchise, and the first meeting was set for October 30 in Minneapolis.

Williamson and Bush presented the economic requirements and franchise obligations of MJHL member teams, as well as the funds and support the league would provide in return. The league then set a deadline for formal applications. The development committee would meet at the end of December and vote on the six new member franchises.

It didn't take very long for critics to come out of the woodwork.

"There has been considerable apprehension among Minnesota high school and college coaches that the proposed junior league for the Upper Midwest could damage their programs," wrote John Gilbert in the Minneapolis *Tribune*.

Some high school coaches worried all their best players would jump to juniors, turning the high school league into a kind of transitional B league. Others worried about the negative effects on the players themselves.

"The junior thing is great for a kid who doesn't want to go to college," said one coach, "but it's ridiculous for a junior coach to take a kid out of school after ninth grade ... What could be worse than being a mediocre twenty-one-year-old hockey player with a ninth-grade education?"

Ignoring their vocal detractors, Williamson and Bush pressed forward. By February 1973, franchises had been assigned to Chicago, Fargo, Minneapolis, St. Cloud, St. Paul, and Thunder Bay, Ontario. Then came their first big break.

Coach Bob Gernander, who'd led Coleraine High School to back-to-back Minnesota High School State Tournament titles in 1967–68, and Coach André Beaulieu, who'd won two Minnesota State Independent Championships with Hill-Murray School, both announced they were joining the MJHL. Gernander signed on to coach the Fargo-Moorhead Sugar Kings while Beaulieu took the helm of the Minnesota Junior Stars. Additionally, Ken Wharram, a fourteen-year veteran of the Chicago Blackhawks, became the head coach of the Chicago Warriors; and Rich Blanche left his post as assistant coach for Denver to lead the St. Cloud Junior Blues.

With four highly successful, well-respected coaches on board, recruiting efforts took off. By April, enough letters of intent had been signed to fill 75 percent of the league's roster spots.

At the same time, Williamson and Bush were in the midst of their own scouting. With an upcoming international junior tournament to be held in Leningrad at the end of December, they were hoping to send a team of MJHL all-stars to the USSR.

Technically, it was an invitational tournament, but with the Soviets, Czechs, Swedes, Finns, and Canadians all competing in a round-robin format, in effect, it would be the first ever world junior championship tournament. Team USA was still awaiting the Soviets' official invitation. But when the call finally came, Williamson and Bush would be ready.

With only a few weeks to prepare, Williamson, Bush, and Mike Radakovich, former assistant coach at Colorado College, began to select their all-star roster. They also scrambled to schedule a two-game series with the Ontario Hockey League-leading Peterborough Petes on their way to Europe.

"Radakovich was instrumental in securing players like Paul Holmgren, Gary Sargent, and several other high school stars who'd been overlooked by D1 college programs," Williamson says. "The tight time frame was far from ideal, but somehow we were pulling it off."

"It's the dawning of a new era."

The invitation finally arrived, and the National Junior team held its first practice on November 22. A mere two days later, they headed north to

Winnipeg to play a citywide junior all-star team. "I think we really surprised a few people," Williamson told the press after a convincing 8-2 win. "It's the dawning of a new era."

The All-Stars practiced for three more weeks, mixing in a handful of exhibition games, including a 2–1 overtime win against the Petes. "I was proud of our kids," Williamson told the Minneapolis *Tribune*. "Even when we were down 1–0, nobody panicked. We stayed within our system."

After losing to the Petes 6–4 in Ontario in the rematch, however, their misadventures began. The team had chartered a bus to New York that was set to leave the following morning. From there, they would fly to Prague for a couple of scrimmages and a few days' practice before the tourney began.

With heavy wet snow coming down the following morning, however, area roads were impassable. The team was forced to fly to Montréal instead. They planned to fly to New York from there and connect with their flight to Prague.

Their first flight was uneventful. But after that, things went sideways.

"It was still snowing very hard when we boarded the plane in Montréal," wrote Doc Nagobads in *Gold, Silver, & Bronze*. "As I settled into my seat, I looked out on the tarmac and noticed our bags on a luggage cart." Nagobads and Williamson managed to get the crew's attention before the plane took off but were told the bags would have to be sent on the next flight.

Things got even worse after that. Low visibility in Prague forced their plane to reroute and land in Bratislava, a full two hundred miles southeast of their destination. With planes grounded indefinitely, the team took an overnight train to Prague. They arrived the following morning—uncomfortable, exhausted, and hungry—only to learn their equipment had yet to arrive. They cancelled that evening's exhibition game against the top Czechoslovakian junior team and hoped for the best.

When their gear still hadn't arrived twenty-four hours later, they were forced to cancel the second game as well. Their bags finally arrived later that afternoon, but all of it was wet. Nagobads and team trainer Allen Mathieu unpacked everything and spread it out in the team's hotel rooms and hallways to dry. Hockey gear was everywhere. The players whose skates weren't too wet practiced on a nearby outdoor rink, while their rest worked out in the gym.

The day after that, bad weather grounded their plane yet again. If they hoped to arrive in time to play their first game, they would have to take a train to Moscow. From there, they would take the Red Arrow, an infamous overnight train that runs between Moscow and Leningrad.

By the time the team finally arrived in Leningrad, they hadn't eaten for hours. Their top priority was breakfast. Unfortunately, the food the Soviets provided was "absolutely inedible," according to goalie Mike Dibble. "Murray stood up to our Russian interpreter and said, 'You get us something to eat, or we're out of here. Then they got in a big fight and we finally got some food that we could eat."

Unsurprisingly, after five days without their equipment—unable to practice and scrimmage—the US Juniors lost four games in a row. They managed to beat the Czechs in their final game to pull out a fifth-place finish in the six-team tournament.

"It was really instrumental that we didn't come home shut out," Dibble says. "We hadn't won a game, and Czechoslovakia was a very good team. All I can remember is that I had a lot of saves, and the Russian crowd was chanting 'DEE-bull, DEE-bull' because they didn't like the Czechoslovakians."

Though they'd stumbled on the world stage, the MJHL All-Stars had laid a solid foundation for future US national junior teams.

"My bag never did show up," says Williamson with a chuckle, "so I had to wear the same outfit every day for two weeks. Still, the thing I remember most is what an eye-opening experience it was for the kids who got to play against the best junior teams in the world. Our primary goal had been to promote junior hockey in the United States. We really had no idea we were getting in on the ground floor of something that would grow so big."

Third-year Gophers coach Herb Brooks saw the MJHL as a tremendous asset, despite their fifth-place finish internationally. The league gave younger players a place to keep developing after they finished high school. For some high-school standouts, a year in the junior league made all the difference. The league's sixty-game schedule provided far greater opportunity— and far more experience—for college-bound players than the Minnesota State High School League's paltry twenty. Ultimately, the MJHL was proving a simple but profound point: if US-born high school players were given a longer season and a bigger stage, they could compete with even the best Canadian-born players.

> *Ultimately, the MJHL was proving a simple but profound point: if US-born high school players were given a longer season and a bigger stage, they could compete with even the best Canadian-born players.*

Unfortunately, not everyone embraced the new league.

With virtually no warning, on August 28, 1974, headlines in the Twin Cities boomed like a shot across the bow. "Junior hockey league is ruled pro by NCAA," said the Minneapolis *Star*.

"NCAA expected to bar players from junior hockey league," declared the Minneapolis *Tribune*.

According to sportswriter Dan Stoneking, "The crux of the NCAA's case against the [MJHL] is that the league received *direct payments* from the National Hockey League instead of through the Amateur Hockey Association."

Before launching the league, however, Williamson had met with Warren Brown, assistant executive director of the NCAA, to avoid precisely such a problem.

"He pointed out some discrepancies at that time, and we changed them to conform with NCAA rules," Williamson said. "One of our principal goals was protecting the college eligibility of our players."

After the league's first season, Williamson and Brown met again. "We gave Mr. Brown a statement which showed financial allocation of the NHL to the Midwest Junior League," Williamson maintained.

"He told us at that time if there were any problems, the NCAA would get back to us within a week. We never heard from them again and naturally assumed there weren't any problems."

Instead, in a secretive closed-door session, the NCAA executive council voted 11–3 to declare MJHL players ineligible.

"We have followed the rules down the line," said MJHL President Ken Austin. "The kids only get car fare and one meal a day. Just what the NCAA allows."

"We were pure two weeks ago, and we'll be pure two weeks from now," added Williamson.

In truth, of the $726, $255 spent by the NHL to subsidize amateur teams in 1973, a mere $59,755 went to the MJHL. Meanwhile, the NHL forked over a whopping $570,000 to the Canadian Amateur Hockey Association to support Tier 1 Junior A teams.

Previously, the NCAA had ruled against giving Canadian Tier 1 junior hockey players eligibility because many of them were said to receive "payments close to a living wage." Objectively, no one could make the same claim against MJHL players.

"We set up the league to help the kids get scholarships," said St. Paul Vulcans Coach Doug Woog. "We allot about enough to equal no more than $50 a month." Either way, the NCAA's announcement put a major damper on recruiting efforts. Clearly, the MJHL had no choice but to fight the NCAA's ruling.

On Thursday, September 5, Murray Williamson, AHAUS Executive Director Hal Trumble, and lawyer Gordon Martin traveled to NCAA headquarters in Shawnee Mission, Kansas. One week prior, Williamson and Trumble had sent a nine-page report detailing the league's finances.

Explaining the role of AHAUS to the press before departing, Trumble said, "The Amateur Hockey Association of the United States has about 10,298 teams playing hockey. It also has a paid staff of two. All the rest are volunteers. No one is making money from the NHL subsidy . . . The NCAA telling us not to accept the NHL financing to help us carry out our programs is like a millionaire telling the poor they can't accept welfare."

Williamson was convinced the whole thing was a misunderstanding.

"Sitting at that long table in the NCAA conference room," Williamson says, "I looked out the window at the rolling green hills and thought, *This isn't hockey country.* So many people connected with the NCAA, especially in leadership positions, came from football and basketball. They didn't understand hockey like they did those other sports. I told them we didn't want to fight. We just wanted to explain our side of things and tell them the truth. I was confident [that] once they understood, things would work out all right."

Williamson and Trumble explained that while the NHL had helped get the MJHL started, no individual player received anything more than what was permitted by NCAA rules. "The NHL money was used for paying the officials and other expenses," says Williamson. "Not a cent ever reached a player."

They also pointed out that the NCAA had been striving to *Americanize* collegiate hockey for many years. The MJHL was a great way to do that, since every roster spot would be filled by an American player.

"It wasn't too many years that the only Americans on the ice in the NCAA finals were the two officials," said Ken Austin. "We formed this league to develop Americans."

"Some of the kids who were given scholarships after the first year *never* would have gotten an offer straight out of high school," Williamson says. "The proof was in the pudding. Our system was working."

Less than one week later, the NCAA reversed its ruling and the MJHL was forced to stop receiving direct financial subsidies from the NHL. Williamson, for his part, put a positive spin on the news.

"I think there is a new degree of cooperation between the MJHL and the NCAA," he said, "and American collegiate hockey is much better for it."

Meanwhile, incoming Gophers freshman Reed Larson, a high-scoring defensive star at Minneapolis Roosevelt High School, was suing the NCAA in US District Court to reinstate his amateur status. At seventeen, Larson had signed an agreement with an agent to negotiate his contract once he turned pro. It was a prudent move, perhaps, but not permissible under NCAA rules. To further complicate matters, Reed had voided the contract three days later. The entire dispute hinged on a seventy-two-hour period in which the amateur athlete had been represented by an agent.

"Maybe the intent of the rule is right, but it seems overprotective," said District Judge Miles Lord, ruling in favor of Larson. "The NCAA doesn't seem to make leeways, and there are a lot of circumstances in this case that the organization should reconsider."

Perhaps stinging from the judge's rebuke, not to mention incredibly frustrated with the sport of hockey in general, the NCAA took the feud to a whole new level. On Thursday, October 10, 1974, a Minneapolis *Star* headline proclaimed, "NCAA may drop hockey," quoting a letter signed by Warren Brown.

"This is to advise you that NCAA officers have placed on the agenda . . . the question of whether the National Collegiate Ice Hockey Championship be discontinued and the NCAA Ice Hockey Committee be disbanded," the letter read. "There is a strong feeling that unless these people dedicated to intercollegiate ice hockey are prepared to take a stand against the NHL–AHAUS subsidy pattern and also abide by NCAA rules in Canadian recruitment, ice hockey will be rejected by NCAA membership."

"I don't think the NCAA understands the development money paid to amateur hockey by the NHL," Herb Brooks told the Minneapolis *Tribune*. "Even the youngest players in Bloomington and Warroad and elsewhere have been getting some benefits."

Brooks had been directly involved both with the NCAA's dispute with the Midwest Junior Hockey League and the court battle over Reed Larson's amateur status, both of which were lost by the NCAA.

"The whole question of amateurism and professionalism has to be examined closely," said Andy Geiger, athletic director at Brown University and one of the few people on the NCAA Eligibility Subcommittee with hockey experience. "There are so many people involved here. I can't say anything more. But it's the damnedest thing I've ever seen."

At the time, only eighty-seven of the nearly eight hundred NCAA member schools had ice hockey programs. Williamson was right. The NCAA's perspective was skewed by other sports, most of all football and basketball. Hockey remained an enigma.

Williamson was right. The NCAA's perspective was skewed by other sports, most of all football and basketball. Hockey remained an enigma.

In mid-October, the eligibility subcommittee met to settle the issue once and for all. Their decision was swift but also a double-edged sword.

"The National Collegiate Athletic Association has modified its rules to allow college athletes to play Junior A hockey in Canada," wrote the AP. "The rules change announced Thursday by NCAA official Warren Brown opened the door for several ineligible hockey players, who were invited to apply for immediate reinstatement."

The ruling was great news for Brooks, who went on to recruit Joe Baker, Paul Holmgren, Mark Lambert, and Ken Yackel Jr. from the inaugural St. Paul Vulcans squad. Former Vulcans Dan Bonk and Jim Boo also joined the Gophers as walk-ons.

All told, fifteen former Vulcans played for Brooks at the University of Minnesota on one or more of his three NCAA National Championship teams. No wonder the Vulcans were known as the "Gophers Hockey farm team."

"Those were the days," said Vulcans Coach Doug Woog, reminiscing years later. "It was a great time for hockey in Minnesota and really a wild ride. I can remember all the ups and downs we went through to get that whole thing going. I was excited to really be a part of it all."

Unfortunately, but perhaps predictably, in its four years of operation, the MJHL faced persistent financial uncertainty. As a startup league with no established fan base, operational costs continually exceeded revenue from ticket sales. Something needed to change. Before the 1976–77 season began, the MJHL reached out to the USHL and proposed a three-year plan that would merge the two leagues.

The USHL agreed to the merger, and the league's board of governors established a two-division format. The Midwest Division would feature the three former junior league teams: the Austin Mavericks, Bloomington Junior Stars, and St. Paul Vulcans. The US Division would feature the three minor pro teams: the Waterloo Black Hawks, Sioux City Musketeers, and Green Bay Bobcats.

Over the next two seasons all six teams played an interlocking schedule. Out on the ice, the minor pro teams dominated their younger amateur rivals, but it was they who eventually folded. Beginning with the 1979–80 season, the league would be composed of strictly amateur Junior A teams.

With a little bit of luck and a great deal persistence, the Minnesota Junior League had essentially morphed into the league Murray Williamson first envisioned: a post-high school development league that gave talented young players a place to get more game experience against great competition while maintaining their NCAA eligibility status.

Four decades later, the USHL is a top junior hockey league sanctioned by USA Hockey. There couldn't be a better or more appropriate legacy for a feisty coach who passionately believed in the excellence of US amateur hockey.

EPILOGUE

Murray Williamson's turn behind the bench with Team USA at the 1974 World Junior Championship was the last time he coached a US national or Olympic team. His hockey career, however, was far from over. Having already rejected an offer to coach in the WHA, he continued serving as director of special projects for the Minnesota North Stars through the end of the 1973-74 season.

In the meantime, he and his partner Bob Peters continued to grow and refine their Olympic Development Summer Camp, which they'd launched previously in 1967. As the first hockey camp of its kind anywhere in the world, its impact on US hockey was both immediate and substantial. Though it was rebranded one year after its founding at the behest of the US Olympic Committee, the Bemidji International Hockey Camp lived up to its original name, producing players who competed on every US Olympic hockey team from the 1968 Winter Games right up through the Miracle on Ice. Williamson and Peters even played a small part in developing speed skater Eric Heiden, who swept all five of his races in Lake Placid, earning an unprecedented five Olympic gold medals.

In 1977, Williamson traveled to Europe, where he coached the Genève-Servette Hockey Club, the oldest continually operated team in the professional Swiss National League. After guiding his squad 14-10-6 record for the 1977-78 season, Williamson offered to buy the franchise, but couldn't work out a deal with the current ownership group.

Williamson spent the following season as a scout for the legendary Scotty Bowman, who was then head coach of the NHL's Buffalo Sabres. In 1980, Williamson was instrumental in founding and helping to steer a committee for the creation of the Hobey Baker Memorial Award. Since 1981, the award has been given forty-one times to the NCAA men's ice hockey player who best "exhibits strength of character both on and off the ice" and "displays outstanding skills in all phases of the game."

Through the US national and Olympic teams he's coached—as well as his youth hockey camp—Williamson has inspired and mentored over thirty thousand young hockey players from over forty-two states, five Canadian provinces, and fifteen countries.

Over time, Williamson's career transitioned to real estate. In the past four decades, he's developed, owned, and managed numerous economy lodging hotels in mid-size cities throughout Minnesota and in Naples, Florida. At one time or another he's had properties in Cannon Falls, Chaska, and Shakopee, but the ones most dear to him have been in and around his beloved town of Bemidji.

Without question, the legacy he's most proud of is the continuing hockey tradition that lives on through his children and grandchildren. His sons Kevin (University of Wisconsin-Eau Claire), Randy (Lake Forest College), and Dean (University of Minnesota) all played college hockey, as have his granddaughters Taylor (University of Minnesota) and Kendall (Colgate University).

Even at age eighty-seven, Williamson laces up his skates at least once a year to play shinny out on the lake with his growing extended family. His moves may not be as nimble as they were back in the day, but his competitive spirit has never waned, even if that means deking out a player seven decades younger.

INDEX

Abbott Cup, 30
Ahearn, Kevin, 148, 197
Ahern, John, 21
Allen, Keith, 181–182
Alm, Gary, 83
Alm, Larry, 83, 84
Amateur Athletic Union (AAU), 7–8, 9
Amateur Hockey Association of the United States (AHAUS)
    during 1930s and 1940s, 7–8
    Bush and, 91
    donation to US Olympic Fund, 120
    Lockhart and, 134
    national team program development and, 140
    1952 Olympics team and, 9
    now USA Hockey, 7, 214
American Amateur Hockey League (AAHL), 90
American Hockey Coaches Association (AHCA), 68–70
Anderson, Rod, 51
Anderson, Stu
    Governors and, 49, 50, 51, 73
    Williamson on, 75
Anderson, Wendell Richard "Wendy," 12
    Des Moines arena opening, 60
    Gophers and, 32
Andolsek, Lud, 109
Armstrong, Murray
    Canadian players on team, 83
    Mariucci and, 85
    top players from powerhouse Junior A clubs and, 54
Austin, Ken
    basic hockey facts about, v
    efforts to form a top-tier junior hockey league and, 204
    MJHL and, 210, 211
Austin Mavericks, 214
Baker, Bill, 76
Baker, Joe, 213
Bates Manufacturing Hockey Club, 9
Bauer, Arnie, 78
Bauer, Father David, 105, 119–120
Beaulieu, André, 206
Bedecki, Tom, 54, 81
Bemidji International Hockey Camp, 215
Bentley, Max, 16
Bertram, Dick, 149
Bessone, Amo, 54, 65
Bierman, Bernie, 15
Bjorkman, Rube, 61
Blair, Wren, 104, 122–124
Blanche, Rich, 206

Blatherwick, Jack, 168, 169
Blatnik, John
    basic hockey facts about, v
    citizenship for Canadian hockey players and, xiii–xiv, 109, 122
Blatzheim, Al, 12
Bloomington Junior Stars, 214
Bobrov, Vsevolod, 112
Bonk, Dan, 213
Boo, Jim, 213
Boucha, Henry
    NHL as choice over WHA, 197
    1970 national team and, 144
    1971 national team and, 147, 148, 154
    1972 Olympic team and, 178
    in US Hockey Hall of Fame, 2
Bowman, Scotty, 215
Brimsek, Frank, 40
Broadmoor World Arena, 69–70
Brooks, Herb
    basic hockey facts about, v, 2
    Gophers and, 83, 213
    Governors and, 49, 50, 51, 73
    on Mariucci's facial wounds, 16
    on Mayasich as hockey style, 20
    on MJHL, 209
    on NHL development money and NCAA, 212
    1968 national team and, 126–127
    1972 national team and, 175
    on Russians' psychological warfare, 129
    Sonmor and, 3
    training style of, 169
    Williamson and, 3, 75, 126
    on winning 1955 MSHSL Tournament, 73
Brown, Bernard, 198, 199–200
Brown, Charlie, 177
Brown, Harry, vi, 204
Brown, Walter
    basic hockey facts about, vi, 8
    development of national team with Ridder, 11–12
    LIHG and, 11
    1948 Olympics hockey team and, 8
Brown, Warren
    basic hockey facts about, vi
    MJHL and NCAA, 209–210, 212, 213
Brundage, Avery, 8
Bryson, Bill, 91
Buchanan, Neill, 81
Buffalo Sabres, 215
Bush, Walter
    AHAUS and, 91
    basic hockey facts about, vii, 89–90
    characteristics, 98

Des Moines arena opening, 59–60
development league for senior amateur players,
    94–95
development of 1956 US Olympic team, 57
Frontenacs and, 92
MJHL and, 205, 206
NHL expansion and, 193, 194
1960 Olympics and, 92
North Stars offer to Mariucci, 104
as president of MAHA, 92
raising money for national team, 62
Sabetski and, 180
Scallen and, 193, 194
senior league hockey and, 90
on Soviet Olympic players, 120
United States Hockey League and, xiv
US 1968 Olympic team and, xiii
on US Central Hockey League teams, 91
in US Hockey Hall of Fame, 2
US 1959 World Championship team, 62
Williamson and North Stars, 203–204
Williamson and Steers, 97–98
Bushnell, Asa, 9
Cahan, Larry, 124
California Seals, 175
Campbell, Clarence, 195
Campbell, Gene, 19, 60
Canadian Amateur Hockey Association (CAHA), 80
Casey, Terry, 117
Central Hockey League (CHL), 90
Cheevers, Gary, 196
Chernyshev, Arkady, 115
Chicago Blackhawks, 29
Chicago Cougars, 197
Chicago Warriors, 206
Chisholm, Ron, 93
Christian, Gordon, 12
Christiansen, Keith Raymond "Huffer"
    Minnesota Fighting Saints and, 197
    1971 national team and, 149–150
    in US Hockey Hall of Fame, 2, 135
Clark, Don
    basic hockey facts about, vii
    Des Moines arena opening, 59
    1967 national team and, 100
Cleveland Barons, 177
Cleveland Crusaders, 196
Cleverly, Harry, 68
Coleman, Jim, 131
Collie, Conrad, 83, 86
Colorado College Tigers, 45, 81, 82–83, 85
Cooper, Jim, 198–199, 200, 201
Copeland, John, 77, 79
Coppo, Paul, 135
Cornell University, 148–151
Central Sports Club of the Army, Moscow (CSKA
    Moscow), 167
Cullum, Dick, 10

Cunniff, John, 2, 112, 113
Curran, Mike "Lefty"
    Minnesota Fighting Saints and, 197–198
    1969 national team and, 136
    1969 US national team and, 137
    1971 US national team and, 154
    1972 Olympic team and, 185
    in US Hockey Hall of Fame, 2, 135
    Williamson and, 185
Davidson, Gary, 192, 195
Dea, Murray, 83
Denver Pioneers and Gophers, 83–84
Des Moines, Iowa arena "The Vet," 57, 59–62
Desmond, Dick, 10
Dibble, Mike, 208
Dirksen, Everett, 122
Dornack, Wayne "Bud," 135, 136
Dornhoefer, Gary, 181
Dorohoy, Albert "App," 36
Dougherty, Richard Leo "Dick"
    Des Moines arena opening, 60
    1955 World Championships, 19
    1956 and 1960 Olympics, 12
    on 1956 Olympics game against Soviet Union, 23
Dulmage, Jack, 119–120
Dupont, André "Moose," 148
Durbano, Steve "Mental Case," 177, 178
Edmonton Oilers, 195
Egers, Jack, 148
Eskenazi, Gerald, 191
Eveleth hockey, 39–40
Eveleth-Virginia Rangers, 34–37, 41, 43
Fair Play Cup, 145
Falkman, Craig, 116, 128, 129
Fargo-Moorhead Sugar Kings, 206
Federov, Sergei, 182
Fichuk, Pete, 151
Firsov, Anatoli
    ability to be NHL player, 173
    on 1967 US national team, 118
    on 1968 Olympics, 131
    1972 Russian Olympic team, 178, 181
Fleming, Bob
    background, 139
    basic hockey facts about, vii, 139–140
    characteristics, 4
    development of 1972 Olympic team and,
        140–141, 142–143
    Kane-Williamson dispute, 150–151
    1962 World Championship, 92
    1972 Olympic team budget, 175–176
Flint Generals, 151
Foss, Paul, 151
Ftorek, Robbie, 2, 187
Fullerton, James, 141
Gagarin, Yuri, 173
Gambucci, Andre, 41
Gambucci, Elio "Papa," 35, 40–41, 42

Gambucci, Gary
  on Karakas's pool hall, 41
  1970 national team and, 144
  1971 national team and, 147
  North Stars and, 175
  in US Hockey Hall of Fame, 2, 135
Geiger, Andy, 212
Genève-Servette Hockey Club, 215
Gerbig, Barry Van, 193
Gernander, Bob, 205–206
Grant, Bud, 166
Greeley, Walt, 12
Green Bay Bobcats, 133, 135, 214
Haddock, William, 7
Harkness, Ned, 54, 149
Harris, Bob, 51
Harris, Ron, 124
Hart, Philip, 122
Hartman, Sid, 19, 103
Hatskin, Benny
  basic facts about, 192–193
  Hull and, 192, 196, 201
  NHL and, 198
  NHL expansion franchises and, 194–195
Hay, Bill "Red," 81
Heiden, Eric, 215
Hewitt, Foster, 193
Heyliger, Vic
  as AHCA secretary-treasurer, 68, 69–70
  basic hockey facts about, vii
  bona fide national championship and, 67–68
  on development of college hockey, 65
  as national team coach in 1966 World
    Championships, 99–100
  nickname, 100
  1956 Olympics team, 18
  top players from powerhouse Junior A clubs
    and, 54
  unified set of rules plan, 66–67
  as University of Illinois hockey coach, 65–66
  as University of Michigan hockey coach, 66
  Western League and, 82
Hibbing Flyers, 34, 36
Hobey Baker Memorial Award, 216
Holmgren, Paul, 206, 213
Howe, Colleen and Gordie, 183, 184
Howe, Mark, 2, 183–184, 186
Howe, Marty, 111, 114
Hull, Bobby, 191–192, 196, 201
Hull, Joanne, 191
Hume, Fred, 193
Hunter, William Dickenson "Wild Bill," 195
Hurley, Tom, 114, 126
Hynes, Dave, 182
Ikola, Willard, 16
  on 1956 Olympics game against Soviet Union, 23
  1956 Olympics team, 20
  Thompson and, 40

International Ice Hockey Federation (IIHF)
  as LIHG, 11, 14
  World Junior Championship Team USA, xiv
International Olympic Committee (IOC), 8
International Skating and Hockey Union (ISHU), 7
Irving, Stu, 182
Jennings, Bill, 194
Jeremiah, Eddie, 18, 55, 89
Johnson, Charles, 86
Johnson, Lyndon B., 122
Jordan, Terry, 151
Jorde, Marv, 82–83
Joyce, Gare, 195
Kairies, Robert "Red," 204
Kane, Bob, 150–151
Karakas, John, 16, 41
Karakas, Luke, 43
Karakas, Mike, 40
Kelley, John "Snooks"
  on early AHCA tournaments, 70
  Governors and, 49
  Mellor and, 161–162
  1956 Olympics team, 18, 21
  top players from powerhouse Junior A clubs
    and, 54
Kennedy, Edward, 122
Kennedy, John F., viii, 93
Kenwood Huskies, 89
Kharlamov, Valeri, 173, 178, 179, 181
Kingston Frontenacs and Bruins, 92
Klinck, Wayne, 83, 86
Kollevoll, Olav "Ole," 54, 55
Konik, George
  1967 national team and, 101, 102
  1970 national team and, 144–145
  1972 national team and, 175
  as pro player, 110
Kostka, Vladimír, 152
Kraftcheck, Steve, 73
Kundla, Johnny, 14
Lambert, Mark, 213
Larson, Reed, 211–212
Lentz, Art, 141
Lethbridge Native Sons, 30
Ligue Internationale de Hockey sur Glace (LIHG)
  international ice hockey in non-Olympic years, 8
  as IIHF, 11, 14
  1948 Olympics hockey team and, 8
Lilyholm, Len, 126, 128, 175
Lockhart, Tom
  AHAUS and, 134
  basic hockey facts about, viii, 134
  national senior amateur tournament and,
    134–135
  1967 national team and, 100, 107, 138
  in US Hockey Hall of Fame, 2
Lord, Miles, 211–212
Lord Roberts Community Center, 28

MacGregor, Clark, 122
MacLeod, Jack, 117–118
Maltsev, Alexander, 173, 178
Manitoba Hockey Hall of Fame, 30
Mariucci, John "Maroosh"
  as "a players' coach," 76
  Armstrong and, 85
  basic hockey facts about, viii–ix, 1
  on Canadian players on US teams, 55–56, 79,
    81, 83
  on Canadian youth hockey, 53–54
  characteristics, 14, 15, 16, 17, 19, 76, 78
  coaching style of, 18
  Des Moines arena opening, 59, 60–61
  development of hockey as sport and, 104
  end of pro career as player, 91
  facial wounds, 16–17
  Elio Gambucci and, 42
  Gophers and
    bodychecking by players, 77–78
    building of team, 72–73
    early seasons with, 14
    fired as coach, 103
    having "Minnesota boys" on, 43
    importance of academics, 71
    leave from, for 1956 Olympics, 45
    skaters going to Olympics and, 87
    Sonmor and, 74, 104
    St. Boniface and, 32
    Williamson signed up by, 47–48
  on Mayasich, 133
  on national team development, 101
  1956 Olympic team, 18
    on expectations for team, 21–22
    leave from Gophers for, 45
    on picking team members, 20
    predictions about, 61
    on Soviet team, 23
    on team performance, 23
  1967 national team and, 102–106, 107–109
  North Stars and, 104
  Olympic medals and, 87
  Penrose Memorial Cup and, 15
  Ridder and, 12–13, 15
  Steers and, 3
  as student athlete at University of MN, 54
  style as hockey player, 15, 16
  on US high school hockey programs, 56
  Williamson and, 42–44, 47–48, 108–109
Mariucci Arena, 1
Martin, Gordon, viii
Martin, Seth, 116
Marvin, Cal, viii
Massier, Murray, 83, 86
Masterton, Bill
  injury and death of, 124–125
  1967 national team and, 101, 102
  as pro, 121

US citizenship, 110
Masterton, Carol, 125
Matchefts, John
  on 1956 Olympics game against Soviet Union, 23
  1956 Olympics team, 12, 20
  Thompson and, 40
Mathieu, Allen, 208
Mattson, Jim, 47
Maxwell, Wally, 80
Mayasich, John
  awards, 32
  basic hockey facts about, ix, 2, 133
  Des Moines arena opening, 60, 61
  Gophers and, 32, 47
  1956 Olympics team, 19, 20
  1960 Olympics team, 40
  1969 national team, 135, 136, 137–139
  Thompson and, 40
Mayoroff, Boris, 171, 172
McCartan, Jack, 2, 17, 85
McCarthy, Eugene, 122
McDonald, Ab, 29
McElmury, Jim, 177, 197
McGlynn, Dick, 197
McIntosh, Bruce, 182, 197
McKinnon, Dan, 12, 79
McLean, Cyrus, 193, 194
McLeod, Jackie, 105
Meade, Lee, 198
Medicor, 194
Mellor, Tommy
  "Snooks" Kelley and, 161–162
  NHL as choice over WHA, 197
  1972 Olympic team and, 177
Melnychuk, Jerry, 115
Meredith, Dick, 60, 89
Miami Screaming Eagles, 198
Michigan Wolverines, 14, 34
Midwest Junior Hockey League (MJHL)
  Brooks on, 209
  finances during operation of, 213
  merger with USHL, 213–214
  Nagobads and, 207, 208
  NCAA and, 3, 209–213
  Williamson and, 205, 206, 207–208, 209–210, 211
Mikhailov, Boris, 178, 181
Miller, Art, 117
Minneapolis Bruins and Frontenacs, 92
Minneapolis Bungalows, 90
Minneapolis Culbertsons, 90, 91
Minneapolis Millers, 74, 91
Minneapolis South Tigers, 49, 50–51
Minneapolis Southwest, 51
Minnesota Amateur Hockey Association (MAHA)
  Bush and, 92
  Ridder and, 1, 9
Minnesota Fighting Saints, 197–198
Minnesota Hockey League (MHL), 90

Minnesota Junior Stars, 206
Minnesota North Stars
  Gambucci and, 175
  Mariucci and, 104
  Nanne and, 122–123
  regional junior teams and, 204
  Ridder and, 1
  Williamson and, 203–204, 215
Minnesota State High School League (MSHSL)
  Tournaments: 1955, 49–52, 53, 73
Missildine, Harry, 119
Molson, John David, 194
Mondale, Walter, 122
Montréal Canadiens, 26–27, 29
Mott, Morris, 116
Moulton, Wes, 18
Murdoch, Murray, 68
Murphy, Dennis, 195
Nagobads, George V. "Doc"
  basic hockey facts about, ix
  Mark Howe and, 186
  MJHL and, 207, 208
  1967 national team and, 113, 115
  on 1968 national team, 126, 127
  on Williamson as coach of 1967 national team,
    110
Nanne, Lou
  awards, 1, 121
  basic hockey facts about, xiii
  1967 national team and, 101, 102
  1968 Olympic team and, xiii–xiv, 122–123
  North Stars and, 122–123
  US citizenship, xiii–xiv, 107, 110, 121–122
National Collegiate Athletic Association (NCAA)
  amateur code, 80
  Championships, 34, 41, 66, 81, 86, 149
  Larson suit, 211–212
  MJHL and, 3, 209–213
National Hockey League (NHL)
  bodychecking in, 78
  as cartel, 191
  expansion franchises, 193–195, 203
  Junior A hockey subsidies, 198, 204
  longest fight on record, 16
  MJHL and, 211
  WHA and, 196–197
Naymark, Len, 34, 36
Nedomanský, Václav, 186
New England Whalers, 197
New York Raiders, 197
Newell, Rick, 148
Nixon, Richard M., 189
Noble, George, 51
Oakland Seals, 193
Olds, Wally, 197
Olympic Development Summer Camp, 215
Olympic Games
  1920, 7
1948, 8–9
1952, 1, 9–10, 35, 41, 89
1956 US team, 18–24
  development of, 57
  exhibition games, 21
  medals, 89, 100
  members, 1, 12, 19–21
  team captain, 79
1960
  Bush and, 92
  US medals, 40, 89, 100
  US team members, 2, 12
1968
  Canadians, 130, 131
  Soviet Union, 129, 130–131
  Sweden, 128–129
1968 US team
  AHAUS donation to US Olympic Fund, 120
  members, xiii–xiv, 1, 122–123, 126
  pre-Olympic games, 126–127
  Williamson as coach, 1
  wins and mark, 128, 130, 134
  See also United States national teams: 1967;
    Williamson, Murray and 1967 national
    team
1972 Russian team
  Czechoslovakia and, 188–189
  exhibition games, 178–179, 180–182
  members, 178, 181
  against US, 187–188
1972 US team
  Czechoslovakia and, 187
  development, 140–141, 142–143, 147
  exhibition games, 176–182, 185–186
  Finland and, 188
  members, 162, 184–185, 197
  Poland and, 188
  qualifying match against Switzerland,
    186–187
  Russians and, 187–188
  silver medal, 188, 189
  Sweden and, 187
1980 "Miracle on Ice," 1
  instability of US teams, 175
  Mariucci and, 87
Omaha Knights, 148, 177–178
Orr, Bobby, 99, 122
Oss, Arnie, 60, 89
Palazzari, Aldo, 65
Paradise, Bob, 2, 127, 135
Parent, Bernie, 198
Parritt, Harold, 17
Patrick, Craig, 175
Pearson, Mike, 71–72, 84
Peluso, Tom, 182
Penrose Memorial Cup, 15
Pepkin, Vasilie, 162–163, 165, 171, 172–173
Peterborough Petes, 206, 207

Peters, Bob, ix–x, 215
Peter's Meats, 91
Philadelphia Blazers, 196, 198–201
Philadelphia Flyers, 200–201
Pleau, Larry, 135
Pleban, John "Connie"
  basic facts about, 35–36
  Eveleth–Virginia Rangers and, 35
  1952 Olympics, 9, 10
  1956 Olympics, 18
  1962 World Championship, 92
Polupanov, Viktor, 131
Port Colborne Sailors, 97
Radakovich, Mike, 206
Ragulin, Alexander, 173
Regan, Don, 195, 196
Regan, Tim, 179, 181
"Regina Ex-Pats," 83
Reichert, Bill, 33
Rendall, John, 112, 121
Rendall, Tom, 47, 80
Renfrew, Al, 79
Rensselaer Polytechnic Institute, 14, 54, 151
Ridder, Bob
  basic hockey facts about, x, 1
  characteristics, 14
  Des Moines arena opening, 59, 60
  development of 1956 US Olympic team, 57
  development of national team with Walter
    Brown, 11–12
  MAHA and, 1, 9
  Mariucci and, 12–13, 15, 23–24
  1952 Olympics, 9
Rigazio, Don, 12, 19
Riggio, Frank, 36
Rigolet, Gérald, 186
Riley, Everett James "Buck," 59
Riley, Jack, 135, 181
Roberts, Glenn, 66
Rochester Mustangs
  1969 national team and, 135
  Steers and, xiii
  US Central Hockey League, 91
Rodenhiser, Richard Peter "Dick," 12
Roseau Rams, 50
Ross, Don, 111, 175
Russell, Lawrence "Spud," 25, 27–28
Ryman, Marsh, 75, 91, 103–104, 141
Sabetski, Günther, 180
Sanders, Frank
  Minnesota Fighting Saints and, 197
  1972 Olympic team and, 177, 178, 187
Sanderson, Derek, 196, 200
Sargent, Gary, 206
Sarner, Craig, 185, 197
Scallen, Tom, 193–194
Schroeder, Julius, 68
Selke, Frank, 26–27

Sheehy, Tim
  New England Whalers and, 197
  1972 Olympic team and, 178, 189
  in US Hockey Hall of Fame, 2, 135
Sinden, Harry, 92
Sioux City Musketeers, 214
Smedsmo, Dale, 178
Smith, Jack, 83
Smythe, Conn, 26
Snider, Ed, 200–201
Somers, Bob, 204
Sonmor, Glen
  basic hockey facts about, x, 3, 73–74, 75
  as coach of Gophers, 103
  Mariucci and, 74, 104
  on Williamson's "hockey sense," 75
Spartak Moscow, 112
St. Boniface Canadiens
  Abbott Cup, 30
  Gophers and, 31–32, 42
  Manitoba Hockey Hall of Fame, 30
  Turnbull Cup, 29–30
  Williamson and, 25, 28–29
St. Cloud Junior Blues, 206
St. Paul Johnson Governors, 49–52, 73
St. Paul Steers
  biggest opponent of, xiii
  Brooks on, 3
  as informal national B team, 121, 142
  Mariucci relieved as coach, 3
  Williamson and, xiii, 3, 97–99, 121, 142
St. Paul US Central Hockey League team, 91
St. Paul Vulcans, 213, 214
Stanley, Ed, 68–69
Stanley Cup
  Chicago Blackhawks, 29
  Montréal Canadiens, 29
  "Russian Five" and, 182
  Toronto Maple Leafs, 27
Starr, John Howard "Howie," 68
Starshinov, Vyacheslav, 131, 137
Stephens, Win, 204
Sterle, Norbert "Norb," 65
Stewart, John "Black Jack," 16
Stoneking, Dan, 209
Stordahl, Larry, 126
Strömberg, Arne, 93
Tarasov, Alex, 188
Tarasov, Anatoly
  awards, honors, and medals received, 174
  ballet and, 166, 168, 170
  basic hockey facts about, xi, 159–160
  development of hockey in Soviet Union and, 160
  dryland training, 156, 160–161, 167
  firing of, 188–189
  importance of training, 156
  on 1967 national team, 115
  overspeed training, 167–169

on requirements of good hockey players, 161
training methods, 174
Williamson and, 153–154, 155–157, 164–174, 179–181, 188, 189–190
Tarasov, Tatiana, 189
Thief River Falls, 49, 50
Thompson, Cliff, 22, 39–40
Thompson, Cyril L. "Cheddy," 68, 69
Thunder Bay–Arrowhead League, 34, 36–37
Tonnele, Theodore, 39
Toronto Maple Leafs
sponsorship system, 26, 27
Stanley Cups, 27
Tower, Whitney, 63, 64
Tretiak, Vladislav, 173, 178
Trumble, Hal
basic hockey facts about, xi
MJHL and, 211
on 1969 national team, 139
on 1971 national team, 149
in US Hockey Hall of Fame, 2
Tschida, Marsh, 115, 116
Turler, Michel, 144
Turnbull Cup, 29–30
Tutt, Thayer
basic hockey facts about, xi
first AHCA tournament site and, 69–70
1967 national team and, 100, 107
in US Hockey Hall of Fame, 2
Williamson in Soviet Union, 161
Unger, Eric, 160
United States Amateur Hockey Association (USAHA), 7, 39
United States Central Hockey League, 90–91
United States Hockey League (USHL)
championship, 98
as feeder program, xiv
merger with MJHL, 213–214
venues of games, 104–105
United States national teams
1950 World Championship and, 35
1951 World Championship and, 9
1954 World Championship and, 11
1955 World Championship and, 19
1959 World Championship and, 62
1962 World Championship and, 92
1963 World Championship and, 92–93
1966 World Championship and, 99–100
1967
European tour, 111–118
Mariucci and, 102–106, 107–109
1969, 135–139
1970, 140–145
1971
Cornell and, 148–151
Czechoslovakia and, 151–153
Finland and, 155
Flint Generals and, 151

members, 147, 148, 151
Omaha Knights and, 148
RPI and, 151
Soviet Union and, 155
Sweden and, 154
West Germany and, 153, 155
1972, 175
instability of, 175
medals from 1961-1966, 100
money raising for, 61–62, 120
1956 and 1960 Olympic medals, 100
reasons for poor performances by, 94
United States Olympic Committee (USOC)
and IOC, 8
money raising by, 61–62, 120
1948 Olympics hockey team and, 8
1956 Olympics team, 18–19
1970 team development and, 141
1972 budget, 175–176
University of Illinois Fighting Illini, 65–66
University of Michigan Wolverines
all-Canadian roster (1955-56 season), 80
Gophers and, 14, 46–47
Heyliger as coach, 66
NCAA National Champions, 81
University of Minnesota Golden Gophers
bodychecking by players, 77–78
1956 Olympics team, 19
Olympic players from, 87
Pioneers and, 83–84
Sonmor and, 73, 103
St. Boniface and, 31–32, 42
Tigers and, 82–83, 85
Vulcans as farm team for, 213
withdrawal from WIHL, 85–86
Wolverines and, 14, 46–47
US Hockey Hall of Fame inductees, 2, 4, 135, 173, 174
US Senior Amateur Championship
1950, 9
USA Hockey, 7, 214
Vancouver Canucks, 193
Vaughan, Richard, 68
Vaughn, Dick, 55
Vladimir Lutchenko, 173
Walter A. Brown Memorial Tournaments, 105–106
Waterloo Black Hawks, 214
Wayne Gretzky International Award, 174
Weber, Vic, 141
Weiland, Ralph "Cooney," 55, 77
West Canada Selects, 105–106
Westby, Jimmy, 50
Western Canada Hockey League, 193, 195
Western Collegiate Hockey Association (WCHA), 86
Western Intercollegiate Hockey League (WIHL), 17, 56, 71, 82, 84, 85–86
Westwick, Bill, 119
Wetzel, Carl

1967 national team and, 112, 116, 117, 118
1972 national team and, 175
Wharram, Ken, 206
White, Maury, 61
Whiteside, Cy, 81
Wickberg, Håkan, 154
Wigen (no first name given), 51
Williamson, Dean, 216
Williamson, Kendall, 216
Williamson, Kevin, 216
Williamson, Murray
    on Armstrong compared to Mariucci, 85
    awards, xiv, 4
    on Blair, 123, 124
    Brooks and, 3, 75, 126
    on Canadian system of advancement in hockey,
      75–76
    characteristics, 4, 28, 142
    Copeland and, 77, 79
    Lefty Curran and, 185
    Des Moines arena opening, 60, 61
    development of 1972 Olympic team and, 141,
      142, 143, 147
    Eveleth–Virginia Rangers and, 34–37, 43
    Elio Gambucci and, 35, 40–41
    Genève-Servette Hockey Club, 215
    Gophers and, 47–48
    on hockey season in Canada, 72
    "hockey sense" of, 75
    on Mark Howe, 184, 186
    with International Milling, 97
    on Jorde, 82–83
    Kane and, 150–151
    on learning from Russians, 182
    Mariucci and
      first meeting, 42–44
      1967 national team and, 103–104, 107–109
    on Mariucci's
      coaching style, 14, 17, 18
      facial wounds, 16
    Masterson and, 125
    MJHL and, 205, 206, 207–208, 209–210, 211
    Nanne and, 107, 121–123
    on NCAA understanding of hockey, 211, 213
    1956 Olympics
      on US team, 20
      on US win over Canada, 22
    1959 national team money raising and, 62
    on 1966 World Championship national team,
      100
    1967 national team and
      budget, 120–121
      as coach, 110
      Nanne and, 122–123
      plans, 100–102, 104
    1968 Olympics
      on beating West Germany, 130
      on Russian team, 130–131
      US team and, xiii, xiv

    on 1969 national team, 135, 136
    as 1970 national team coach, 142
    as 1971 national team coach, 147–156, 157
    1972 Olympics
      development of team, 140–141
      exhibition games, 176–182, 185–186
      on game against Russians, 188
      on Rigolet, 187
      silver medal, 188, 188, 189
    as 1974 junior national team coach, 215
    North Stars and, 203–204, 215
    Olympic Development Summer Camp and, 215
    Philadelphia Blazers and, 198–201
    post-hockey career, 216
    Sonmor and, 3
    in Soviet Union, 161, 162–174
    St. Boniface Canadiens and, 25, 28–29
    Steers and, xiii, 3, 97–99, 121, 142
    on Stu Anderson, 75
    as student, 72
    Tarasov and, 153–154, 155–157, 164–174,
      179–181, 188, 189–190
    as typifying "Canadian player problem," 56
    US junior program and United States Hockey
      League, xiv
    on West German 1968 national team, 126, 127,
      128
    Winnipeg Barons and, 29, 32, 33
    on year-round state sponsorship of Olympic
      teams, 119
Williamson, Randy, 216
Williamson, Taylor, 216
Winnipeg Barons, 29, 32, 33
Winnipeg Blackhawks, 33
Winnipeg Jets, 192, 193
Woog, Doug, 2, 213
World Championships
    1950, 35
    1951, 9
    1954, 11, 133
    1955, 19
    1959, 62
    1962, 92
    1963, 92–93
    1966, 99–100
    1967, 105–106
    1969, 133
World Hockey Association (WHA)
    Hull and, 192, 201
    NHL expansion franchises and, 203
    players' salaries, 196–198
Yackel, Ken
    Gophers and, 32, 46
    in US Hockey Hall of Fame, 2
Yackel, Ken, Jr., 213
Yurkewicz, Al, 12
Zikulov, Vladimir, 181

CONTRIBUTORS

When John "J.J." Schaidler was young he could only imagine two possible futures: becoming a writer and playing hockey. Much like his boyhood idol, Tony Esposito, J.J. became a goalie when the older kids needed somebody to shoot at. Mimicking Tony O's "butterfly" style as a four-year starter in high school, J.J. earned MVP honors twice and was named to the Wisconsin All-State team his senior year. Sadly, his NHL dreams ended there. Not coincidentally, his childhood nickname J.J. was also left behind. He never stopped writing, however, and has made a career of it for over three decades. Working professionally as John Schaidler, he's written and edited everything from TV commercials and corporate videos to grant applications, press releases, website copy, stage plays, academic papers, and billboards. His eclectic resume includes a wide array of memoirs including *Gold, Silver, Bronze: A Doctor's Devotion to American Hockey* by the legendary George "Doc" Nagobads and *Warda: My Journey from the Horn of Africa to a College Education* by scholarship winner Warda Abdullahi. He's also had the pleasure of editing numerous children's books, including the award-winning picture book, *Gizo-Gizo: A Tale from the Zongo Lagoon*, and the graphic novel, *Lake of Tears*.

John resides in Monterey, California, where he can often be found tide pooling, hiking through the redwoods, playing board games, or questing for street tacos.

Beth Gibson Lilja has specialized in organizing, training, and preserving memories for over twenty years. As a certified professional photo manager, she has helped 750-plus people and companies save, organize, and share their photo legacies, including Murray Williamson.

Through her company, BGL & Associates, LLC, Beth creates photo management plans that she, or her clients, carry out. These plans transform print and digital photos and memorabilia into treasured memories with stunning photo displays. This work has inspired an events business, where Beth hosts gatherings and retreats to assist others with their photos and projects. She is a Golden Circle member of the National Association of Productivity and Organizing Professionals (NAPO). A born leader, Beth has served as president of numerous boards to help grow and improve various nonprofit organizations, which has also led to a public speaking career.

Beth graduated from St. Cloud State University. She lives in Golden Valley, Minnesota, with her husband Patrick and their dog Caribbean (Cari). She loves travel, photography, and making new friends.